Newtown Naughty Boy

by

Richard Blackshire

ISBN: 978-1-326-28968-3

Contents

INTRODUCTION

One does wonder why anyone wants to write a book in the first place. For me there was a number of reasons for embarking on writing my memoirs at this particular time. Believe me, it does take a while – but I would hope (like myself) that most writers see it as a labour of love.

This is, after all, my own personal time capsule – and you, dear reader, are that person who has just discovered it and dug it up.

I'm hoping that you're going to find this book a can't-put-it-down one. I have read books myself like that and I want my book to be like this too, where the reader gets involved with the stories and the characters and just wants to know what happens next.

My intention is to entertain and inform you, as you might just say to yourself at times,

"I remember that," or "I used to go there," or "My God, did he really do that?" If you do then that's great, as I will have reached the audience I wanted.

Feel free to just laugh out loud (as the modern saying goes) because there will be some humdingers within these pages for sure, I promise you that. I have described a bit of history and how my family came to be in Hemel Hempstead. I have then interjected episodes from life that happened, using the characters who were there at that time. Their dialogue is as close as I can remember to what was actually said. Sometimes I can remember the phrase exactly: other times I know how it would have been said.

All the people in this book are real. Most of them I have a real fondness for, especially those who are mentioned several times during the stories. I must say though at this point that if I have misremembered anything that this is not intentional by any means. I hope you like these characters too, and that you feel their joy and sadness at times.

I'm going to take you on a journey through my life and through the decades from the end of World War II and into the funky seventies. I'm going to tell you about what it was like to live then and how people thought and what they did. We will look into the depths of a new town created to house people from London and the impact that this had on the locals. I will take you through my school years and into work: my teen years and my fascination for shooting, discos, and girls. I had to end this story somewhere, and I decided to stop at a convenient point: before I met my wife. After all, this is about growing up … and I hope my wife will concur in saying that by the time I was married I was indeed a grown-up. Some may of course say differently: my mum would have for sure.

That brings me quite painlessly to the title of the book. There is a famous bit of family video footage taken one Christmas Day at the family dinner table. It involves my mother (who was at that time reaching her final time with us, unfortunately). She still enjoyed herself, mind you, and on that day she was her usual buoyant self.

The subject of star signs had come up and she was in full flow, telling the family why I was so like a Sagittarian. My brother was feeding her questions to provoke more (let's say) interesting dialogue from her. We were all laughing as she spoke the immortal words,

"They never grow up, you know."

"Who don't?" responded my brother.

"Well, you know. They get a thing in their heads and they just can't let go of it."

"Who?" repeated my brother. "Who are you talking about?"

"You know. Those with that sign … those Sagerteranian people," as she now incorrectly called them.

"So are you saying he has never grown up, then?" responded my brother.

"Nooo … that boy has never grown up: he's always been a very naughty boy." It was as if I wasn't in the room, and yet I recorded all this on a camera not fifty centimetres from Mum.

So you see I had to add into my title for this book those immortal words spoken by my mother on her last Christmas. I came up with

Newtown Naughty Boy. You need to decide yourselves if indeed I am or was that naughty.

I had some inspiration a while back when I came across a book written by someone I knew from school. I know he won't mind me mentioning this: Reg Stickings's book *Searching for Soul* was something that just hit me out of left field one day. Here was a guy who had found it difficult to read and write at school, just like me, and now here he was: a published writer. When I read Reg's book I found it so easy to read and it did indeed help me to realise that maybe I could write a book too. I do owe Reg an awful lot for the inspiration and drive to do something myself. I would recommend his book to anyone, even if they have little interest in the northern soul scene. Thanks, Reg. You're a star, and I hope in this book I can do justice to the time that you also wrote about.

So ... back to the book and its content. It is a collection of stories from my past, interwoven with a bit of history and a few observations. When I think back to events in the past – say, back over fifty years – the images conjured up are like some old black-and-white film footage from the 1930s. Past history always reminds me of that sepia tone on film. Some events are like stills – like a picture you might look at and reflect upon, while other events in life play like a video. They play in short clips in my head and have a great deal of detail and emotion attached to them. I don't quite understand why we sometimes have these video clips in our minds or why some seem more important than others. Of course, the ones in this book are the ones I can remember – and they are also the ones that have, for some reason, run repeatedly over time. I will call these snippets from the past video flashes.

To give you an example of one of these video flashes let's go way back in time ... let your mind come back with me, and try to envisage a wobbly grey misty picture which slowly clears and then becomes full colour.

It's a warm summer's day and I'm out in the backyard, which is a small area of grass with a path running through it to the bigger back garden much further down. This area is no bigger than someone's living room, I expect, but shaped like a triangle. There are a few plants in a flower bed here – lily of the valley, if I remember rightly: one of my mum's favourite scented flowers. It's midweek, and I know this because I can hear the children playing in the nearby junior school. They are excited and I can hear cheers and clapping quite easily. They seem more animated than usual and I suspect something is going on.

Apart from the noise from the school in the distance there is a kind of almost silent summer background sound you get … just the air moving and the insects and birds adding to that summer effect.

I'm obviously not school age, as there is no family dog running around my feet. So I'm around four years of age, I would guess … playing in the warm surroundings of the back garden, quite safe and contented.

I look up to the sky on impulse. It's a vivid blue canvas, as blue as your eyes can take: an almost aquamarine. Could it really have been this blue or has my vision of the past enhanced it so much within this video flash? There are no contrails here from Luton Airport jets. Luton Airport already existed (from 1938) and had been an airfield for fighter squadrons during the Second World War, but air traffic was still low in the fifties and was confined to just a few holiday flights with propeller-type aeroplanes.

No clouds here, just blue and warmth from the sun and that almost-still silence. Why is it that the passage of time always makes you think that past days were always warm ones? I have no idea. Do we always see what happened in the past as more idyllic than it actually was?

I stared into the sky for some time then turned, and my eyes widened as something caught my young eyes. As I looked my arm instinctively rose up and stretched as far as it could towards an object I had seen but couldn't reach. Too far for my short arms and frame to grasp it … and I stretched out as far as I could, even on to tiptoe to get those last few inches. It was hopeless. I just could not reach but I wanted it and it was beyond my grasp. When you're young and you see something, you really want it bad.

"Best get Mother out here," were my first thoughts, and so I ran indoors and screamed for her to come out. "Quick. Come outside quick and bring the chair. Bring the kitchen chair, Mum."

Mother obliged for some reason and didn't even ask me why. She just blindly followed orders, wiping her hands on her pinny, then took hold of the stool that sat in the kitchen. In fact the stool was a strange object. It was my old wooden high chair from when I was a baby and the legs had been cut down to make it more acceptable for adults to sit on in the confines of the kitchen. It was well-worn and the paint was scratched off. I get the impression it was a lovely scratched yellow colour with the wood showing through in places – very distressed, and what we might call shabby chic today. Father had done a really good job at sawing off the feet as none of them were the same length, and if you sat on the stool it rocked on its uneven supports.

I ran first and Mother followed with the high chair stool.

"There," I said. "Place it there." She sat it down and I climbed up on it and I stretched my arm up. The stool rocked on its wonky legs and I had to steady myself on Mother. It was only at this point that she started to take any interest in what I was trying to do. She looked up into the blue and followed my tiny hand upward to the object in the sky. I was on tiptoe by now and still unable to reach. My mother, now understanding what all this was about, took hold of me and put me back down on the ground. Smiling at me she took the stool and went back into the kitchen.

Well, I screamed my head off.

"I want it," I demanded. "I want that now," still pointing to the sky. At this point, and probably to save the neighbours' ears, I was taken inside and in no uncertain terms told to calm down. This usually entailed a little shaking by my mother and some variable toned crying whilst this was performed.

My little video flash now fades to an end. The image fades away and the rest of the day and what happened is as blank as a white sheet of paper. The memory goes from full-on detail to nothing instantly.

THE END, role the credits.

To this day I have never understood why this flash plays in my head from time to time. It's in there and holds some importance, but I have no idea why. I'm guessing we all have these flashes in our head: some will be important and very relevant. One I would guess that everyone has is their first day at school. I think everyone remembers that – and I will be, of course, relating more on mine later. But some of these clips don't seem to be that important, although maybe they were at the time. I'm thinking that maybe through life we replay these so much that they become more relevant and more repayable. It's like a painter applying more oil paint to a picture, making it thicker and making it stand out from the canvas more. You get to a point where the vision is so infixed in your mind that it will never leave.

Oh, and the object in the sky? The one that had me all excited? I expect as a reader that you would like to know what exactly I had seen. Well, you need to read the rest of the book and maybe I will divulge more. Read on, folks, and enjoy.

Hemel Hempstead: A Potted History

Although Hemel Hempstead is my home town – and, indeed, was a new town under the New Towns Act 1946 – it has been on the map a very long time. We can go back to the fifth century, to Anglo-Saxon times, just past that point in history where the Romans had had enough and withdrew from Great Britain for good – and after leaving quite an impression on us, too. The settlement was known by the name of Henamsted or Hean-Hempsted. This loosely translates to High Hempstead. If we now spring forward to Norman times and 1066 with William the Conqueror, the name has changed to Hemel-Amstede. The *Domesday Book* of 1086 records the area as Hamelamesede.

There now seem to have been some changes down the centuries whereby Hamelamesede became Hamelhamsted, which is not too dissimilar from how it is today. In Old English the word stead was used to denote an area of pasture or a clearing within a wood. We now see the word stead added to towns such as Hemel Hempstead and Berkhamsted.

The word Hemel is a bit more difficult to pin down. It probably came from the word Haemele, which was the name of the district in the eighth century, and is most likely to be the name of the landowner at that time.

Strangely enough, until the Second World War the locals called the area Hempstead – but now, more commonly, it is just called Hemel.

Henry VIII granted the town a royal charter that gave Hemel Hempstead the right to start to rule itself through a bailiff. A market was allowed to operate on a Thursday. Henry and Anne Boleyn are reputed to have stayed in Hemel at some point too. I bet they didn't consider it to be anything else but a stopover to some other grander place.

After the Second World War the government designated Hemel Hempstead to be one of the proposed new towns in 1946. There were to be several new towns created and, as part of the first wave, Hemel was created along with its close neighbours Stevenage, Welwyn Garden City, and Hatfield. Places further away, such as Harlow and Crawley, were also to become a designated area for rehousing from bombed-out London.

The Blitz had caused the displacement of a great number of people, and there was also an issue with slums: they had to be cleared, and the redevelopment of London was to take place. So on 4 February 1947 the government purchased 5,910 acres of land with the aim of creating one of these new towns, which would surround the small town of Hemel Hempstead. This was the third candidate for development, and the decentralisation of people and industry from London was to take place quickly.

There was, however, a lot of opposition to this new town from the local residents of Hempstead. In a lot of ways I can understand this, and if you compare this to current-day developments where there is opposition you can sympathise with the locals. After all, Hempstead was a small sleepy town with nearby villages that would now be swamped with noisy, brash Londoners. I think if I lived in those times I would also have been in opposition. Nonetheless, the town got the go-ahead following a public inquiry and officially became a new town on 4 February 1947.

Plans were drawn up by a Mr G A Jellicoe (later Sir Geoffrey Jellicoe), and his vision of Hemel was said to be a "city in a park". One wonders if this was to differentiate it from Welwyn Garden City. His plans were, however, not fully appreciated by – again – the locals and the Ministry of Town and Country Planning. It's a great shame, really, because on one side the locals obviously didn't want any change at all and were in complete denial of having a new town imposed on them. But on the other hand it would seem that old Jellicoe had devised something of a wonder.

Jellicoe's original plan included not just one water garden (as we have today) but seven, and centrally-located recreation areas where canals would be intermingled with large open spaces. There would be civic and public buildings combined with restaurants, offices, and a theatre. God, we would have had a theatre. We were also going to get an expansive lake covering the land to the west of the Old Town. A heliport was discussed, along with a grotto. Can you just imagine how different Hemel would have been?

Jellicoe's vision was clearly too expensive, and in some ways didn't fit into others' ideas of what a new town should look like. Jellicoe became disenchanted, but was persuaded to develop the layout of a new park along the river. Today we have a lovely park, Gadebridge, which just goes to show how skilled Jellicoe was with his vision of how things could be. If only the original plan had been agreed – and if only the local people had not complained so much – then maybe Hemel would have been far more than it is today.

Work began on the new Hemel Hempstead in 1949, just four years after the end of the war. Apart from the development of a new town centre, two other areas were designated for the development of council housing. These were Adeyfield and Bennetts End. Adeyfield was located on a hill to the east of the old town. The first four families of the new town moved into their new homes in February 1950. Bennetts End was located on the rising ground to the south east. Construction began in 1951, and 300 houses were occupied by autumn 1952. One of these 300 houses was going to be the one I was to be born into. Bennetts End was just one neighbourhood made up of streets of council houses. It had its own set of shops called Bennetts Gate, which opened in 1954. Until then local people shopped from mobile vans, which served the district until the shops were built.

Of course, other estates were to be built following on from Adeyfield and Bennetts End. Highfield, Gadebridge, Warners End, Chaulden, Grove Hill, and Woodhall Farm were the largest developments, whose construction spanned several decades. Other areas that were already outlying villages such as Apsley, Leverstock

Green, and Boxmoor would be expanded to become part of Hemel Hempstead, although they would retain their village names. Schools were built, as well as an industrial estate called Maylands Avenue, whose first factory was erected in 1950.

Hemel had always been an industrial town and it was famous for its papermaking facilities at Apsley, notably the John Dickinson paper mill – and the less-known Frogmore Mill, which is famous for being the first place in the world for making paper by machine. We also have to add Kodak to the list, which monopolised the town so much that at one point there was some talk of the town being renamed Kodaksville. One other notable company was the famous firework manufacturer Brocks, which occupied the fields where the Woodhall Farm estate is now.

All in all the stage is set for my entry on to this earth and the part I have to play. I wanted to set the scene and explain a little about the history of Hemel before we got started upon my upbringing and the things that took place.

The Stork Arrives

1954

And so on 9 December 1954 I came out of my mother's womb. Not in a cosy hospital, of course, but into the back room of 18 Lower Barn. I had arrived in style directly into the house that was going to be home for some twenty-five-odd years. Of course I have no recollection of any of this, and so anything that's written here has had to be pieced together from other family members. My mother blames, if that's the right word, my total indulgence in and fanaticism vis-à-vis science fiction on that very day I was born. For her, lying on a bed down in the back room on a Thursday the TV must have been on. She always maintains watching a film on TV before my birth. The film in question was *1984* by George Orwell.

Now for the life of me in later years I could never understand how such a film would be playing on TV on a Thursday. In fact the first film of *1984* didn't screen until 1956, two years after my birth. She was however most insistent on this fact. Things didn't add up, and so I had to do a bit more research.

This, I found out, was a television adaptation of the book – which I'm sure everyone knows was published in 1948 (the title is a reversal of the date used for the future *1984* date). The TV adaptation, which was adapted by Nigel Kneale, was apparently hugely controversial. In fact questions were asked in Parliament the very next day. It would seem that the date of the transmission was in fact Saturday 11 December and not my birthdate after all. My mother must have been sitting in a chair with me watching the adaptation when it was first televised on 11 December. In some way I'm quite pleased I was born just before the transmission: my first ever science fiction programme.

I suspect I was an easy birth with no complications. I'm an uncomplicated person and I don't think I would have given any resistance. Maybe I was eager to get out to watch *1984*. Who knows? I sometimes wonder if the film did have some effect on me, and that it did in fact give me that fascination for science fiction that would stay with me.

I nearly wasn't born on 9 December. I was running late, it would appear, as we headed for Christmas. There was talk from the midwife that if I didn't come out soon then I would just "jolly well have to wait until after Christmas". In those days if things didn't happen in the order prescribed then you'd better jolly well wait until another time that was convenient to everyone else. I suspect the midwife had other things to do, like baking cakes and making paper chain decorations. I would need to wait: that was the order given. Thank God that *1984* came on the TV and gave me a push because I would have been devastated to have had my birthday in January and to have missed the adaptation.

I was born into this street where I lived, a street of just twenty-four houses … twelve on each side: even- and odd-numbered either side of the road. These houses formed a cul-de-sac: a dead-end street, if you like … a place that would be good for playing outside when older.

Lower Barn was a typical new town build with its red brick houses on two stories. The road curved slightly before finishing with a T-shaped turning area. The road had a special significance in the new town's development plan, as the occupants of this road had been singled out. Yes, that's right: we were special people, and I didn't realise this until much later on in life. Those who occupied the houses in this street had to meet two important fixed criteria. One was that they had to be a local family who already resided in Hemel Hempstead or the surrounding area and the other was that they had to have had one child. So no Londoners here, then: this was a road – to coin a phrase – for local people. It was no surprise, then, that many of the people in the road already knew each other. In fact a couple of people had been to school with my mother in Apsley.

There was a nice feeling about this road with its local people: everyone got on well and everyone helped one another out. People then were so pleased to have a nice new house in a new town and they looked after their environment very well. The Second World

War had given people a sense of pride in those days and families wanted to be seen as keen, tidy, and helpful. It was the war and its ways that had formulated this instilled way of thinking with people. Those from London who occupied other streets were also very grateful for having been able to move into such a lovely clean new area. Many of these Londoners would have either have been made homeless from the Blitz or would have come from one of the cleared slum areas. Londoners knew too well that moving to Hemel was a huge improvement from what they had had previously. The air was better and the opportunities for work would bear fruit. It was a better standard of living all round, and it showed in people's faces.

As a baby I don't have any clear recollection myself until the age of four, but I do feel I remember sitting or lying in my Silver Cross pram. I was often put outside in the fresh air, as it was seen as good to have your baby aired outside like the washing. I can remember being left outside unattended for a while and would have been strapped into the pram. Some sort of harness was fitted to me which would restrict my movements and stop me from tumbling out. The pram was high: it had huge wheels and the carriage sat on its own leaf springs. The maker of the pram was considered at the time to be the Rolls-Royce of prams – and so I expect it was not only me being shown off outside, but the pram too.

We had good neighbours either side of us, who would be known as Auntie and Uncle for years to come. In fact I was quite upset when I got a bit older to hear that they weren't in fact my real auntie and uncle. They were good people and I know they helped out in troubled times – and there was to be trouble within the family in those early years – trouble that would affect my parents and me in later life.

Our House
As a child I always felt the house was big, but on returning in later years as an adult it feels quite small now. Yet a family of four

lived here, and we seemed to have enough room back then. As already mentioned this house was a council house, and therefore my parents paid rent each week to a man who knocked on our door. A nice man, as it happens, with a smart dark pinstriped suit with large lapels and a trilby hat. He always had a clipboard with papers on it. He had a nice smile even though, I suppose, his job was difficult at times. After all, who wants to see the rent man each week?

Rent was always kept in the sideboard drawer at home in an old tobacco tin. Sometimes money was borrowed out of it to pay for something urgent but it was always put back, and we never got into a position where we could not pay our rent. No credit cards then, of course, so if you wanted something you saved up or raided the rent tin.

Renting meant that you had to furnish yourself and decorate the inside. Outside maintenance was covered by the rent and the council would be responsible for fixing things that went wrong with the building and the heating system.

The house had no central heating back then: no radiators in those days. There were two fireplaces in the two reception rooms and a coke boiler in the kitchen to heat the water. Outside there were three brick outhouses: a shed with a coke storage area, a coal shed and an outside toilet. I'm never sure why we had an outside toilet because there was one inside upstairs, but I guess this was a hangover from the old days.

The front garden was massive, with a path dividing the two separate patches of lawn. Each of these lawns had a flowerbed in the middle. One was round, the other square. Around the edge of the grass were borders for plants. The whole thing needed some looking after, I can tell you. The back garden was just as spacious, in a way. A long path went down to an open area at the bottom where fruit and vegetables were grown. There was even a chicken run here with a number of chickens all happy to lay eggs for us.

During the war families were told that they needed to grow food. "Dig for Britain" was the slogan, and every house and patch of land – however small – had to be used to grow food. There were no cattle and other animals then, as animal feed could not reach the British Isles. Therefore what you could grow was what you would eat. After the war this already-instilled mentality and the skill of growing just continued. Food was more plentiful but we had not as yet reached the point where farms could produce as much as was needed. I was born in 1954, ten years after the war had finished, yet rationing of food had only just stopped when I appeared on the scene. All our potatoes and vegetables and some fruit were grown down on the bottom garden. Mums and nans made preserves, jams, pickles, etc. from what could not be eaten. Things you ate then were very fresh indeed and very good for your health.

All this gardening, of course, was hard work – and in the summer my father was usually outside in the garden, digging and planting all the time. He would sweat buckets down there as he double-dug trenches for potatoes and other crops. He used to use this old army battle dress to do all this gardening: he called it his gardening clothes. He wore the trousers out in the end but I still have the top, which is still in good condition. People then didn't have the money to spend on clothes so anything like army issue would be put to general use. Your old clothes became gardening clothes.

Of course my dad would not be alone down in the garden. Many men would be down in their gardens doing exactly the same. Lots of conversations would strike up over the garden fence: there was certainly a social side to gardening, and much gossip would take place during this time. And, of course, gardening meant that quite a lot of waste would be produced: some would be composted and some would be burned on bonfires. It was quite common for someone in the street to start up a fire to burn off some dry old stuff that had heaped up over a season. Washing would need to come in when bonfires started, or we would end up with smoky clothes. I so loved a good bonfire, and any excuse was used to start one up. I think my dad loved them too.

The house was carpeted but carpets were not wall-to-wall in those days. They were really large rugs, and some were threadbare too. Carpets were still a luxury and fitted ones almost unheard of.

Lino was still used in kitchens as a hard surface. Stairs had a strip of carpet running up the middle of the stairs and held in place by stair rods: these were metal rods used to hold the carpet in place, effectively trapping the carpet and keeping it tight. Everything had to last until it was completely worn out because money was very tight.

In the winter one of the fireplaces would be lit in the morning and fed with coal all day. This was the only source of heating in the house during winter, and although the chimney would transfer some heat to the rest of the house it was still basically cold in all the other rooms … therefore in the winter you gravitated to the living room and stayed there, only venturing into the kitchen and up to the loo when you really needed to.

One aspect of the open fire that stays with me even to this day was that during the winter the fire could be used to cook a spud for tea. This – believe it or not – was a real treat for me, and if you have never tasted a baked potato cooked on an open fire then you really have missed out. A sizeable spud would be placed under the fire grate (the place where the ash falls through). The spud would have to be turned two or three times over a period of an hour. At the end of the process you had what looked like a burned black stone. Mum would take a tea towel and wipe the ash off the side of the spud and place it on a plate in front of the fire. Copious amounts of butter and grated cheddar cheese would then be applied to the two hot halves that had now been cut open. It's an unbelievable taste … a crunchy outer shell, and the soft white spud and cheese inside. Pure heaven.

The rest of the house was cold, but you didn't really notice it then because you were used to it. Beds had loads of sheets and blankets on, so once in bed you were as warm as toast. Your nose, though, was maybe freezing as it peeked out of the top.

We loved our house. It was home, for sure – and it had a good feel about it, generally. It's so important to feel that home is home and somewhere safe when growing up. It's only bricks and mortar in reality, but I do feel that a good home has a soul. This one did, for sure. It was a happy house.

Meet the Blackshires

As best as I can I will describe my family so that you have some idea of the people and personalities that made up the family network around me. This chapter is about those who brought me up and a little of their background before I was born. The facts are as accurate as I could obtain, considering that most have now passed on. I am part of a family of four: Mother, Father, and my brother Robert.

Mum

My mother was born on 5 February 1921 and lived in Apsley all her young life. She lived at 54 Weymouth Street – which had been purchased by my great-grandfather Joseph Andrews, a gas fitter by trade. He purchased this double plot in 1894 – Lot 20 on the list – for the tidy sum of £35, for which he tendered just £4 deposit. Joseph was already living at number 29 Weymouth Street and obviously saw a very sound investment here.

The family were aware of a connection to John Bunyan the English Christian writer and preacher, but it was not until my brother performed some extensive research in the sixties using a book authored by a Dr Brown on Bunyan that a more formalised family tree was developed. This was all before the Internet, of course, and records had to be pooled together over a period of time. It would seem that John Bunyan is in fact my eight-times-great-grandfather.

Granny Andrews, Joseph's wife (my great-grandmother) had some extraordinary artefacts from past generations in her family. So important were these items that they were donated to the Bunyan museum in Bedford. I am not a religious man by any means but to have an important famous ancestor as a relation does give one a certain sense of pride.

Mum went to school at Two Waters school in Apsley and left around the age of fourteen. She then worked at Apsley Mills in the card department and eventually came across my father at an evening class at John Dickinson's. Dad made the naffest of chat-up lines you could ever want to imagine,

"It's wintry weather, isn't it?" My future existence was written in the stars from this point on. I have the impression that my dad would walk down to see my mum and date her at the Weymouth Street house. Mum played the piano a bit and I think this was used as a bit of a smokescreen for their courting. Mum's family found my father a bit of a London smoothie – who drank pints of beer, of course – and who had unchristian ways. That said … they liked him, and accepted him wholeheartedly into the family.

Mum got called up at the start of the Second World War and joined the WRAF and, I believe, was stationed in Leighton Buzzard and involved in information from the long-range listening posts sited in that area. She became pregnant with Rob in 1944 and was therefore forced to accept a life living with my father's parents at number 87 Deaconsfield Road. She had Rob there and between Mum, Nan, and Granddad they helped to bring the baby up while my dad was still away in Europe fighting the dreaded Hun.

Around 1957 my mum fell ill. I was only three or four at the time and don't remember anything at all, at least not consciously, although I have been told that subconsciously I took some things on board during those very stressful times.

Mum had a lot on her plate and had been diagnosed at the young age of thirty-six with glaucoma – a nasty disease of the eyes which, unless treated quickly, would render an individual blind. She had to then undergo tests frequently and take eye drops for the rest of her life. In addition to all this she was told soon after the glaucoma diagnosis that she also had breast cancer. The prognosis then for breast cancer was never good and she underwent some really extensive and drastic surgery to remove one breast and the lymph glands under her arm. I remember seeing the scars on her upper arm. They were long and wide and looked more like a stepladder reaching up her arm. The butchery was extensive and there was no cosmetic surgery in those days. She was a long time recovering from this and I do remember drawing pictures for my dad to take into hospital while she was convalescing. I never visited her at all, as visiting was not seen as a priority in any way for children in those days.

She recovered fully from the cancer but a choice sentence from one of the senior nurses at the hospital was going to unsettle her mind for the rest of her life. In an attempt to reassure her this nurse said,

"Although you are cured, Mrs Blackshire, you have to understand that we will be looking after you for the rest of your life." I suspect that at the age of thirty-six this was not really something you want to hear. In actual fact as far as the cancer was concerned it never was an issue and never came back. What did happen was that Mum had a minor mental breakdown and left home one evening without telling anyone. She was found the next morning roaming the grounds of Shendish House an area of landscaped farm land near to Apsley Station.

Rob can't remember much about this either as he was shielded somewhat from the proceedings that had taken place, but he said that there was maybe the first adult conversation that took place between him, Dad, and Granddad to try and understand what had happened. They appeared very worried for her, Rob says. I'm sure my young brain was taking some of this in like a sponge during those awkward times, and for several weeks after this incident Auntie Doreen my Uncle Sid's wife came up from Apsley each day to ensure that we had a good square meal. After all, men were hopeless at cooking – and cooking was deemed to be women's work in those days.

Mum recovered enough to cope on and off after this but she was on medication – mainly antidepressants – from then until she died, aged eighty-six. She became agoraphobic at one point but managed to work through this problem once Dad got a car and they could drive to places. She had a bit of a raw deal all round, really, but she was a tough thing to have survived the cancer like that and to have lived to a ripe old age.

Dad

Dad was born in October 1919 in Acton high street, London. He moved to Hemel at the age of sixteen in 1935. His family must have been one of only a few Londoners who came to Hemel before the development of the New Town. Dad's first job was working for the British Brush Company in Ebberns Road. His dad (my Granddad Charlie) also worked there – and they both befriended a Bill Pickard, who may well have been the manager there at the time, and who helped them establish themselves in the area.

Dad then moved on to work for a company of paper merchants in London called Gidney Rourke. At that time they were situated in Tooley Street. He was not there long before he was called up for active service in the Royal Artillery as part of the start of the Second World War.

Dad landed in Normandy six days after D-Day (D plus six) and progressed through France, Belgium, Holland, and Northern Germany. He passed through Osnabruck and Munster in the Ruhr along the way and ended up in Celle.

Celle is situated near the notorious Bergen-Belsen concentration camp where many thousands of Jews were either gassed or experimented upon. Current estimates put the number of prisoners who passed through the concentration camp during its period of operation from 1943 to 1945 at around 120,000. These included 20,000 Soviet prisoners of war.

Although Dad never went to the camp he did see some survivors along the way in transit. He told us how dreadful it all was with the sight of these poor fellows with sunken eyes.

Rob had already been born at this point and Dad didn't see his first child for some nine months. I do have a letter that my dad sent my mum from Europe about the birth of Rob and how my dad was going to work so hard when he got back to ensure that he had a good life. The letter is very tenderly written and shows what a passionate, kind-hearted individual he was.

When my dad came back and was demobbed from the army he rejoined Gidney Rourke, who were now resited in Southwark Street, London. Dad was what was called then a commercial traveller. These days we would call anyone working in this sector a salesman. Travelling then meant getting on trains and buses and seeing – at the most – one or two customers a day. Most of Dad's day would be spent travelling. He always had a smart suit, a raincoat, a brolly, and a leather case with samples of paper and board inside. To top all this off, on his head was a trilby hat. He looked the proper business man and always had this smart appearance for the whole of his working life. He sported a moustache, which always seemed a mix of salt and pepper even in the early days. In later times there was a tinge of yellow there from all the cigarettes he smoked.

Money was tight, of course, but he still had to look smart for his job. He only had two white work shirts to wear but each would have a set of separate collars. You could then just change your collar on your shirt as it got grubby. You would then wear a vest next to your skin, and it was the vest that took the hit from your body odour. So you changed your vest every day (well, maybe), and your pants, but your shirt had to last you. Baths were, of course, just the once a week affair – and in between times you had what was called a strip-wash in front of the sink. When I look back it all seems slightly backward but it was how it was then and no one knew any differently. You didn't really think people smelled ... maybe because you were used to it. Most people smoked then, and this added to people's odour. Mum and Dad both smoked, and the house constantly had a smell of smoking inside it. We just didn't think anything of it.

On October 8 1952 something terrible happened to my dad. I, of course, was not around (I was yet to be born) but I certainly felt the aftershocks for many a year in my life. Dad had caught the local steam train – the 7.31a.m. from Tring to Euston, a local slow passenger train that would more than likely stop at every station between Apsley and London. It consisted of nine carriages and my dad was in the middle somewhere among the other 800-odd passengers. The train was busier than normal as the last service had been cancelled due, I believe, to heavy fog. The train my dad was on switched over tracks to the fast line just before Harrow and Wealdstone. The train was stationary at Harrow while the guard was checking the last two carriages. Then at 8.15 a.m. my dad's train was struck from behind by the express from Perth travelling at sixty miles per hour. It had passed two semaphore signals set at Danger before colliding. Sixty miles an hour does not seem much these days but steam trains were heavy and the energy within something like a steam train hitting a stationary carriage does not bear thinking about. A second or two after this collision the 8.00 a.m. express to Liverpool from London Euston was passing on the opposite fast line at sixty miles per hour and it derailed in the station. Sixteen carriages were destroyed in all. Thirteen of these were compressed into a space of just forty-five yards.

There were 112 fatalities and a total of 340 people reported injured. My dad walked out of his carriage alive and gave help as best he could to the injured and the dying. I can't imagine the scene that was presented to him that morning. My dad told me that when he came to after the impact he looked around and there was just nothing left of the carriage he was in. It had been sliced in two behind him. His seat escaped being crushed by inches.

Dad returned home at some point. He walked up the path from the station to home, his raincoat splattered in blood from the injured and dead. He had seen the aftermath of the death camps in Germany but what happened that day was, to him, far more horrific and disturbing and it bit hard into the depths of his soul.

He had a few days off – I suspect, with severe shock – but basically he had to continue work after that and that meant he had to get back on the trains and travel. He told me that many a time when he was walking to Apsley station, maybe along the path that took you over the canal, he would have a panic attack and have to hold on to the iron railings by the side of the path and get his composure. He told me that the sound of the express's whistle sounding so loud before it hit was in his head. He could not supress that sound for a long, long time. Dad took medication to get through this. Doctors freely gave out all sorts of mind-bending drugs in those days without any consideration of the consequences that might impact on people.

Although my dad's history seems a bit doom and gloom from the passages above he did have his fun times too, and this shouldn't be forgotten. Dad was a well-liked man. He always had a story to tell – and had lots of friends in the street and down at the Boot, the pub he frequented. He never really moaned too much about anything and always tried to keep a happy face on when times were tough. He used to say to me that he treated every day as if it was Christmas Day, which is something I try to do to this very day myself.

Rob

My brother Rob was born in 1944, ten years before me. There being ten years difference between us was quite a noticeable gap. I kind of had a brother to play with but he was mostly too old for some of the games I wanted to play. He lived at Nan's in Deaconsfield Road with Mum and Dad till he was eight years old. There was no TV then for him and no books, either. You had to be very self-sufficient as a child then and find what you could to occupy your mind. Rob suffered with quite a bit of childhood illness and struggled to keep up with his schoolwork.

At that time, while living with Nana and Granddad, the school he attended was the notorious Corner Hall. Rob said that the teachers there were very stern and I suspect really old-school compared to today's teachers. Things improved for him once he moved away to Lower Barn, aged eight. The attitude at Belswains School was very different from that at Corner Hall and he began to thrive in this new school, which still smelled of fresh paint when he started there.

My recollections of Rob as a child were that he always seemed to be shut in the dining room studying, with the door shut. I was never allowed in but I would poke the odd message to him under the door. He seemed to study non-stop in the evenings and weekends but he did take some time out to enjoy his passion for bike riding. From the age of nine he rode all over the place with the aid of one of those old cloth OS maps to Chipperfield, Flaunden, Bovingdon, and even out to Leighton Buzzard. It was all safe then ... nothing to worry about. You could let your children just play out anywhere with the knowledge that your kids were safe. Let's also remember that there were no mobile phones either for contacting parents and friends if your children did get into danger. But nobody worried then.

Rob did well at school and progressed to Apsley Grammar School where he also did well, but always had to work hard for it.

He finally gained a place at Nottingham University to study chemistry was the option he took and then he had a number of jobs in research.

He met his Scottish wife Agnes on a holiday to Spain and after a brief spell living in Hemel they moved to Leighton Buzzard.

Granddad Charlie

All of us in the family have a certain fondness for Granddad Blackshire. He was a lovely, lively big guy with a great sense of humour and the ability to take the mickey without causing offence. To me he was always a larger-than-life character and fun to be with as a child. In his early days he managed a grocer's shop in the high street, Acton and it was from there that during the First World War he joined the Royal Inniskilling Fusiliers on the front line.

You see films and read accounts of what it was like then in the trenches of this "war to end all wars". I still can't imagine what it really could have been like for him then. By all accounts he kept most of it to himself and it was only later (a long period of time after his passing away) that by chance I found out some information about his time in the trenches.

Granddad and my dad would have a bit of a tussle sometimes about who fought in the worst war. Granddad would wind Dad up by saying that the Second World War was just a walk in the park compared to the first, and so the conversation would go on. He said it wasn't a proper war at all, and my dad was always trying to prove him wrong on many points. As a child I don't remember him actually giving out any real detail about his experiences. He was a proud man and I think he wanted to take whatever happened to the grave with him.

What we did know had happened was that he had been gassed by the mustard gas the Germans used and then was captured by Jerry (as he described the Germans) in France. He was sent to a labour camp to work down an iron mine. You see films made about the Second World War prisoner of war camps like *The Great Escape* and wonder how these compared to what my Granddad experienced. Hollywood seems to glamorise these things and in actual fact I suspect none of it was like the portrayal on the silver screen. I suspect that reality was a lot harsher than that portrayed in these films.

The Internet makes it an easy job to inspect records of birth, deaths, and marriages. I was enjoying myself on one of the paid-for sites that deals in such records and I could easily inspect registers and certificates from past family members. I then noticed that the website I was using also had an area to search for possible war records and it was just a simple task to put in the name Blackshire and press a button. I didn't expect anything, to be honest, but what came up astonished me. There was a record for Granddad.

"What could this be?" I thought. It was clearly to do with him. I think I had to pay an amount to see a PDF version of this record from the national archives. What I then had in my hands were two documents. One was an account: it was a report my Granddad had had to make when the prison camp was finally relieved. It was in his words as to what took place there … the conditions and the beatings that took place. All this was in his own words and none of this had been seen by the family until I discovered it.

Here is a small snippet of what I read of Granddads report in his own chilling words :

"I was sent to Munster where I arrived about a week or 10 days after my capture. I was sent to Metz on the 9th June. The mine there is called the Moutiers Mine. The work was filling wagons; we were about 100 British, a small number of Italians and two or three hundred Russians. The work was very hard. At first each shift did 8 wagons a day then it got to 12 wagons and then 16. If at the end of the shift our total waggons filled was 14 instead of 16 the next morning we would be punished. The punishment was to stand by the wire facing it, standing to attention and not allowed to move for 2 hours. Sometimes we had to hold a bowl of soup in our hands for 2 hours. We were hungry but not allowed to eat it. Sometimes we were shut in a dark room for the whole night."

"I was under a man named Patlos. He was a German subject, a civilian, a very big man, employed there to see the work was done. If we were in Patlos shift and incurred his displeasure he would line us up and call out each man's name and beat us with a piece of solid india-rubber. Formally he had used a hammer for testing wheels but broke so large a number of them on men's shoulders that he took to using the piece of rubber."

"On one occasion Patlos was knocking me about with such violence that my lamp went out and I stumbled and fell. Then he struck me once or twice on my face before I was able to roll over and protect it. As a matter of fact I had done our full number of wagons the day before but as often happened, a couple were stolen by removing our chalk numbers and substituting another. We were credited with 14 instead of 16."

Another prisoner at the camp; A Rifleman A Launder No 593058 writes in his report –

"I should like to mention the case of Charles Blackshire. I saw this man bought up from the mine on one occasion; his face was so bruised it was impossible to recognise him owing to the thrashing which he received from Patlos."

Regarding past atrocities, I sometimes think that our existence potentially hangs in the balance. If Granddad had died in that camp – and it was very likely that he might have – then this book and I would never have been. It's very chilling to think about this even now.

Granddad remained at the rank of private throughout this campaign, refusing to take any promotion. He was offered it but declined. He always maintained that it was a far safer option since enemy snipers would always take out the first or last man in a column of marching men, recognising these as either officers or NCOs. He would also never take the third light from a match to light his fags – saying that the rule in the trenches was that at the first lighting of the cigarette the sniper would take notice, on the second lighting of the second fag the sniper would take aim, and on the third lighting the third man would be shot. Superstitious, maybe, but Granddad lived well into his eighties.

The bravery of this man didn't stop there. When a world war broke out for a second time he was too old to join up and fight so he joined the fire brigade at Hemel Hempstead, and for a large period of time was senior officer at the Apsley substation. Some of his duties during the war took him to Cambridge to fight fires there. He remained in the fire service for some twelve years in total until just before I was born. In my life I knew him as a greengrocer and he worked at the grocery store along at the parade of shops at the top of The Marlowes. Stainforth was the name, and I often went in there to see him working.

To me he is a hero: a true hero who fought against the most awful atrocities humanity can throw at you. He was the best Granddad you could ask for.

Nan Dorothy (Doll)

Nanny Blackshire was a lovely lady, short and always a little overweight but she had a heart of gold. She had a certain way about her in as far as she had come from quite humble beginnings but liked to think and show she was a cut above her peers. It wasn't anything nasty, mind you, just some mild snobbery here and there. They lived in in Deaconsfield road all the time I knew them … but never really let on to anyone that they didn't own the house, but rented it. It gave Nan some satisfaction to think that others didn't know this. She was a dab hand at cards and enjoyed many a round of cards with the family while smoking her Player's Weights cigarettes.

Nan took in some children during the war. One was a London lad – the boy's name was Gerald – and another time she had a family from the Smoke. She actually put the whole family up for a while but in the end the adults went back to tend to their business, leaving the boy with Nan till it became safe in London again.

During the war Nan worked down at John Dickinson's in the munitions section. She crafted the papier mâché auxiliary fuel tanks for the RAF. These tanks could be attached to aircraft, filled with fuel, and then jettisoned when spent. She never worked after the war. She retired and tended their extensive garden in Deaconsfield.

Nan was about the kindest nan you could ever have. She was always there for you with a smile and some reassurance. She passed away in later life in her eighties while resident at the William Crook House in Warners End.

Nanny Brandom (Nan)

My other nan on my mother's side was a different nan entirely from my father's mother. Nanny Brandom was a much more serious character indeed. She was kind and loving in her own way but she was not someone who might endear herself to a young boy. It's a great shame because her husband (my other Granddad) died before I was born. I never knew him but guessed from what people said that he would have been a great person to know. So this nan lived in the house in Weymouth Street along with her son – my Uncle Sid – and his wife Auntie Doreen and their two children, Paul and Teresa.

Nan would come up to our house every other Sunday for dinner and I was always expected to entertain her by playing cards. It's not like I didn't like playing cards, because I did. It's just that playing with Nan was a bit uncool and I would have rather been outside with me mates.

Sometimes Nan would babysit for my parents if they went out down the pub. I would be left with Nan in Weymouth Street for the evening. It was not so bad, usually, as Nan had a TV set that had ITV on it and a shove-halfpenny board game. She also liked a drink called Sanatogen Tonic Wine. This wine was labelled as a tonic wine and the excuse was given that this wine had special medicinal properties. I believed that Nan had to have this wine as it was good for her and kept her well. She also used to give me a very small amount of this tonic wine when I visited her. How nice it tasted, and this was a real treat for me. I knew the wine was doing Nan some good as the colour – a nice rosy red – would return to her cheeks, and she seemed jollier on this medication. Of course now I realise that this wine has alcohol in it, and the company doesn't state that the wine has any medicinal qualities at all.

Nan was a good sort, really, but she didn't take centre stage in my life as a boy. That role was given to my other nan and granddad, who were to me at times like second parents.

On reflection

Something that occurred to me on reflection of those times and adds to uniqueness of this period. Almost everyone over the age of say 40 would have served in the armed forces in some capacity. A good percentage of those would have seen front line action. Some would have killed or seen others killed. Every grown up man and woman you passed on the streets was potentially battle scared in some way. There certainly hasn't been a generation since that has grown up among so many ordinary people who have also fought for their country. The war had a huge impact on folk and it took quite a time before people stopped talking about it.

Playing Outside

1958

My first recollections of playing outside in the street are a bit vague. As soon as I could walk I was allowed to walk up the garden path to the gate at the top, and I'd been able to do that for some time at the time of this story. The front garden had a low wall and I was trapped in, so to speak. I could walk up and walk back down as many times as I liked. I would have been about four years old and at preschool, exercising my legs and growing stronger every day.

I was encouraged to be out as it was seen as healthy to be out as much as possible. If my parents were gardening then I would be out there messing about among the plants pulling up things that maybe I should not have been.

One day when I was doing my toing and froing up the path, two faces peered at me through the garden gate. One was taller than the other and much older than the smaller one. I was mesmerised, to say the least. I had had no interaction with anyone my age till now … no nursery for me: my parents did try and get me in somewhere but to no avail. I suspect that the baby boom meant that nursery places were scarce. This was like the first contact between man and something else. For a start, I didn't know what to do. I was frightened in a way but curious – very curious to know who these boys were. They spoke to me to come to the gate. I did as I was told. It was not an order at all but more of a friendly way of saying,

"Hey … come and join us. We are fun." I can't remember the exact dialogue here but I know they told me that they lived a few doors down. They were brothers, and they were allowed to play in the street. They wanted me to open the gate and join them. I didn't. I could hear my parents' warning,

"Don't go outside the garden. Ever." My father was quite firm with the rules and I always (well, nearly always) took on board what he said. His stern words were enough in those days. My father would always end one of his rulings with the statement that if I didn't do whatever it was I would die. It was never that you might injure yourself or you might get knocked over. It was always

"You will die if you do that." That was usually enough to stop me wandering.

Our conversation ended and the boys left to carry on their play outside the fortification that was 18 Lower Barn. This first contact was important for me: it established life outside the garden, and I wanted a piece of the action. It didn't take long ... days ... maybe a week or so, and I was outside the gate – with my father's permission, of course. The death curfew had been lifted and a new one put in its place. "You can now go outside the garden, but if you go outside the street, you will die". I had friends now in the street, and I had taken those first steps into another world. It felt liberating, and the world just got a whole lot bigger and hugely more complicated. Meeting people when you are a child is of course an important part of development ... but, boy, why is it so damn complicated?

Pete and John were my first friends in the street. They lived further down the road and they had an older sister, with a younger one to come quite soon. I suspect the approach to knocking for your friends may have changed a bit since the sixties. In those days you went to a friend's door and you knocked on it. We had no doorbells then: each door had a knocker to make a loud clacking sound. Someone would almost always come to the door – either your friend or one of the parents or siblings. If it was you friend it was self-explanatory. If it was the parent you would say,

"Is XYZ coming out to play, please?" You would either get fobbed off with,

"He/she's having dinner or is busy," etc.. Or you might be asked to come in and wait. Going around to your mate's house was a hit-and-miss thing ... no mobile phones here for asking in advance. In fact no one really had a phone, anyway. The only way you knew if your friend was available was to walk around and ask.

If it was sunny we would spend all day out in the street, playing. Only mealtimes would interrupt the fun, and even then meals would be taken as quickly as possible so as not to miss any of the fun with your mates. Sometimes I would be munching down my grub at the dinner table and watching my mates playing outside, shoving food down like there was no tomorrow. Winter was a different situation: while you might still wrap up and go out you might not be so inclined to go out if it was raining hard. Light rain never put us off and the cold would never deter us. We were hardened little buggers and we had no reason to stay inside the house. All the fun was outside with your mates.

I can't say that we were engrossed in play all the time. There were periods when we sat about trying to think of what we might do. This generally led to some trouble somewhere along the line. At other times we knew exactly what we wanted to do and spent all day doing it.

In those early days, when I was four going on five, play consisted on me riding up and down the street pavement on my little three-wheeler tricycle.

The street was free from worry, as far as parents were concerned. It would be a highlight of the day if a car drove along the road. If one did it was probably a tradesman of some sort. Out of all the twenty-four houses in the street there were probably only four or five houses that had a car. This gradually increased as time went on but in the late fifties to early sixties people were still finding their feet from the war days. We didn't have a car until my brother purchased a Morris Minor in the early sixties. Even then not many had a car, and my father certainly didn't have one until the late sixties.

Therefore in those early days of playing outside there was no real danger. The road was clear and, when you look at pictures of that time, it all looked incredibly clean and tidy. It's surprising how cars parked on roads makes a road look messy. The area of play was just the street at this time. I was not allowed to go further. I guess that the threat of death was pushed out to encompass outside the road by my father was enough.

Time marched on and once I had reached school age things begin to change a bit. I suppose once you start school you feel independent of your mother and father. I was five when I started at the infant school and with the independence of being able to walk to school I could also do other things too.

Playing in the street progressed to a hierarchy where certain groups of kids would play with certain other kids. This was generally based around age. There was, however, something else that divided up how we played. It was not until some years later that I realised the road had a north-south divide, in that one side of the road didn't mix well with the other. In fact this was so apparent from the ages of about six to ten that a war existed between the kids in the even-numbered houses and the kids in the odd-numbered houses.

This war raged on for years. Sometimes it would subside to peace and tranquillity, and at other times it would be gang warfare – but on a very small scale, of course. We were small kids, after all. It's difficult to understand why this happened or even if this was normal within other roads. We kids in the even numbers just didn't get on with the kids in the odd numbers. The time when it was worst was during holiday times where we kids just had loads of free time to do just about anything we wanted, and we bloody well did as well. We got bored and when you're stuck for things to do you tend to get into trouble, and trouble was something that came easily to most of us then.

Meet the Gang
1958-1966

Our gang consisted of four or five kids at any one time. The two brothers Pete and John, my friend Baz (from when he arrived on the street at about the age of seven), and a young girl (Jenny) who lived midway along the road. Anyone else might join at odd times but we were the core, and we would sit and plan our attacks on the odd numbers.

It's not like we really meant any real harm, but we felt we needed to rule the road. As a gang we would play, and our play was usually about getting up to no good. One aspect of this play revolved around fire. We were so preoccupied with lighting fires at that time that it

40

was like an obsession. This was basically because it was not allowed and seen as dangerous by grownups.

The problem we had was that you just couldn't go to Scott's the newsagents and ask for a box of matches. There is no way you would ever have wanted to go there to test out the wrath of Scotty. Besides not selling them to you he would probably have told your parents.

However, there was another way to obtain matches. For those kids who had parents who smoked cigarettes – and that was nearly all of them in those days – it was easy. All you needed to do was to sneak indoors and steal a couple of matches from the main matchbox. No one would miss those, or would they? Actually having something to strike to light the matches with was not an issue. The pavements were so littered with cigarette packets and other stuff that you could easily just find an empty matchbox laying in the street.

Once you had come out of your house holding up the possible magic for making fire you were king. You were brave and you were the boss. Kids would jump around for joy just at the sight of fire sticks in your hands and the possibilities this might lead to. It was the rawness of humanity coming through. We were like cavemen getting excited at the prospect of heat and light. They say that the only thing that distinguishes us from other animals is the ability to make fire.

So where would one go? Well ... the end of the street had plenty of cover and bushes, and if you went further down the path along by the side of house number twenty-four the bushes were thick, and the back of the communal garages cut you off from sight. Lighting a fire was a big deal but you had to get it right. Getting found out could be disastrous. Striking the matches and not getting fire was a disaster too, and your reign as king would end rapidly.

As already mentioned, there was plenty of litter around to use. Paper and card were not difficult to simply find in the street and some dry wood in the bushes would help. A small pile would be assembled and all the kids would gather around ... the gang, mainly, but sometimes some of the youngsters would be there too – and they

41

would have to swear on the pain of death not to say a word. They never did. By the way, the threat of the pain of death always works.

The fire-starter would be the one who owned the matches. Paper would be lit and then other things piled on until a small fire was going. Flames were good … smoke, less so. Smoke would find you out. Someone might be appointed lookout and be half in, half out of the bushes. Any noise from possible walkers on the path might instigate a furious flurry of stamping on the fire to put it out. The lookout would shout,

"Someone's coming," and everyone would know what to do. We would perform a dance on the fire to extinguish it as quickly as possible, as acted out like some Native American war dance. Even the little ones learned how to do this and joined in the stomping. As soon as the danger passed then another fire would be lit. The issue was always getting the matches and although I could get a few out of the house I didn't have an endless supply, and it did matter where the matches were stored in the house.

Baz came from a house where no one smoked but matches were used to light the fire and cooker. The problem Baz had was that his parents almost counted those matches, and if he took too many then he would really be in for it. Time and again his sister, who was a few years younger, would come trotting over to us and gleefully say,

"Barry, Mum wants you." This always meant that Baz would indeed be going off home to be told off and we would not be seeing him for the rest of the day, and maybe also for the next few. I always got the impression that someone in that family was acting as a spy, and it never took too much working out as to who that individual might have been. I always wonder now how we didn't get found out more often, as we must have all come back home from playing outside stinking of smoke. Maybe as we lived in houses with coal fires this was undetectable. We clearly must have stunk.

One day Pete and John came and knocked for me and said they had something to show me. We raced around to their house and into their back garden, where a small hole was evident in the ground.

Like all the houses in the street the back gardens ran parallel to each other and were separated by a chain-link metal fence. You could always see next door through these fences. There was no privacy here.

"Wow," I exclaimed. "How did you make that?"

"With these," was the answer, and each of them pulled a shiny penknife from their pockets. I stood there open-mouthed. They then proceeded to open the blades on each knife and started to dig further. It was unknown why the digging was taking place, but just the fact that they had knives and could dig was making my head spin. They let me have a go but then informed me that if I wanted to be in their gang I needed to get a penknife.

"Oh," I said. "But I can use yours, can't I?"

"No," said John. "You have to have your own knife if you're to be in the gang. That's how it works."

Well, I don't know how many sleepless nights I had thinking about the knife. I would have to ask my parents about having one. This was a big issue. I was frightened to broach the subject and feel the disappointment that I would most certainly get when Dad started on about knives, the war, and – most certainly – death. Scott's sold the penknives and they cost about two shillings. That was quite a bit of money then, and not something I would have had in my piggy bank. I had seen the knives before in a display case by the door of the tobacconist, and I almost coveted them as I passed by them each time. It's a boy's thing, of course, and if you're not a boy you probably wouldn't understand this passion for pointed sharp things. I can visualise them now sitting there waiting for young boys to own them.

I had to ask Mum first. She would be the soft touch. I really almost felt sick before asking her. I so wanted a penknife … and I so expected disappointment. But I asked, and of course the answer came back that Dad would decide. So when Dad came back from work the subject came up and I filled in the gaps. He wanted to know what I wanted it for and I said,

"Digging and sharpening sticks." Dad said,

"Yes ... OK." Wow ... was I pleased? It was like a huge rock had been lifted from my chest. The very next day I was pulling my mum up to the four to Scott's. As kids we nicknamed these local shops the four, as in,

"Are you going up the four today to get some sweets?"

Although the newsagents was named Scott's across the top of the front of the shop. The manager of the shop wasn't actually called Mr Scott. We as kids always thought he was of course and so in this book he is affectionately known as Mr Scott.

Old Scott's eyes blazed as my mum told him that her son would like to look at the knives in the widow. He looked at me with one of his narrow-eyed stares. He knew something. It was as if he was thinking,

"Are you mad woman, are you really going to give this boy such a sharp thing?"

My stomach was churning. I wanted the knife as quickly as possible and to get out of the shop, away from Scott's laser stare. There was a blue one or a brown one for sale. I chose the brown one and my mum paid and I left the shop quickly. I was given some stern advice later by my father about how to open the knife and close it. This was in fact good advice, as the single blade on that knife was extremely sharp. The knife always fascinated me as it was made by a company called Richards from Sheffield and there was a little picture of a lamp post on the blade.

The next day I went back around to see Pete and John. They looked at me with knowing eyes.

"Well ... have you got it?"

"Yes," I said, and showed them the new penknife ... the same design as theirs but in a different colour.

"You're in," they said. And I was taken to the hole to start digging.

One has to understand that when we talk about knives in those days there were never any thoughts of these things being used as weapons. It was unheard of among young boys. It just was never an

44

issue. Boys carried knives about as a tool, either for camping or for just making things out of wood. Along with a hankie, some copper coins, the odd Bazooka Joe bubblegum, and a few airgun pellets, there was always the knife. It was part of how we were.

I never really had a problem with the penknife. It served me well and I always had respect for its blade. Of course all that digging soon blunted the blade and I then I had to resort to trying to sharpen it on our brick wall. It never was as sharp again as that day it came out the cabinet but sharp enough to cut sticks and things – and then, of course, it would also suffice for a game of Stretch.

I have no idea where the game Stretch came from. It could well have been dreamed up by my friend Baz – who would, I'm sure, agree that he always won. For Stretch you need a lawn or grass area, a penknife each and some good shoes. You face each other on the grass with maybe a foot or two between your toes. One person would then attempt to throw the knife into the ground a short distance to the side. If the knife didn't stick in then your go was over. If it did stick into the mud then your opponent had to move one foot over to where the knife had landed – in other words, stretching out one foot from the original position. Then it was that person's go and they might be able to land their knife a bit further out. The game would continue till – of course – you could not stretch any further and you probably fell backwards in a heap on the ground. Being a small lad with short legs and a blunt knife, guess who didn't win at Stretch?

The penknife was always in my pocket and it served me well until the countless games of Stretch and the sharpening of sticks made the rivets loose and a danger to use. It was replaced several times over a period of time. I still to this day own a knife, albeit a Swiss Army one. Anyone fancy a game of Stretch?

In the bushes we made what we called our camps. It was the easiest way to be out of sight of grown-ups and for us to make our plans. We had bushes at the end of the street and also a small wooded area a short distance away called the dell. The dell, from what I can find out, was in fact – way back in time – an opencast mining pit for chalk. It had a low-level chalk face and was surrounded by trees and bushes. There was lots of cover here to make camp and play at whatever you wanted. We spent many a time here in the deeper bushes either lighting fires or sharpening sticks or making things that could be thrown. In those days you had to entertain yourself and, although you had some toys and books at home, the outdoors was always the pull for us kids. We found things to do: games or making things … whatever we wanted. Yes, OK … some of it was sometimes a bit naughty, but by and large we were good kids. We had a respect for things around us. Well, nearly all the time.

Throwing things was always a bit of a game. Throwing things at tin cans or just throwing stones at objects could be fun. Sometimes it was seeing if you could hit an object or maybe we would see who could throw the furthest. These were all games in a way but one of the games we played at was a bit rougher than some of our parents would have liked. War was war and we needed things to throw at the odd numbers in the street. Stones were an option and were readily used and plucked from the gardens to use.

This all worked quite well but we always thought that there could be something better to use – something more like a real bomb going off that had a cloud of smoke or something like that. The gang – four boys and one girl – sat one evening on the pavement outside my house, all deep in thought about what we could use. As we sat and played with the contents of the pavement one person said,

"What about this stuff?" and handed out a handful of grit dust that made up the hard-standing between road and pavement. There was indeed a lot of it about, both just loose on the ground and formed into piles in places where the rain had swept it.

"Try it," said one of the lads. With a handful in his hand Pete hurled the contents down the street as far as he could and managed to nearly blind us all with the grit dust as it blew back.

"Oh, bloody thanks," said Baz, spitting out grey spit on to the pavement. We were all covered.

"That's no good," I hollered. "We can't throw that. It's not going anywhere apart from over us."

Dusting ourselves down, we returned to the pavement to talk some more. Sulking, and dejected by our attempts, we stayed in near silence until the young girl in her pretty dress piped up,

"What about this?"

We all looked at her in astonishment. The girl was holding up an old discarded ice lolly wrapper. These were numerous and were everywhere along the street, wind-blown into every crevice and corner. There were loads of these: they were just dropped after the ice cream man had been. Baz took the wrapper. He knew exactly what the girl was suggesting. He filled the little disused ice bag with grit and dust.

"Not too full," I said. "It needs to be sealed."

"OK … about half, then," said Baz. He then twisted the top to seal the contents into the bag.

"Great," we cheered. "What should we call it?:

"A grit grenade," I said. "It's a grit grenade."

"Try it out, Baz," said one of the others. So Baz, who was our best thrower, launched the grit grenade down the road on its practice run. Thrrrrup… It landed some thirty yards away, still in one piece. You could hear the moans as we realised our attempts had failed. Those bags were tough. I suppose they had to be for the contents they once held.

"I know," I said swiftly. "I think I know how this will work. You know, on the films … like when the British are fighting the Germans and they use a grenade. They pull the pin out first, don't they?"

"Yes," said one of the younger gang members, "But our grit grenade doesn't have a pin, does it?"

"No," I said, "It doesn't … but we can improvise. Bring the grenade back and we can have another go with it…"

"OK," I said. "Baz, take the grenade." Ready to throw it, Baz took the grenade. "Baz, stick your thumb into the bag, like. Jab it."

Baz did as he was told and made a small split in the Tonibell Orange Mivvi bag.

"OK … throw it, Baz. Throw it really high." Baz threw it high and we all looked in astonishment as a cloud of dust seeped out in a trail. Like a Brocks rocket it arced and then hit the ground, this time expelling all its contents like a bomb exploding.

"Hooray," we shouted. "It's worked! It's worked!'

"We need to keep this under wraps," said John. "This is our secret weapon."

"Yes," I said. "No one says a word, OK? And now all we need are some victims."

Well … it wasn't long, before a victim arrived. By the next day we had made a number of grit grenades and had hidden them along the road in certain strategic places where we could quickly get to them in people's gardens, in bushes, and down drains. You name it: we had our secret weapon stash ready there. Soon there was some conflict one evening: not from the odd numbers this time. No, this was from outside our world. The ginger-headed lad from around the corner had had the misfortune to actually think he could ride his bike down our road.

The audacity of it … he didn't get far before he realised that he had overstepped the mark and as he turned, realising his mistake, I shouted to Baz to arm the grit grenade.

"Arm the grit grenade, Baz," I shouted so that our bike-riding target could clearly understand the situation he was now in. Baz moved swiftly: he pulled a grenade out of a hole in the pavement where the gas mains shut-off tap was hidden. With one swift movement he had primed the bomb with his thumb and was launching it at Ginger.

Ginger was peddling like billy-o at this point, with his bottom clearly off the saddle. Hearing the words about the grenade and Baz arming it were clearly enough to turn him into some sort of Olympic cyclist. He could not, however, outpace the secret weapon and the velocity Baz could throw it at.

Pwhaaam. It hit the brake bar that you pulled under the handle bars to stop the bike. You could hear its impact. It actually split the Strawberry Mivvi bag in two, much to our delight, as a cloud of dust enveloped old Ginger. We heard him yell out and pedal faster. We cheered and hooted for ages. Ginger sped off and was not seen again for some time to come. What a triumph it had been.

The weapon had worked and we had scored a point for the road. It would be a few years before Ginger would get his own back on Baz. He did, of course. We were much older and the situation would be different and the tables would be turned.

Summer holiday times were a really good time to play out and have some fun … six or seven weeks of sheer delight with school a distant memory after the first few days. I would relish those weeks and lie in bed counting how many days had gone and how many were left. The start of the next term seemed a long time off and we made the most of playing anywhere we could get to. With school out all the kids would be outside, and in between our battles of war with the odd numbers there would be some times of peace where we would play in a more friendly way.

Having time on our hands meant that we would often get up to no good, but we had some games that we would play in the street – and these were well organised and structured and fun, of course. I have no idea where these games came from. I guess that they are just handed down over the years from elder brothers and sisters. Some had names and some didn't.

Ting Tang Tommy was a hide-and-seek game where one person would face the lamp post at the end of the street and count slowly – say – to fifty. We would all run and hide. The idea here was that the hiders had to get to the lamp post and touch it before the seeker could also touch the lamp post and say out loud,

"Ting Tang Tommy … I see XYZ running towards me." Of course the seeker could not find people unless he left the lamp post to search for them. So as he moved out in search of them in one direction maybe someone behind him could make the dash. If he was away from the post and saw you he could do nothing and you were safe.

Another game was Peep Behind the Curtain One, Two, Three. This was a game where you all lined up facing a catcher, who was facing you to start with. The catcher would then face away from you and say the words,

"Peep behind the curtain … one, two, three," out loud. These words could be said slowly or fast, or a mixture. The idea was that you didn't quite know when the catcher would finish the sentence and turn their head. The idea was to move towards the catcher while the words were being spoken. If the catcher had finished the phrase and turned and spotted you moving then you were out. You stood like statues until the catcher faced away again to repeat the process. If you wobbled and were seen you were out. The idea was that one person would eventually get to touch the catcher's back before they could finish the phrase. Then that person became the catcher.

One game – which was just odd, to be honest – was another where we lined up facing a single person, the caller, who was maybe twenty yards away. The caller shouted out commands or codes so that the designated person could move towards them. Some examples of these might be,

"Baz … do one lamp post, four pigeon steps, two fairy steps, and a watering can." Baz would then do all of these. First he would lie down flat towards the person shouting the commands and place his hand where the top of his head was. Then he would move his position to that place. That was the lamp post done. Then he would do the prescribed pigeon steps – which were extremely small steps – followed by the fairy ones, which were a little longer. Then Baz would do the watering can. This was something to behold. You held your arm back in a loop as if it were like a teapot handle and you held the other arm out like a spout. Then you spat as far as you could. You would then move where your spit landed. That would then be your moves completed.

The next person would then be given – say – ten pigeon steps and a helicopter. The person after that might be given just one command: the blind man's buff, where you – as the opponent – ran towards the caller and the caller ran towards you. Both of you had your arms interlinked in front and you bumped into each other at some midway point, so that's where your new position would be. A strange game indeed – and, really, the caller had full power over who would win – but it was a bit of fun and we liked the spitting. That was fun. Sometimes you could hit the caller if you were close enough and they were stupid enough to call out "Watering can," in spitting range. Baz actually was not a good spitter. He never could get the hang of it, and although he could throw anything miles he certainly could not outspit me. I was the king of the spitters.

Other games in the street included the usual things kids played. Hopscotch was something the girls liked to play and because there were plenty of chalk bits in the garden you could easily mark up some of the pavement flagstones with borders and numbers. I can't remember ever playing this as it was typically a girl's game, and some girls would play this on their own.

Kicking a ball about was something that we might try from time to time but we would usually get told off at some point after it had either hit a car or gone in someone's garden. There were a few people along the street who would not give balls back at all. They would retain them and stop us kids from playing again.

Another pastime we would perform was to traverse the length of the road via the low brick walls that stretched from one end to the other and formed the boundary between each house and the pavement. The only interruption was the garden gates, which would be leapt over. The wall was only a couple of feet high and its width was that of a house brick, so you had to have good balance and not fall off. If you fell off then you had to start again from the beginning. Some grown-ups would thump on the windows and say,

"Get off my bloody wall…" You didn't actually hear this. All you saw was a red face and the words mouthed out. We took no notice, of course, and continued our trek to the end of the road. If they came out of their house then it would be time to leg it.

We played marbles on the pavement a few times. One area at the end of the road had some good places to play, with some cracks and unevenness. A few paving slabs stretched on to the playing field and we sat cross-legged at each end, firing marbles at each other. Areas of the pavement were given names: for example, one that might entrap your marble was called Dingly Dell. Baz was good at making up names for things. He seemed to have a passion for it. He called me Titch for ages until the name Dick was adopted later on when someone heard my Uncle Sid say it. It seems in those days that most kids had nicknames and you had to put up with whatever name you were called.

Bush Camp
1961-1964

One of the activities we liked to perform in the summer was nettle bashing. There were bushes running along the path at my end of the road, and among these were the dreaded stinging nettles which grew through the summer. We hated nettles with a vengeance. They often stung our legs and arms. Being in short trousers most of the time didn't help matters – and playing in bushes certainly didn't, either. These weeds needed to be punished, and we would really take great delight in bashing them to bits. First we would find a suitable shrub in the bushes that would have some nice long flexible woody stems protruding out. There were plenty of these available, but to this day I have no idea what they might be called. We called them whippy sticks, and these would be cut out using our penknives. We might then improve (in our minds) the sticks in some way by whittling points on to them or stripping off the outer covering. This served no purpose whatsoever but it looked good to us. We then swiped at the nettles and thrashed them in some strange furious whirling dervish way. Large areas would be decimated and flattened and patches would then be trampled to make sure there was no chance of regrowth, at least not for a while. Then when you had done you could sit in your camp and admire your work sting-free.

Making camp was important. It was not so much how you went about it: it was more about owning an area for your gang. Camp was always in thick bushes, and it was always hidden from the eyes of our parents. It seemed important to us that some of our play at least was private and concealed. Sometimes it was naughty play and other times we would just sit in a circle on the ground, chew some grass, and discuss the world as we knew it. Our world then was very small indeed. We might make plans or we might just relax, but it was a special time to all be together and to bond. Camp was almost always a summertime thing: it was only really feasible to do this when the bushes were in full bloom. Camp had one entrance so we could not be surprised by other gangs. It was cleared of any dog poo, which was in abundance then.

Of course the bushes were used for other things too … things us kids didn't really understand at all. We sometimes came across a condom in among the bushes. We had no idea what these were, but instinctively we kind of knew they were dirty and should not be touched or talked about. Someone would find a stick and flick it away, usually exclaiming "Yuck…" as they did it. The other item that was found from time to time was the dirty magazine. Again, we didn't really understand much about this – but we knew books like this were something to keep hidden, as they were naughty. We had no idea why these books were in bushes, either, but it gave us great delight to flick through the pages and look at the images of almost-naked ladies in undies. In those days about the most risqué thing you would see in a magazine like this was a pair of women's breasts. Everything else was either blurred out or covered up. There were certainly no images of men and nothing that gave any inference to a sexual act. It was just women's breasts – which we all thought were funny – and we giggled away at these objects of delight until someone shouted,

"Someone's coming. Quick, put it away…"

The Trolley
1964-1965
A huge passion during the ages of around seven to ten was the trolley. This was a handmade go-kart that you could use to run along the street with, or run it down hills. The trolley was a simple affair: a plank of wood with a hole bored in the middle at the front end. This then had a bolt put through to hold a cross member piece of four-by-two. The bolt allowed the wooden four-by-two to pivot when you sat on the plank, which was long enough to allow you to put your feet on the cross member.

Then one set of pram wheels was needed – ideally, larger wheels on the back and some smaller – say – pushchair wheels on the front. The wheels would already be on an axle and would simply be attached to the cross member by bashing nails around the axle to fix it to the four-by-two wood cross member. The whole thing was a lash-up, but it worked. Interestingly, the hole to be bored through the plank and the cross member had a largish diameter – larger than my dad's hand drill could create. So the only way for my dad to make this hole bigger was to heat a metal fire poker up on the gas stove and then burn a hole through the wood. You would immediately think by comparison with today about popping down to B&Q and getting a drill bit. But none of that was available then. You had to improvise, and use what you had.

The carts or trolleys as they were more fondly known had a string to attach to the cross member to aid steering and to also give you something to hold on to. The idea was that someone would sit on the back with their back against yours and they would push with their feet on the ground to push you along. That was all well and good on the flat, but it was much more exciting to go down a hill.

Fortunately the path running down at our end of the road sloped enough for us to ride quite fast and then perform a ninety-degree turn into the road. You could pick up some speed here and you hung on for grim death as you accelerated around the ninety-degree turn. Sometimes people came off and invariably the whole cart rolled over. There were grazed knees and ripped trousers and there was often crying if you carried a younger person on the back and they had been flung out. It was fun all the same. We took the knocks, and our arms and legs were always bruised and scabbed. We spent many an hour pulling the trolleys up to the top of the slope to run them down to the bottom again.

The trolleys in a way were a status symbol and you really had to have the best wheels in the street. I had this trolley which had some hardboard sides to it so that your passenger could sit inside a box and be more secure. This in some ways made the thing more stable but Baz and I wanted something else: we wanted power, and we wanted something that would look impressive. We wanted an engine and flames … a jet engine … Yes, a jet engine was needed for the trolley.

We found an old metal tube around the back of the garages. It was rusty but substantial with a wide end to it. At about four feet long it was perfect for the jet engine. We strapped it to the side of the trolley with chicken wire and Baz thought this looked the business now. Even so I thought it needed some further work: we needed this to look like a jet engine … we needed a fire inside this metal tube.

"I'll fry," said Baz.

"No, you won't," I said. "The metal will protect you. Just don't touch the metal: it will get hot."

"OK ... so how are we going to build a fire inside this tube?" said Baz.

"I have an idea," I responded. We went into my shed and in there were a few old rags (my dad's old vests, if I remember rightly). I pointed to the lawnmower.

"We need some petrol out of this..."

"How we going to do that?" said Baz.

"Let me think," I said. I went indoors and had a root around in the kitchen. I needed something to put some petrol in, and something small enough to hold so that it didn't get noticed. What I came up with was a Marmite pot, which I found in the bin. We cleaned out the residue and went back into the shed to manhandle the mower and get some petrol into the small black pot. We now had everything. I spied a small leather bike bag in the shed which wasn't being used so we put this bag on the other side of the trolley to keep our supplies in: rag, petrol, and some matches.

Finishing off, we took the trolley out into the street. We were not going to run it from the top of the usual slope. No: this needed something special for its maiden voyage. We pulled the trolley up to the top of the Coronation Fields, right up to where the Bennetts End shops started. This was a vast downward slope on grass and was perfect for the run. It must have been about half a kilometre. I was unsure if we could stop at the bottom, to be honest ... if not, we might end up in the dell at the bottom. This had not been tried before. There was uncertainty here.

"But what the heck?" we thought. "In for a penny..."

"OK, let's fire it up," I said. I had pushed some chicken wire into the metal tube already. I knew what would happen if there was nothing in there to hold the rags back in place: they would blow out as we rode down. We then dunked some strips of rags in petrol and inserted them into the metal tube. Our fingers smelled of fuel but we were so excited. I was to ride the trolley this time: Baz would pilot on the second run.

"Right," I said. "Once in position light the jet, Baz, and jump in quick."

Baz lit a match and held it near the back of the tube. It popped as the fumes ignited and the rags were alight.

"Get in quick, Baz," I shouted. He kicked off the trolley and jumped in the box like the four-man bobsleigh team does at the winter Olympics. Well … that slope was steep, and we gathered speed quickly. This was as quick as anyone would want to go on a handmade trolley. Baz shouted,

"Have you seen the jet, Titch…?" I looked back and there was a three-foot stream of orange flame and black smoke coming out of the back of the tube. The air rushing in the front of the tube was causing the fuel to run like a jet engine. It was magnificent. I think we made a whooping noise almost all the way to the bottom.

The trolley jerked and bounced over the rough grass. It felt like I was trying to land a wounded Lancaster bomber (in my head that's what we were doing). We screamed down that bank and past a woman who was carrying two bags of shopping back from the shops.

"Wooohooo," we exclaimed as we sped past the old lady, and I swear she dropped her shopping as she saw the sight in front of her. Two young boys about eight in a trolley that was, it seemed, being powered by a jet engine.

The Möhne dam was coming up quick … or was it the bushes of the dell? I clearly could not tell as I piloted our Lancaster bomber low over the Coronation Fields. We were running out of field. There was no let-up in the speed … we had to stop and I was running out of time. Baz shouted,

"Use your foot, Gibson…" using the name from that very famous Dam Buster, Guy Penrose Gibson.

I inched the sole of my Clarks sandal over the top of one of the front wheels of the Lancaster and smelled the rubber burn as the tyre ate into it.

"Not enough," I shouted back to my co-pilot and rear gunner.

"Turn, then," said Baz in a panic as the line of trees loomed up in front of us. "Turn the bloody wheels, Titch, for God's sake…"

It was the only way to stop. I turned sharp to run the trolley parallel to the bottom of the field. The trolley went with the front wheels to start with but the back end slipped and we did a 180-degree turn on the grass, finally the Lancaster came to a standstill with a lurch pointing back up the field.

"Wooohooo," we shouted. We looked at each other with beaming smiles.

"That was the best," said Baz.

"Yes," I said. "Do you want a go?"'

"Sure do," he responded. "Let's take her back up."

Well, I don't know how many times we shot down that hill that day. It was a few – and it was all good fun, taking it in turns to drag the trolley up to the top of those Coronation Fields. At one point the Marmite pot jumped out of its satchel and bounced on the ground for several yards like a Dam Buster bouncing bomb. Thank God for the tough glass those jars are made of. We soon ran out of rag and needed to get back home. Hopefully we had not been reported …

and hopefully my dad still had enough petrol in the mower for the next cut.

Hot Wheels
1958-1962

From a small toddler I had always had wheels of some description. First I had a small trike and a scooter, then around the age of five or six I had a hand-me-down metal pedal car which was lovingly painted up by my dad with some spare paint from the shed. I was so impatient to drive it after the paint job that my dad had to tie some rag to the door handle because it was still tacky.

A lot of people had two-wheeled bikes in the road. It was a natural progression from the three-wheeled variety of transport you got as a youngster. You started off with three wheels and then progressed on to two.

One of the other hand-me-down items was a two-wheeled bike with a nice red frame and twenty-inch wheels that my cousin used to ride. At first I was too short for it and it sat in the shed with some old sacks over it until I grew tall enough for it. The saddle was right down on its lowest setting and my toes only just reached the floor. I convinced my dad that I was indeed ready to ride this out in the street. I loved that red bike so much and got my dad to buy me a futuristic Pifco electric horn for it.

Learning to ride a bike was easy, really. Someone held the back of the saddle and you rode back and forth like that until you could go on your own. It didn't take long for me to learn, and riding on the pavement area was easy and safe. We didn't go on the road much at all, and we didn't really go out of the street. To make the bikes sound like they had an engine we would place a playing card or a cardboard strip into the spokes, which would be held on to the front forks by a clothes peg. This then caused a clacking noise to be made as the bike was ridden. If we all did this in the road at once it made quite a din. Pete and John's dad used to work nights and we were often berated for making too much noise outside. We would race the bikes up and down the street and sometimes take them up the fields to ride. However, it was something else that Baz and I had which was far better than the bikes.

Baz came around to me one day and said he had something he needed to show me.

"It's the best," he said. I went outside the garden gate, and there outside on the pavement sitting on its own push-down stand was a two-wheeled scooter ... a bright red monster, not like the baby ones we had had a few years back but a bigger and meaner affair. Baz pointed out its brake. I looked and, sure enough, it had a step-on brake on the back of the footpad that pushed into the back wheel. The wheels were quite big too and would, I suspect, gain some speed. He pointed to the front and there was the scooter's name: Firefly.

"The scooter has a name? God, you lucky git," I said. Baz smiled and then asked if I would like a go.

"Sure I would, Baz," I said. He let me have a few goes but I wanted my own. I really coveted Baz's scooter. It was the business.

Well, I don't know how long I waited. I don't think it was long at all. I came home from school one day and I saw my dad running down the path into the house with a large item under his arm. He had spotted me and was trying to get back to the house without me seeing what he was up to. But I had seen. I kind of knew ... my own Firefly. I ran into the back yard and there it was: not red like Baz's, but emerald green.

"Wow," I said. "This is fantastic." I looked at the front. The name was Tornado. I was around to see Baz in a flash with my green version of bliss. Basically we had the same type of scooter but they were different enough to be our own.

We rode those scooters everywhere. We would run them at speed and then jump on the back brake to make a skid, leaving a black mark down the pavement. You could just ride somewhere, park, and play. No one bothered to steal anything in those days. It was unheard of. The scooters were our mode of transport for a few years until we grew out of them. They finally lay rusting around the back of the house until the rag-and-bone man took them away. It's strange how as you grow things come and pass through your life but that's how it is. The golden age of scooters soon passed, only to be replaced by some other fascination.

A Trip to the Four and Beyond
1955-1962

The only shops (for a while) that I was allowed to walk to were in the small parade of shops that existed at the top of Hobbs Hill Road. These four shops helped to supply the local area with produce. Hardly anyone had a car in those days. The only way to obtain food and essentials was to either walk to the local shops or have things delivered, if possible. The Hobbs Hill Road shops consisted of Scott's the tobacconist-cum-sweet shop, then Skelton's the greengrocer, Ludlum's the wool and haberdashery shop, and finally (at the end) was Garment's the grocery store. The names of these didn't change for many years and the format of the stores didn't, either.

The long summer holidays were great but we did have days when we just could not think of what to do. In desperation the option to walk up to Scott's was always there as long as you had a bit of money. We never had pockets with money in – it always got spent as soon as you had it – so a trip indoors for maybe a tanner (six old pence) was all you needed. A tanner would buy you a multitude of sweets. Most things in Scott's were priced at an old penny each or maybe two or four items for a penny.

Sixpence, then, would buy you enough. It would buy you the world, almost. You might have six pennies in your hand or two threepenny bits or a single tanner – the shiny silver coin that my nan would call snow. It mattered not how you had your sixpence: all that mattered on the trip up to Scott's was the discussion about what you would buy. Would you spend it all on sweets, or maybe half on sweets and half on Brocks' caps? Caps for cap guns were always needed, but I will cover that later on.

The trip to Scott's took no more than five minutes but it sometimes felt like a trip to the top of Everest. In midsummer the walk up the hill seemed a relentless slog and many a time you would be persuaded to spend your money on an ice lolly or a pyramid-shaped carton drink called a Jubbly … now, they were excellent.

Old Scott was an impatient shopkeeper. He liked the trade from the kids but it all seemed to take too long for his liking. He would stand behind that counter, his black Brylcreemed hair slicked back on his balding head. Each of us in turn would decide.

"I'll have one of them and one of them," we would say, and this went on until the sixpence was used up and the money exchanged and the bag handed over. Of course if you could not quite decide on what you wanted and didn't say,

"I want one of them," etc. etc. quickly enough, then old Scott would get irritated and he would glare at you.

"Come on. Come on. I haven't got all day to serve you pesky kids," he would say. We took no notice, of course: he usually had an empty shop. It wasn't like he had an urgent packet of fags he needed to sell. But all for our moaning about Scotty, we did really like him. After all he was the sweet shop seller and that was a good enough reason to like this guy. We then would walk out the shop and inspect what we had: mostly penny chews of all sorts of flavours. Black Jacks were popular as they turned your tongue black and, along with Fruit Salad sweets, these were all four for one old penny. These were good value, and if you spent your sixpence on these types of sweet you ended up with a full bag with twenty-four sweets.

I would like to get one or two pieces of Bazooka Joe bubblegum. This was a large block of pink gum for a penny but it had the added bonus of having a miniature comic page inside the wrapper. I once unwrapped one of these to find an invitation to the Bazooka Joe club, where for one shilling I could have a club card and a secret siren ring. Wow, I sure wanted that. I sent away for it as soon as I could persuade my dad to get me a postal order. When it arrived the ring turned out to be really just plastic junk and not what I was expecting. It didn't look like it looked on the picture, where Bazooka Joe was using it to call all his mates.

None of us bought any bars of anything: it was all small items in those days. You just wanted to get as many sweets as you could for your money. Once or twice you might splash out and buy a sherbet fountain by Bassetts. They were three old pence each. Another option was to buy what was called a Lucky Bag. These were also three old pence – and a bit of a swizz, to be honest. A Lucky Bag was a bag that you could not see the contents of and which, once opened, had a small number of sweets and a plastic toy inside. We always hoped for more in these bags but once opened they always disappointed us.

There were also barley sugar sticks and toffee lollies, flying saucers, gobstoppers, and Refreshers. As a treat I often liked a packet of Spangles. These were in a packet like Polos were but square in shape, and they came in all sorts of flavours. I liked the Old English flavour ones and Mum liked the barley sugar flavour. I once was addicted to a sweet called Parma Violets … a bit of a girl's sweet, really, but I liked these mauve sweets and their strange flowery taste.

There were also sweet cigarettes (which these days are not allowed), so you could buy your own cigarettes from Mr Scott and look like your dad with a fag in your mouth. How cool was that? Scott's was a frequent haunt for us, and sometimes we would make the trip there only to find that he was shut for lunch. We would have to sit on his brick wall and kick our shoes till he came out and opened up again. Baz's Auntie M worked in Scott's sometimes. She was a lovely lady, and much loved by the kids who went in the shop.

If you wanted anything more than these shops provided then you would need to walk to the Bennetts End shops. The trek to the Bennetts End shops was about a fifteen-minute walk, and my mum would perform this journey maybe two or three times a week. We had no fridge in those early days and, therefore, to have fresh food meant a trip several times a week. My mum would carry bags of food back from the shops and complain about the weight she had to carry.

There were no plastic bags at all in those days: they just had not been invented. The best disposable bag available was a paper-based carrier bag, but most people had their own shopping bag to take to the shops … how environmentally friendly we were in those days. Carrying the food must have kept my mother fit as she did this relentlessly for many years and until my father finally got a car.

In the kitchen we had what was called a larder room where a cement shelf would keep some food cooler than the ambient temperature in the house. Keeping cooked or raw meat past two days would have been a tricky ordeal and several times I heard my father say,

"God, that meat's gone off. We can't eat that." Eventually we got a fridge and then meat could be stored for longer and the trips to the shops were less frequent.

Milk and bread were delivered to the house on a daily basis. The general groceries were also delivered once a week from Garments at the four by a man in a van. The goods would arrive in a cardboard box. They were generally tins of stuff and the heavier items that my mum didn't want to carry. The cardboard boxes were great, and these would be used for all sorts of things around the house. Nothing was thrown away: everything that could be used would be used. If the four or Bennetts End shops could not meet your needs then the only other option was to travel into town or go to Watford. When I was a young lad Hemel town centre was still being developed. The long new town shopping centre known as The Marlowes stretched from the bottom of Queensway right down to what was known as the Plough roundabout (which we would nickname the Magic roundabout later on).

For getting into town two options were available by bus: either walking down to just opposite the Boot pub at the bottom of St Albans Hill and catching the 314a double-decker or walking down to Belwsains Lane and catching the 322. Both walking distances were about the same from our house, but we kind of favoured the 322 as the bus trip only took ten minutes. Getting a bus into town was like a treat. After all, we had no car, so this was like a ride that us kids enjoyed. It was a little adventure on four wheels.

Any motor vehicle ride was seen to be something to look forward to: a treat to relish and savour. I loved the single-decker 322, as the driver gave you a ticket from a machine that seemed to be clamped to the door where the driver sat. To see the different-coloured tickets fly up out of different slots and your change given into a dish-shaped part in the driver's door at waist height ... how cool was that? On the other hand the double-decker had a conductor with a machine for dispensing printed tickets on white paper. The number of people, adults, and children were input into the machine and the conductor would turn a handle on the side. This produced a long strip of tickets all connected to one another. If you had several people in your party the ticket strip would sometimes reach the floor of the bus. I always collected these tickets. They were treasures and reminders of the trip out.

Trips into Hemel or Watford tended to happen when clothes were needed or something else specific that could not be purchased more locally. In the fifties and sixties Hemel's new high street looked almost futuristic. It had that modern look to it, with a fresh clean appearance. Shopping in town was a luxury as people really didn't have a lot of spare money to spend on trivia. What you bought definitely was required and had to have a purpose within the house. You went to town to buy something specific. Window-shopping had not been invented then: that was something the seventies would bring.

One of my favourite shops in town as a boy was Woolworths – or Woolies, as it was most fondly called. Woolies changed over time but in those early days it was a place where you could buy a multitude of things quite cheaply. It was a lovely store to go into and walk around and there were different smells from different counters. A lot of my clothes then came from Woolies and one of the favourites was the Ladybird brand, which went on for many years. I had a few T-shirts with a Ladybird label in the back. I thought this so cool at the time. Other shops were visited, of course, but one structure down in the town always excited me as we approached it. That was the viaduct that ran over the Plough roundabout. The tall multi-arched structure looked like some giant to a five-year-old – almost menacing in a way, but awe-inspiring too.

The Nickey Line and Trains

The Nickey line, which opened in 1877, provided passage by railway between Hemel and Harpenden. It passed high over the Plough roundabout in Hemel and twisted up towards the industrial estate and beyond to Redbourne, and finally to Harpenden. As a little boy trains were a huge fascination. They were objects of excitement: things you could ride on and also admire from a distance. Throughout its life the Nickey line carried people as well as goods up to the last train to pass down its tracks in the late 1970s. The track was taken up in 1982. The demise of local train tracks all over England was a concern to people but some trains were just not making the money and they had to go.

Mum and Dad used to call the train that shunted back and forth on the Nickey line Puffing Billy. This, I think, was just a nickname used by my parents for a very small boy who was enthusiastic about trains and who probably wanted to know what the name of the engine was. Puffing Billy was in fact a much older locomotive produced in the early 1800s.

I remember I was about eight years old at the time and I was with my father down in the town. He told me that he wanted to show me something quite important and that it would be something I should remember. To this day I do remember it very well. It has stuck in my head as an important event, as my father instructed me.

We walked up from the town up Midland Hill. In those days it was more like a country lane than a road. Part way up the hill (of course) was Hemel railway station, as it was called – or Midland Hill station, as it was known to some. Dad paid for a platform ticket as we were not going to travel on the train. We walked on to the platform. It was quiet and peaceful and the only noise was from the overhead trees swaying in the wind. We walked for a bit down the platform in the warm sun.

"I wanted to show you this, son," said my dad. "It's something that's part of our history but it's not going to be here for much longer."

"Why?" I responded, with a worried look on my face. I loved trains and the thought of no more trains here was something that was deeply disturbing to me.

"It's shutting down," said Dad. "There is no money so it will be gone soon. I want you to look at this place, son. Take it all in and remember it as it is now, as we won't be retuning here again."

I did indeed take in the scene. I recorded it as a video flash in my mind and it still remains there today, ready to be played whenever I like. True to his word, we never did return – and the only reminder to me now is when I drive past the Midland Hotel pub which still stands where the station was.

My brother was a keen trainspotter in those days, and I remember him having a number of trainspotting books crammed full of the numbers of the different steam trains. The idea was to go out and check off numbers on the old steamers you saw passing by. Rob would mark the ones he saw using a coloured pencil. He often went into London and to major train junctions just to collect these trains in his books. This was something I did too to a certain extent, but not as enthusiastically as my brother.

Sometimes Rob would take me down to Apsley and we would stand on the bridge that spans the main railway line between Euston and Birmingham. The bridge was always the one that led up to Shendish. We liked to wait for the steam trains to come and Rob would lift me up so I could see the engine heading our way and billowing out steam from the top of the funnel. The sooty smoke would engulf us as the train sped past under our feet. It was an exciting, special time and I still miss the old steam trains. I'm so glad I witnessed their use.

Cards and Games

1958-Present

In the fifties and sixties you really did have to make your own entertainment at the weekends. Television was an option, but with only one or two channels at the most the choices of entertainment through that medium were limited. For my family at least the only real entertainment to take part in was a good old game of cards.

Playing cards had been used as entertainment by families for donkey's years, and during the war (when there was nothing much else to do in the evening) a pack of cards seemed to solve the problem. It was apparent that my mum and dad and their respective parents had been brought up to play a variety of games.

Now it should be noted that neither family were hardened gamblers by any means, but some low-denomination coins were always used to make it more interesting and exciting. I was introduced to playing cards at a very young age (maybe four or five) and I was expected to hold my own against the grown-ups, too. This introduction to cards was, in fact, seen as a good way to educate me in numeracy. When you play cards of any description there is an element of fun, of course, but you are learning how to add and subtract numbers and also to make some judgement based on risk. I loved playing cards and it was always a fantastic fun time. I sometimes wonder if other families did the same, and I could not bear to think of a childhood without cards or games. It's what binds a family together.

The usual set-up for a session was with my Nan and Granddad Blackshire, either at their house in Deaconsfield Road or at our house. We always played on the dining room table so everyone had lots of room to pile their money up and have a drink beside them. We played a variety of different games, and as time progressed we integrated more games. Knockout whist was a firm favourite in the early days, with rummy and Nine Card Brag being two of my Granddad's loves. Rob brought back two new games from

Nottingham University: Hunt the Lady (sometimes called far wor-se) and nomination whist. Both of these were a little more sophisticated and required paper so we could keep the score. My mum and dad's favourite by far was solo whist and cribbage. Solo needed four players and therefore was difficult to play with five people. I think we did have a way around this, but it escapes me now. Cribbage required a crib board to score, and we used matchsticks to move the scores along in the holes in the board. Crib is a good way for a youngster to learn addition because you scored when you made fifteen with your cards.

There was always a party atmosphere at the weekends with these card events. There would be huge amounts of laughter as – say – my nan would think she had the winning hand at Brag and would play her final cards, only for Granddad to have what he called a prile of priles, (three 9s) and take the pot of money. The room would erupt and everyone would laugh – even the losers – because it was fun and no one worried about a few pennies. My nan would laugh so hard that she would then have a coughing fit from all those Player's Weights cigarettes she smoked, and we would have to get her some water.

Money in those days was interesting for me as all the pennies and halfpennies had different kings and queens on them. Sometimes you got a really worn penny with a young Queen Victoria on it and when I was a little boy 1860 seemed an awfully long time ago. These coins had been around over a hundred years and were worn to almost nothing. Copper coins were heavy in those days and if you had a shilling's worth in your pocket you certainly knew about it. The thruppenny (threepenny) bit was a lovely coin. It was worth three old pence and had twelve sides. This brass coin had replaced a silver round version just before I was born. The silver ones were real silver and were commonly placed in Christmas puddings as a sort of mystery gift. The sixpence was silver in colour and commanded a bit of respect during cards. As I have already said, we played cards using pennies and halfpennies but sometimes the kitty or the pot grew for whatever reason and someone might have run out of pennies and had to change a larger coin. If someone had to place a silver sixpence in the kitty and take five pennies out there would be a notable "Oooh" from the players and my nan would always say,

"We have some snow in the kitty." If things really got bad there might be the ever-so-special silver shilling too. It never became more than that, though, as our family was never rolling in cash.

Another firm favourite (and it was easy to play) was Newmarket, where you placed bets on horses (cards) and then played to achieve a win. Sometimes I might lose a bit of money from my piggy bank but mostly I was up a little, and I think the grown-ups ensured that I was OK.

Christmas was a bit special, of course, and although we played lots of other games then there were a couple of firm favourites that we played when there were a few more of us around the table. Chase the Ace was one of these, and although it was a very simple game that used only one card it never ceased to cause laughter and noise. Another was the more notorious Pontoon, which was only to be played at Christmas because even with pennies you could lose a bit of money here.

All in all the cards and the games played in those days have never left me completely. We don't really play that often now but Christmas is always about playing games and the TV is never on during that time. I still play bridge now and like the competitiveness and challenges from this game.

Starting School

1959-1961

I wonder if it's the same for everyone. You're growing up and getting stronger: you can talk and walk and generally you know right from wrong. Your day is pleasant, playing in the house and garden. It's a fun time and a careless one with no stress and no real worries. You jump from one activity to another with total freedom. The only things that structures your day are mealtimes and then bed. You're very carefree and very safe … and then all of a sudden the dreaded bomb hits. School.

I was five years old when I was told about this dramatic change to my life. I didn't think much to it, to be honest. Change then for a young child was a massive issue. I would protest, of course, when the day came and my parents would relent for sure. Having no nursery schooling prior to going to the infant school I had no exposure or indeed vision of what was to come. If I got upset enough then that would be fine: I would stay at home. That was my plan.

Needless to say, that whole day of starting school was a complete nightmare. Mum had dressed me in what was to become my school uniform, and I was told in no uncertain terms that I was going to school that day and that I would be staying there till she collected me at lunchtime. School was less than a five-minute walk from us. I could see the school easily from my bedroom window. It was just a matter of walking up the path by the side of the school fields and then turning right at the top along Barnfield Road and into the school: there were no roads to cross and it was completely safe. It could not have been any easier.

As the school was in close proximity I kind of had an idea about what school was all about, as from a distance I often watched the kids playing out in the playground from the safety of my own home. This school was new, and I had actually observed it being built as a toddler. It occupied the same playing field as the junior school, which I would migrate to after the three-year stint at Infants.

Once I was ready to leave home my mum took me by hand, and we walked the 200 yards or so to the school. The new uniform itched my skin. These were not my familiar play clothes and this new venture felt alien to me. I had no real idea what to expect that day and I felt anxious and frightened, almost sick. This was not a good day for this particular five-year-old. I felt that my freedom had been ripped away from me and what I had enjoyed for so long would never return.

We went through the school gates and into the reception area where a kind lady instructed my mum on what would take place next. I would be placed in Class One and my new teacher would be a Miss Young. I was not happy. In fact I was distressed to the point where I broke down and cried my head off. Mum would have to leave and I would be left with a bunch of strangers. I lay on the floor and bawled my eyes out, almost pleading not to be left. But it was useless, of course. The enemy had captured me and they had ways of making you feel better … at least, they had a whole armoury of things they could use to get you to comply. I was led into the Class One by the young teacher (we were her first assignment) and my mum promptly left. Mum had assured me she would return at lunchtime to take me home. When you're young three hours seems an eternity.

In Class One I surveyed the scene. There was a multitude of boys and girls all running about, playing and talking.

"Hey, this doesn't look so bad after all. This might be fun," I thought. The teachers were clever, of course. They knew how to slowly indoctrinate their new intake into the ways of the education system in a very careful, subtle way. They had organised fun play activities for the children. There was a large Wendy house in the corner, some play bricks on the floor, and a water play area too. I was told to go and join in the others and play. My eyes were dry by this point and I was taken in hand by an equally small boy called Michael who seemed to want to be my friend. He had funny sticking-out ears which were also full of wax but he seemed nice, and we played well together on that first day.

I sometimes think back to that first meeting in Class One and the small chum who took my hand and introduced me to school. Unfortunately Michael would never see adulthood. He would die at the age of eleven in a terrible carbon monoxide poisoning accident along with some of his siblings. We all have fond memories of Michael, who was part of our school life for a short while. Life plays its hand and no one really knows who the winners and losers will be.

I'm not sure if I had been brought in late to school on this day but the class seemed to be already quite full, and after I joined only one or two others followed.

This was my first ever day of having to interact with many children at once. It was quite stressful, and I remember it so very vividly. Up to now only the brothers John and Pete had been my friends in the street. Pete was yet to join school and John was a year older than me, anyway. Interacting with so many different personalities all at the same time was a huge growing-up experience. For one thing there were girls here, and I quickly learned that girls were completely different from boys in how they play and react. I soon found out that when a girl is playing with something you leave well alone. You don't go barging in and try to take over.

I got off to a rough start with a fiery redheaded girl who quickly told me that the play pool was indeed hers and that I had better clear off sharpish. It was a bit dog eat dog on that first day. The structure and pecking order of the class was being defined in front of my young eyes. Boys and girls were vying for positions in this social order, and some would be top dog and become dominant contenders in the class. Others would become bullies and control weaker individuals and some were passive and tried to keep things easy. This was play of course, but in reality this was war – and the important thing here was that no one had filled me in on the rules before I started. No one sat me down before I went to school and said,

"OK ... this is what school will be like. Just do this and do that and you will be fine." No, no one bloody bothered to say any of that.

They just stuck me in the stadium and someone let the lions out. Thanks a bunch.

The infant school was structured into six classes in all. Each child would spend three years in total at Infants and therefore there were two classes per year. Classes One and Two were allocated to the new children. The whole school was run by a nice but strict headmistress: Miss Gardner. She certainly knew her stuff and she ran a very tight ship in those days. If you had to go and see Miss Gardner for any reason then you were in some really deep trouble.

I didn't know anyone in Class One and so this was going to be an exercise of making friends and, to an extent, (as I found out) of surviving. The tables in the class were arranged so that five or six of us could sit around in a circle facing each other. This formed a good little community in the early days, and later on we would be moved to the more traditional side-by-side desks structure. The school didn't want to upset its new starters, and this way of structuring us in groups to work was a very good and – broadly speaking – new idea.

For the first few weeks at least we would perform fun activities like colouring in and learning the alphabet. We were given two break times – mid morning and mid afternoon – and during these times we had to go outside into the playground. This gave us an opportunity to talk to other kids in the school and mix with boys and girls we maybe knew. This was an opportunity for me to talk to John and later on Pete when he started in the next year. Even if it was raining we would be let out to play. We all had coats and hats and the rain was never an issue for us. We played come rain, snow, and hail.

The testing started a few weeks into school. We were scrutinised and inspected by the teachers. I had little idea of what was going on, of course. It was not so obvious then, but we kind of had an idea that something was afoot. The general nice fun play sessions gave way to more not-such-fun educational set-ups. We were given the very simple *Janet and John* reading books to start with. These books had about fifteen pages each and were mainly made up of a picture on each page with one line of writing underneath. If you had difficulty with the words at the bottom the picture would give you a clue. "See John run" might be the sentence at the bottom, with a picture depicting John running, or "See John kick the ball", and so on.

The words from these books were compiled by the teachers into a ladder of words on the class wall. Periodically you were tested by sitting with the teacher and working your way up the ladder of words, reciting each word one by one. The words got progressively more difficult as you moved up, so at some point you would probably fail to read a word. You then had a marker with your name on next to the word where you had failed, so this meant that you had a good indication of how you were performing in relation your classmates. Some of the girls, the redhead included, managed to just zip up this ladder in one go and their names would appear right at the top. As for me, I struggled. I didn't know it then and would not find out until later in life that I was dyslexic. The books were easy to read to the teacher as they had the pictures, but when the words were taken out of context to some action on the page I was lost.

These tests on the word ladders were used to split and stream the children into different classes. Therefore classes One and Two were reformed part way through the first year. It's difficult to understand what the intentions were here, and I have to make a judgement based on what I know now and what I have heard from my old school chums. It would seem that those children who were deemed to be bright were put into a class with a more experienced teacher. It's not something I can categorically say happened but it seemed like it at the time. Certainly the brighter children were separated out, and even at that very young age it was very apparent indeed. I began to feel my worth was less than it should have been. Playground banter didn't help, either, as kids quite easily pick on situations to reinforce how they are in fact better than you.

So it followed that the two classes were mixed up, and the friends you had got used to in your class were switched into the other class. We therefore had some new kids come into our class. It was disruptive to say the least, and it unsettled the class no end.

The school day started with the register first thing where your name was called and you had to say,

"Yes, miss." Your name was then recorded in a long folder of names with neat ticks down the side. This was the only record of attendance and it was quite an important document for the teachers. Absence (like holiday and sickness) was recorded and monitored.

After the register we were marched into assembly, where we all sat on the floor of a big hall in lines. We were then instructed on some readings from the Bible and were told to pray while the headmistress read out a prayer. Our eyes would be closed and our hands held in front of our faces in a clasped way that people do when they pray. God forbid if you had your eyes open or your hands were not clasped. You would be marched out of the room and have to take the wrath of Miss Gardener later. Assembly was also a way in which we could all be told of important news about the school as a whole. We then listened to a small piece of classical music. The whole thing only lasted half an hour at the most: we would be fidgeting by then, anyway. After assembly we were led back to our classrooms. We then had a lesson until break time and then another lesson until lunch at twelve o'clock. My mum would be at the gates at twelve o'clock to meet me and on that first day she was quite a welcome sight, I can assure you.

A short while after starting at school we acquired the devil dog Ricky. He would accompany us back and forward to school, constantly pulling on his lead and almost choking himself. I always panicked a bit as to whether Mum would be there or not. She was only late once or twice, but that did make me quite frightened. I had lunch at home and then would be marched back to school. The afternoon was more low-key – usually with a story for us all at the end of the day, which was read by the form teacher. In fact all the lessons you had were with the form teacher, which in the infant school was always a woman teacher.

It was not long before I was told that I needed to walk myself to school and back. Again this was a big step for me, and way outside of my comfort zone. The distance was small – 200 yards – and there was no real threat. I managed it OK and got used to the walking. It's all part of growing up and just pushing the boundaries out little by little.

I realised early on that I had been tricked, of course … that school was not really the nice place it was purported to be on that first day, but something like a child prison from which there was no escape. I figured out in my very young head that there would be school and then there would be work after that … and then that would be it until retirement. I thought about Granddad. He was retired, and he looked old. It felt like a long time to wait for some rest and a return to how things were when I was four years old.

As time progressed there was even more work to do at school and it became harder in lots of different ways. I'm not sure what instigated the change but at some point I was moved out of Class Three and into a new class headed by a new Canadian teacher: Mrs Evans. The class was small: maybe ten to fifteen children at the most. I didn't know why this change had come about, but clearly (on reflection) this class had been set up specifically for kids who had some learning difficulties. It wasn't like I was backward in any way but I certainly had issues that were not understood then. We sat in rows and my desk partner was Billy. He was a bigger, stouter chap who talked with a slight speech impediment. It was so slight that you could hardly detect it. It was not until many years later that I learned that he did have some hearing difficulties. Poor Billy. He must have found things really difficult too.

I'm not sure if our lessons were any different from the other classes, as we were a bit more isolated from the usual form classes. Mrs Evans was a nice young teacher: she was strict and she knew how to keep the kids in control. She loved reading the Bible and she had a large pictorial children's Bible that had stories and lovely pictures inside to show during the reading. In those days there was a lot of emphasis on religious education. The Church of England version was the only one we were told about at school. The Roman Catholic kids were exempt from assembly, because they were excused the singing and the praying.

In the last year of Infants I was moved out of Mrs Evans's class into Mrs Stevens's class in Class Six. Mrs Stevens was an elderly teacher with white hair and a reddish face. Now she was strict and old-school. There was no nonsense with her and she ruled the roost, for sure. Again the tables (if I remember rightly) were placed in groups, and I was situated in the middle of the class.

By the window was a set-up where all the girls sat and there was a bit of a distinction here, again if I remember rightly. It was obvious from where I was that the girls in the window got favoured. They always got any goodies going around and they never got shouted at. This group was, I believe, the very bright bunch who would ultimately be singled out for grammar school. There was definitely a divide going on here, and for a small child to pick this up it must have been very obvious. I kind of coasted along here, neither being great nor bad at lessons.

I know that one day in Mrs Stevens's class we were asked to bring in (for an afternoon session) one of our hobbies that we liked to do at home. Well … this was right up my street, and whereas a lot of kids brought in either painting stuff or jigsaw puzzles or knitting etc., I of course brought in a bag of wires, batteries, switches, lights, and bells.

Yes, that's right. My spelling might have been poor but I damn well knew at the age of eight how to connect a simple electronic circuit. Of course, laying all this stuff out on the desk caused quite a stir. Firstly the kids had no idea what all these items were, and some excitement ensued. The teacher had no idea what all this stuff was, either. It was beyond her ageing brain. She didn't know anything about electronics or, indeed, if any of my goodies were safe. Mrs Stevens brought Mrs Gardner in to check what I had brought in. The two were puzzled. How could a boy of eight be interested in electronics at this level? I was left to play and make up circuits in which light bulbs would light or bells would ring. The kids in the class were very impressed. I think at that point that I showed them I had something going on in my head. You could call it a light bulb moment.

Another situation that arose which had an effect on me later was during a week in assembly where Mrs Gardner decided to read out passages from the book *The Pilgrim's Progress*. I do remember sitting there on the floor cross-legged, listening to this tale of a guy who carried a burden on his back that got bigger and bigger as he went along. I'm not sure what effect it had on me but it did stay firmly in my head for a long time. Of course I had no idea at the time while I was sitting there looking at Mrs Gardner recite from this book that she was actually reciting the words written by one of my relatives. How proud I would have felt if I had known. It would be a few more years yet before that part of the family's history was known to us all.

I didn't have any really firm friends at that time. I mixed with a few different guys out in the playground. Playtime was a time to let off steam, and one of the ways we did this was to form trains and run about. What you would do would be to form a link of carriages by holding on to another boy's jumper (girls were of course not allowed). Then, forming a long line, the first boy would run off and you would all have to follow in a line like a train. Where the first boy went then the rest of the train went, and sometimes the end of the train would go careering off in another direction.

On one occasion we were told before break that we must stay on the hardstanding and not go on the wet grass. This was impressed on us as something we must comply with or there would be trouble. So when we got out there someone had the great idea to play trains and I was on the end of a long link of boys. We started off OK, but as the first boy turned towards the grass the rest of the train had no option but to follow in an arc heading towards the dreaded danger zone. Of course I could have just let go of the guy's jumper in front but I had no sense of the danger at all until it was too late. I was over the line. I was on the minefield. Instantly the whistle blew and the guards came out of the sentry post. I was commanded by the playground teacher to come over, where I was duly told off and told to wait outside Mrs *mein Führer* Gardner's office facing the wall.

You see … I was not a naughty boy at all, and to have the humiliation of having to stand facing the wall in the reception area outside Mrs Gardner's office was just too much. To say I was pooing myself is an understatement. I stood there looking at this blank, dark wall wondering what the head would do to me. There was some talk that she had a cane…

Now if Mrs Gardner had come out of her office I would have probably crumpled up and cried. What happened next I wasn't expecting: at least, I had partly forgotten what might happen. Because what happened next was that my mum came through the reception door from outside.

"Oh, God," I thought. "This is even worse."

I had forgotten that as my mum now worked as a dinner lady at the school she was going to be in at some point to work on the school dinners. I didn't expect this and she didn't expect to see her son facing a blank wall. She came over.

"What are you doing there, ducky?" she asked.

"Erm … I've been naughty," I explained, telling the truth and saying what had happened. Tears were in my eyes. I was clearly upset by the whole incident. Mum had a few words with the staff and I was told I could go back to my class. I never saw Mrs Gardner that day, thank God. I don't think I really got into trouble again after that. I was a good boy: at least I was in school.

Mum had decided to take a part-time job, and being dinner lady at the school fitted in nicely for her. The unfortunate thing was that I then had to stay at school and have school dinners.

It has to be said that after talking to some of my old school chums about the subject of school dinners that some of them found school dinners OK. Well … more than OK, actually. Some found this grey pap to actually be a delight. Believe me, it was bloody awful.

My mum always conceded that actually the food was quite good, and that Mrs Sells the head cook could make a decent meal. The problem was that this was not kids' food. There would be a main course and generally this would be either a stew of some kind with potato and some greens. Quite often the veg was something like cabbage or even Brussels sprouts. Sometimes it was even the deadliest of deadly veg: the God-awful butter bean. Even as I type butter bean it makes me wince, and something goes "Twang" in my neither regions. Sometimes the meat was the horror of horrors: corned beef.

Let's get this straight: to any adult who had just been through a world war any of this food would be fruit from the gods. People had not had anything like this five years prior, so meals of any type were considered to be something you should eat up (yum, yum). A circular issued in 1955 updated government advice on nutritional standards and stated that the school meal should be 'adequate in quantity and quality to serve as the main meal of the day.' The puddings were kind of OK and I guess I mainly lived off these. But one day you might get the dreaded pink and slimy semolina, which was like pink frogspawn.

You were waited on by the dinner ladies. You had a plastic beaker in front of you with two inches max, of water, so that even if you wanted to try and push the food down your throat with a gulp of water you couldn't. It was, it seemed, all part of the torture. You then were presented with whatever was on the menu that day. There was no choice: you had what was there. There was no option to say "No thanks," either. The plate was put down and you were instructed to eat. Plates had to be cleared as much as possible.

I didn't know this until later on when I talked to my mum about dinner times at the school. She said that Mrs Sells would not accept any plate back into the kitchen unless it was empty. There were no exceptions here. All the dinner ladies were in fear of this cook: she was a large woman and had that typical cookhouse mentality and look. I knew that my mum would look after me, and she did. Although I was told to eat up, and I wasn't the best of eaters at all – I hated veg for a start – when my mum thought that I had at least made a good stab at the dinner she took the plate away. She would also, along with her colleague Barbara, take other kids' plates away who either could not manage or who were making retching noises at the table.

So … one wonders how the dinner ladies managed to get the wasted food past Mrs Sells. Well, it appears that the solution was simple. The dinner ladies took the plates into the toilets first and flushed the contents down the loo before returning to the kitchen with the empty plates. Mrs Sells never knew, thank God. If she had found out I think that the dinner ladies would have been sacked.

The torture that was school dinner persisted with me for quite a while, and when I moved school it followed me there too. I hated lunchtimes with a vengeance. I remember that sometimes I would even have to load my handkerchief up with food from my plate just to get rid of it. It was like something out of *The Great Escape*, loading food up into your pockets and then dumping it outside in the playground so that the Germans – sorry, the teachers – would not detect it. Even the smell before you got into the canteen areas sometimes made you heave. Kids would go,

"What is it? What is it? Can you see it yet? Is it Spam? Oh, God, it's salad … with cold beetroot." Then there would be some retching noises and some green faces.

For the record there were no chips, there were no burgers, there were no sausages: there was nothing actually nice in that canteen. It was devoid of anything a kid might like.

One of the highlights of the year was Sports Day. This was an organised day in the summer where all the classes would take part in certain types of races. There was the egg-and-spoon race, the sack race, and the accident-causing three-legged race, where one of your legs was tied to another person's leg and you had to hobble fifty yards to the line trying to hold on to each other. I was always strapped to either a lanky guy or some tubby kid. I was never going to win.

If you came first, second, or third you got a really smart rosette. I really did covet these. I desperately wanted to win one. They were so lovely. I watched each race. One of my friends, a striking redheaded girl, won the egg-and-spoon race and came over to me showing off her lovely red rosette.

"OK," I said. "I'll be getting one of those soon enough."

Of course, I never did. There were more powerful guys than me in the class – and, really, this kind of sport came down to size and strength. My friends still tease me about this even today, telling me how many lovely rosettes they still have. Thanks guys. I'm already scared.

Towards the end of my spell at the infant school we were informed by our class teachers which class we would be going into at Belswains Junior School. I remember distinctly the last day and being in the playground in the afternoon. We were all discussing which forms we were going into at the new school. Again there was clearly a streaming aspect to how children were chosen and selected for classes next term. I was going to be part of a new class headed up by Mrs Evans again. She was moving from the infant school and following us down to the primary school. The class would be E1. I suspect the E was for Evans although the other classes were other alphabetic characters: A, B, etc.. You can guess what the other kids thought the E class meant, and we were laughed at during that last day. But that was Infants and the next school would have its own terrors to deal with. One of these would be the dreaded games lesson. Oh, joy of joys. Bring it on.

The Foxy Arrives

1958

Ricky arrived out of the blue one day when I was approaching the age of five and almost ready to start school for the first time. He was a lovely wire-haired fox terrier a few months old and still in his puppy stage. The dog was for my mum, who was suffering from anxiety and depression at this time. I didn't know this at the time, of course, but she needed someone or something at home for company when I started at the infant school. As far as I was concerned he was my dog and not my mum's.

Ricky had some character. He was a male dog and if anyone knows what fox terriers are like they will understand full well what I'm about to tell you. We tried to train him, for sure. God, we really did try hard. We took him up to the Coronation Fields first off and got him to come and sit on command. He was excited, and he loved to run around on that open field. We had some treats to ensure he came back when we called him. We took him a few times and let him off each time when it was safe to do so. We could even let him walk to heel sometimes up the path and he did that really well.

Then the fateful day arrived. We had taken him off the lead and he was doing his usual running and bouncing about, fetching a ball to command and really enjoying his puppy stage of life.

Then he saw it: a big black dog way up at the top of the fields. This other dog was almost out of sight but Ricky saw it OK. He was off like a shot – and boy, he could run. Although my dad ran after him it was hopeless.

"Ricky, come back here…" he shouted. But the dog was gone and was already sniffing around the backside of this big black stray dog at the top of the fields near the shops. In those days, although people would take their dogs for walks it was not uncommon to see stray dogs or dogs just let out by their owners to roam freely. This dog Ricky had found had no owner. It was just roaming the fields. My dad finally caught up with our dog and pulled him away. He certainly was not going to come away to any command, and not even when the chocolate drop tin was rattled. Dad put him back on the lead and pulled him back down the fields. Ricky was rubbernecking all the way down, constantly looking back and choking on the lead. He wanted his new pal back.

Well, that was it after that. There was no going back or putting things right. Ricky had an obsession with the playing fields and with that black dog he had seen up there – so much so that his mind was fixated on escape from the house at all times. If he got out, that was it. He would bolt up the path through the gate and then up the path that led up to the playing fields. He knew exactly where to go and he knew exactly what he was after: that black dog. He was an expert on escape and he knew all the weak points he could exploit in the house and garden. The back garden was surrounded by the usual council chain-link metal fence which was about five feet high. It was quite new, and still quite shiny and rigid against its metal posts. Ricky didn't need to dig under like any conventional dog. Oh, no. He just chewed through this metal fence till it gave way. We didn't believe it till we saw the hole in the fence, and when Ricky was caught again after his exploits up at the field his mouth was inspected.

Dogs have a large canine incisor tooth either side of the upper jaw. On inspection of Ricky's mouth you could see perfectly carved indents into both canine teeth where the chewing of metal had worn the teeth into perfect curves. He had made a pair of wire cutters. We had to then restrict his access to the garden, and Dad built a gate which stopped access down to the bottom part of the garden. Ricky was restricted now to the back yard and the brick wall. There was no way he would get out now. Or would he?

Ricky had a plan in his head. He had devised this, I'm sure, through observation. He knew the only way out of his prison was through the back door or, better still, the front door. He knew this because he sat and watched what went on. He knew that certain people came to the door and that sometimes people went out. It was at these times that he would try and make his break for freedom. He knew, for instance, that when the postman came that maybe the door would be opened. As soon as he saw post coming through the letter box he would take a running jump at the door and wrench whatever was coming through out of the flap before it even had time to drop, sometimes still while it was in the postman's hands. This was no mean feat for a smallish dog as the slit in the door for post was not, as usual, halfway up and horizontal but even further up and vertical. He tore whatever came through and ripped it to sheds, or if we got to him soon enough then maybe you could read your post with just punch marks through it. My dad filled in forms to send off to people countless times, and the forms would have punch marks in where Ricky had inspected the post first.

On the times I came home for lunch from school I would sit and have my lunch and the radio would be on (I was a creature of habit), and as soon as the programme *World at One* came on I would leave to return to school. Just before the programme started the radio would announce it was one o'clock by sounding the pips over the radio... Pip, pip, pip, pip, pip, peeep... Well ... as the pips sounded, that was it. This was the alarm for Ricky to start. He knew the pips meant that I would be leaving and that the door would be opening for an escape run. All hell broke loose every day this happened. It even got worse when Ricky also started associating the telephone ringing with the pips. So every time the phone rang there was barking and jumping and all sorts of mayhem. Anything sounding like the pips would cause him to go bonkers.

He did of course escape a few times, either pushing past our legs when the door was open – or someone just forgot to close the gate or door. He would go, and that was it. We used to try and find him but we had no idea where he went. However, he always returned after a few hours. It seemed he knew his way back home. But in almost all his returns he had managed to roll in mess from another dog. My dad was furious, as this meant a full dog bath. One time he returned and there was a bite mark on his tummy. Something had bitten him and we had to inject penicillin into quite a nasty wound for a week or so. Another time he had been run over and could not walk back.

Someone carried him back but after an inspection by the vet we were told he would be fine. The dog was indestructible.

Another time he went missing and we awaited his return, and then by chance I heard some noise coming from the shed. The shed was a brick house where all the tools were kept and there was a large workbench covering a brick compartment where the coke was kept. The coke hole was substantial and held enough coke to fuel the boiler for maybe six months or more. Water was heated using a boiler in those days and this was situated in the kitchen. It ran almost permanently in the winter and at odd times in the summer. It was our only source of hot water until an electrical immersion unit was added to the hot water tank in later years.

Coke was poured into a top hatch in the shed and then to shovel your coke out there was a small hatch by the floor, which you opened. The coke would then move down and level out as you used it. Well, Ricky – in his bid for freedom from Stalag XVIII, 18 Lower Barn – had, of course, found an open door in the shed. The coke door near the floor had been left open and he had dug himself inside. Then, finding no exit in the dark coke hole, his only option was to claw his way through a mountain of black rubble until his head popped out at the top of the workbench. This was the sight that met me as I opened the shed door. A pile of coke with a dog's head on top of it. A dog who was now not white, black, and tan but black … black all over … as black as they say a coal hole is. You can guess what my dad said when I brought him in.

"That bloody dog," he would say. "Joan, get the bath ready…"

I paint a poor picture of Ricky but he was a well-liked dog, and he sat with us in the evening soaking up the heat from the coal fire. He would sit and get so close to the fire that his muzzle would fry and he would paw at it to try and cool it. In the winter he would sit in the kitchen on the stool which had been my high chair and cut down. The stool was next to the boiler so was really warm, and he liked this position. The stool had two problems. Firstly, its smooth seat was not meant for a dog to sit on and his front paws would constantly slip towards the edge. Secondly, the legs of the stool were uneven so as he slid and shifted weight on the stool the stool would rock on its wonky leg. Ricky had a constant fight to remain on the stool, but he never gave up his position.

After about a year of having Ricky – and after there had been a trip to the canal for a walk – he contracted a nasty infection called Leptospirosis, which is usually picked up from wet places and riverbanks where other animals have been. Ricky was very ill – very ill indeed, for weeks – and the vet said that he might not live a very long life. Well, Ricky was made of stronger stuff than that and lived till he was over fifteen years of age. No rats' pee was going to stop his fun.

Ricky was a pedigree dog and had had good parents. When my school ran a dog show one year my dad suggested that Ricky should go in for it. I went with my dad and we paraded Ricky around for a while for the judges to see. Thank God we didn't have to let him off the lead. He would have been off like a bullet. He had been washed and clipped in the correct way for fox terriers: a close-cut body and saddlebag legs with his beard combed down and slightly forward. He looked the business. We just had to hope there were no postmen there or, indeed, black dogs. The judge looked him over and looked into his mouth. Luckily this was in the pre-chain-link fence-chomping days, or the judge would have had a fit.

Ricky won best dog of the show. Can you believe that? I couldn't. We got a silver cup with his name on, and I was so proud of my dog … and I was so proud as well at school when I was asked to take the cup in to show them all. Thank God they didn't want to see the dog as well.

Ricky was a great dog and it was sad when he finally had to be put down. He was ill and obviously in distress. It had to be done and I came home from school one day and he was not there any longer. His wooden box was empty. He was off now, chasing black dogs in wherever dogs go when they pass on. Maybe even the odd postman too.

Uncle George

1958-1968

There were nans and granddads to visit along with aunts and uncles, but above all those trips to see relatives there was one place that was pure magic. This was Uncle George's ... and the strange thing was that he wasn't even my uncle.

I think I was maybe four when I first went, and I continued to go most years up to about the age of ten. Nan and Granddad had some friends out in a village called Buckland Common, which is a small hamlet, if you like – not really a village. Situated between Berkhamsted and Wendover, this place was a sleepy old country area of fields, farms, and old country pubs. The nearest village to Buckland Common was Cholesbury, about a mile away, and this too was a small sized village.

George and Doris were friends of my nan and granddad from way back, when they lived in London. Nan and Granddad had moved to Hemel and George and Doris had moved to this place in the countryside. Now unlike the rest of the family – who settled in Hemel – Uncle George (as he would become known) went about things in a completely different way. I never saw the start of this but I understand that they bought the land they lived on and then built the house there while living in the sheds and outhouses which would later be where they kept livestock. Uncle George literally built his own place with his bare hands – and what a place it was too. A lovely two-storey thatched cottage in its own grounds surrounded by woodland and fields. If you think of those chocolate box-type cottages you see on tins of chocolate or maybe those jigsaws showing a lovely country cottage then you would not be far from the vision of Uncle George's place.

It has to be said that a trip to stay with Uncle George was something that triggered excitement from the point when one heard one was going. I would be excited for weeks. I would be beside myself and unable to sleep. My parents would not be going on this holiday and I guess now that maybe this was set up as a way of giving my parents a bit of a break.

No, I would be going on this short holiday with my nan and granddad … and it was the best ever. It really was. Uncle George would first pick Nan and Granddad up from their house and then he would drive down to Lower Barn to pick me up. You could hear his car coming from a long way off. He had a hissing side valve Ford Popular and he had a way of staying in a low gear for longer than he really should have. It drove my dad to comment,

"Oh, I can hear One-gear Willy coming, Richard. You'd better go to the door and watch out for them."

I think the name One-gear Willy was something he had called a friend in the army who also had the same affliction. Uncle George would park the Ford Pop while it was still hissing, even with the engine off. It shuddered as the hot engine attempted to shut down completely. They would all come in to see my parents, of course, before packing me off. I was never nervous about going. This was exciting, and Nan and Granddad were the best to be with. I relished being away for the two or three nights which were usually either over Easter or one of the bank holidays.

We all piled into the Pop: me and Nan in the back and Granddad up front, with Uncle George driving. It was a small car, for sure, by today's standards – but it was a luxury to us. I hardly ever got to ride in a car and just having this trip was a huge novelty.

Now Lower Barn to Buckland Common is fourteen miles. I know that now and, by today's standards, that's not a great distance at all. But way back then it was a huge adventure and it seems to me that it took hours to get to the smallholding that was Uncle George's. We would chug along at a steady thirty miles an hour. We drove out of Hemel and headed towards Berkhamsted and then into the countryside. My nan would always say at this point,

"Over the hills and far away," as we hit the lanes and the smaller tracks. Fourteen miles felt like 400 miles to me.

The Ford Pop took its time, and when Uncle George turned a corner a huge knob on the dash was turned to the right or left which then pushed out orange flags from the side of the car that lit up and then flashed. These were the indicators, and sometimes they would get stuck out and Uncle George would have to wind the window down and pat them back down into place. It was fantastic to sit on the leather seats next to my nan. As we drove through Cholesbury there was a petrol garage there and this was always a landmark for looking left across the fields to see our final destination.

"There it is," my nan would say, and we would all crane our necks just to see that glimpse of the farmhouse through the trees. After another few minutes more we would drive into the smallholding that was their home. Auntie Doris would be waiting outside the double-gated kitchen door with a huge smile on her rosy face. I guess like the rest of us she had heard the Ford Pop approaching from several miles away, maybe even as it left Hemel Hempstead.

Now to describe what this place was like and how it felt at the time I can only sum it up by quoting a TV programme that would be on television several decades into the future. It was like *The Darling Buds of May*. Uncle George was in fact Pop Larkin almost to a tee. In fact when I first saw the programme in later life I just could not get Uncle George out of my head. How different all this was for me, coming as I did from a council house in Hemel Hempstead to a smallholding in the country. I may as well have been transported to a different planet. For a child of any age there was just so much to explore here. The only downside of visiting Uncle George was that they didn't have a television, just a wireless radio to listen to. You made your own entertainment and that was just great for the days I was there.

Uncle George was a tall skinny Londoner who spoke in a deep guttural way. He was an odd mix as you kind of thought before he opened his mouth that he would be talking in a country voice. But no: he was as London as you could get. In contrast Auntie Doris was the other end of the spectrum: a very poshly-spoken woman ... almost aristocratic. What a strange but lovely mix these two were. They had no children and I never really found out why this was or even questioned it. This was just George and Doris and this was how they were.

The smallholding was a delight. It had a few acres of land, maybe fifteen in all. I know Uncle George rented one of the fields for additional cattle. They had cows and pigs, chickens, ducks, and grew quite a few vegetables in a field near the house. It was a small place and I would guess it didn't make too much money. Uncle George did have a day job at ICI and the smallholding was an additional income, but it would never have made that much.

Leading up from the main house you could walk through a grassy paddock to a series of outhouses along the boundary fence line. I'm quite sure that some of these were used while the house was being built for George and Doris to live in. These were now used for all manner of things: as workshops, for storing animal feed, tools, woodpiles, and all sorts. The smell in these sheds was amazing: a true country mix which I will never forget ... not a nasty smell at all, but a kind of nice fresh smell. My council house nose just had not smelled anything like this ... a mix of farmyard dung and animal feed along with the smell from the pine trees that surrounded the house. Just standing there and taking it all in was like magic. There was a pigpen further down the line at one end and you could always hear the pigs grunting away. At the other end was a large barn with hay stacked up in bundles. Also in the barn was an old truck that didn't work. Wow. What a play thing to have: a whole truck that I could play around and pretend to drive.

I used to help Uncle George feed the animals, turn the mixer in one of the outhouses, and create the pigswill. I would be able to just roam about and do what I wanted. And do you know what, reader? Just like the TV programme, the sun was always shining. It never rained at Uncle George's. It was always the perfick blue sky summer day.

On my first visit I was playing in the hay and suddenly had a sneezing fit. I was told in no uncertain terms that I had hay fever now and that I needed to stay out of the barn for good. This was the start of my condition with pollen which stayed with me for many a year. It didn't, of course, put me off playing around the farm but I had to stay away from the haystacks.

To my great delight Uncle George had a gun. He had what I was informed was a real gun, just to make sure I understood it was not a toy. In actual fact it was a small garden gun, maybe a .410 shotgun. I was actually allowed to carry and play with this gun, aged four or five. There was no real issue then with me doing this and everyone was OK with me playing with it. There was, however, a bit of a panic when my nan caught sight of me apparently loading a cartridge into the receiver. I had found some old spent cartridge cases but they didn't know that. There were a few shouts at that point asking me to put the gun down. That must have worried them enough because after that the gun was put away. My brother, however, was allowed to use this gun on the crows whenever he came over to visit. Being ten years older he would have been seen to be responsible enough to handle a gun. I don't think he hit anything, though.

Life was good on the farm and there was usually enough going on around the place to keep all of us occupied. We did however have the odd trip out, and this was usually at lunchtime to the pub. Just down the road were two pubs. The Boot and Slipper seemed to be the most popular although we also went to the Horse and Hounds too.

Pubs back then were very different from today's establishments, which tend to cater for families now with food provided and many soft drinks. Back in those days the pubs like these at Uncle George's were small inside. They might have two bars: a public bar for the labourers and farmhands and a saloon bar for those who could afford a bit more luxury. I say "could afford" because the drinks were different prices in each bar. There was never any food served in any of these pubs. Food and pubs were not connected back in those days, and the nearest you might get if you got lucky was a packet of crisps.

Pubs served ale or beer, spirits, and the odd modern posh drink like Martini from a bottle. There were no cocktails, no wine, and no food: it was a pub. The other aspect was that no children were allowed inside, not even to use the toilets. Nope: if I wanted the loo then someone would have to take me to a bush or I would have to hold it in till we got home. There was no way I would be allowed over the threshold of a pub until I was fourteen.

I would sit in the pub gardens and wait for a Coke to arrive with a packet of Smith's crisps if I was lucky. Nan would sit with me until the men arrived with a large silver tray of drinks: pints for the men and pale ale for my nan. I have to remark that to this day I can still smell those drinks in my nostrils from way back then... It was just the stillness in the air of those summers, just the insects and birds, and the gentle warmth from the sun on your skin. It all seemed a magical time and my senses were keen. We all sat in the sun and enjoyed the countryside scene. The word idyllic comes to mind but this very vivid scene of tranquillity, I have to admit, belongs in the past. It's something, sadly enough, that I don't think could ever be found again today: it was just the time and the place.

One of the only downsides of going to George and Doris's was the food. I was not a good eater, anyway: I was very fussy as to what I would eat. Although all the food was fresh – too fresh, sometimes – I would complain about some of the food on offer. One time in the evening the cold meat on offer was tongue. I think that even these days I might say a firm "No" to this, but having this presented to you at age four or five was not a great way of introducing you to new foods.

Uncle George was always busy in the day but he did have some time off to do some more exciting stuff with me. We played cricket in the field sometimes or took rides on the tractor – or once we had a trip down the lane to what appeared to be a waste tip where there were huge pits in the ground full of rubbish. Uncle George and Granddad took me there to try and find some wooden dowels to make into arrows for my toy bow.

Usually during our stay there would be a fete on Hawridge Common: a very low-key affair where a number of stalls would attract locals to try their luck. One game involved bowling small balls over the grass towards a series of score boxes lined up in a row. I think if you were the winner that maybe the highest score would win you a piglet. I have a notion that one year when my parents came over that my mum nearly won the pig. I'm not sure what we would have done if this had happened. I guess Uncle George would have looked after it. My favourite stall was one where a pointer was rotated on a table and segments were marked out with numbers. You bought a ticket with a number on and if the arrow stopped on your number you got a prize. I did well at this, and sometimes I wonder if this started my liking for roulette later on in life.

The time came when it was time to go home, and I hated going back. It wasn't that I hated home itself: it was just I loved the countryside and just seeing new things. Of course the trip back meant a last long ride in the car, but it all seemed to go too quickly and I was back in Lower Barn and packed off to bed. I used to lie in bed thinking about all my adventures. It would still have been light outside then. The curtains never shut the evening summer sunlight out. I dreamed of what I might do next year. It always seemed a long time to wait.

We're All Going on a Summer Holiday

1958-1970

It's no surprise to hear that we as a family enjoyed a summer holiday away at the seaside once a year. This is a very British tradition which had started in the mid 1800s and expanded to the more working-class throughout the early part of the 1900s. I would guess that even in the 1950s after the war maybe not everyone could afford this holiday away from home, but I would say that those at school whom I knew usually went to the coast during the six-week break we had in the summer.

My dad had two weeks' holiday from work each year but he could afford only to take one of these weeks away. Dad being Dad made it perfectly clear that the location where we went on holiday always had to be travelling south or east from where we were.

"We," he said once, "Will never be travelling up to any of those working-class sea resorts." My dad was no snob, by the way: he was to an extent from a working-class background himself but there was something about the northern seaside towns that, I think, frightened him. So it was Bognor, Brighton, Bournemouth, and the Isle of Wight, mostly, with a few trips further down to Dorset, Devon, and Cornwall.

The week's holiday away for me was almost as exciting as Christmas itself, and nearly as exciting as going to Uncle George's. A holiday at the seaside came a close second, and I can remember our holidays vividly from the early days when I was just really a toddler. In those early days Rob, my brother, came with us until he reached that age where you just want to do your own thing and parents are just naff and you don't want to interact with them any longer.

In the 1950s and to an extent the 1960s if you wanted to check out where to stay on holiday you looked in the national newspapers

– maybe the *Daily Sketch* or the *Daily Express* – at all the adverts which promised you sun, sand, and entertainment galore. You might cut out little adverts and then you would painstakingly write a letter to the PO box detailed on the advert. Weeks later a brochure would arrive in the post. It was a lengthy process to find out where to go and where to stay. There was no Internet then to look up locations and we had no phone, either. So letter post was the only communication you had. It took a very long time to sort out.

I don't think I was told till the last minute when we were going because I just got too excited. In fact I think I can remember one year just waking up and Mum saying,

"We going on holiday," that very day. I would have had sleepless nights otherwise.

Now holidays of course are still exciting today for all sorts of reasons – mostly, I guess, because you're away from home and you're not at work or school. Back then in the 1950s and 1960s a holiday was a huge adventure. It wasn't just the staying away somewhere. Oh, no. For me, as well as all of that, it was the getting there … and it took ages, and it was a truly awesome adventure for a little chap like me.

We had no car so the only way to travel was the train, and that meant maybe several changes across London. As far as I was concerned the adventure had begun even before we got to the station. You see, you either walked to Apsley train station or if Dad was flush with money we got a taxi. The issue here was that a taxi meant a trip over the dreaded Durrants Hill. I had this problem with my tummy doing a somersault when driven over hills and I really dreaded the Durrants Hill one as it was a humpback bridge and not really designed for modern cars. I would plead with Dad to either ask the taxi driver to go a different way or to go over it at a snail's pace. Once over the hill I was OK. I was a happy little boy. That is, of course, until I got into London.

The next obstacle in my way was the London Underground. If you're going to the coast on holiday and you're travelling south then you're going to have to hit London at some point and a trip on the

Tube was a necessity. The issue for me was that some stations had not yet been fitted with escalators, and that meant a trip in a lift with more tummy-churning antics. Again I would plead with Dad to find a route around London where we would not need to take one of those deep lifts down to the station platform.

Even some of the Tube trains frightened me a bit, and a certain type – the older ones – I didn't like at all. The hand grips suspended from the ceiling to me looked like skulls jumping and swinging about.

"Why would anyone touch a skull?" I thought?

Eventually we would get to one of the London stations that would take us to the coast. Sometimes we had a closed compartment to ourselves. There was no corridor here and you really had to make sure you had been to the loo before you got on. Once or twice Dad risked getting out to go to the loo when we stopped at a station. It was a close call sometimes, as leaving Dad behind at a station would not have been a good option.

When we reached our destination a bus or a short walk was usually needed to get to where we were staying. Dad liked as much as possible to be staying on the seafront with a view of the sea. Then this usually meant staying in a private hotel, which was more like a boarding house in those days.

I remember that one of the best trips we had was to the Isle of Wight. This entailed a train to Portsmouth, where we got down from the train to see – to one side – the boat we needed to catch that would take us over to the Isle of Wight. The boat trip was great, but the added bonus was that the boat docked at the end of the pier at Ryde and then you got on the pier train which took you to your final destination. I loved this trip, as it was full of special rides. My recollection was that the train on the pier was a little steam engine, but on a later trip it had become electric.

Food was an issue as well for me. I wasn't a good eater then and rather fussy with any grub that was served up, but I managed somehow – and, anyway, I was on holiday so I could leave what I didn't like.

Sometimes we went on holiday with the grandparents and aunts and uncles. It was fun being in a group, and even more of an adventure being a family all together.

I loved being on the beach and this was mainly where we were every day. We would rent some deckchairs and that would be it for the day. I would play in the sand and make sandcastles, then go down to the sea to fetch a pail of water. The first purchase for me was a bucket and spade of course: the obligatory equipment for any child on the beach. We always took these tools back home but they never returned to the beach after that because Dad always used my beach spade for picking up the dog poo off the garden ... so a new one was always bought each holiday and the rusty, smelly one left in the yard.

One thing my dad did on the beach really did cause a stir and sometimes attracted a few kids to come and look. He marked out a shape on the beach, then from the sides he shovelled up sand to form a mass he could then mould into a shape. The shape was usually either a steam train or a steamship. Once he had the shape in place and had cut in extra bits and pieces he then made a place for me to sit at the back so it looked like I was driving whatever he had built.

Of course, whatever the vehicle was had to have a funnel. He then cut into the mass of sand from where I sat and produced a boiler area, which would then feed up inside the sand through the chimney he had made. It all had to be done with careful hands and precision or the whole thing would collapse. All that was then left to do was to take a few pages from the *Daily Sketch* newspaper, shove it into the boiler and set light to it, and quickly block the boiler up with a little more sand. Hey presto! I was sitting on the sand in my little train or boat with real smoke coming out of the chimney. People would walk past us almost tripping over things as they stared in disbelief at the vision that presented itself. Kids would tug arms.

"I want one of those," they would say. I sat there smugly, knowing that I was the only person on the beach who would be sitting in a real sandcastle train that actually worked.

I also loved to fish off the pier for crabs, and another bit of equipment either brought with us or bought there was a hook, line, and sinker: a simple line to toss off the pier into the sea and see what you could catch. Of course you needed bait for the hooks, and bait was obtained beforehand by digging on the beach for worms. You found one of those funny worm casts on the beach and dug as fast as you could till you got the worm inside. These would then be put in my little bucket and kept for the duration of the holiday to fish. I never caught much … a crab or two, and once I got a small dab – but I loved sitting there and pulling up the line to see if there was a worm or a fish on the end.

My other major love was the arcades. I loved penny arcades with a passion, and wanted to be in there all the time. My favourites were the penny-pushing machines which were new in the sixties. There were also many machines where you flicked a metal ball into a cup which said either "Win" or "Lose". It was all fun and my dad had a passion for it too, which probably didn't help the holiday spending fund too much.

We sometimes ventured out to other areas on the bus to break up the week's holiday. I can remember that when we were on the Isle of Wight we took a trip by bus to Alum Bay on the west side. Wow. What a surprise that was, to see a beach made up of various colours of sand. In those days you were not restricted as you are today. You could clamber over the coloured rocks and sand and collect whatever sand you wanted for your little glass bottles made to look like street lamps or lighthouses.

Once or twice we took the option of going to the newly-started holiday camps. These were then completely new and modern. The experience was different to what we had done before. I loved the fact that where you slept was basically a wooden shed. There was entertainment at night too and I could stay with my parents at night to watch acts on the stage. Yes … the camps were a bit like what the Germans constructed in the war to keep prisoners from escaping, but they were fun all the same.

Yes ... holidays were always great, and I got the impression that Mum and Dad really needed this week's break. It was the only time of the year that they had a break from their very hard lives – and they were hard in those days, too. Dad worked a long day and my Mum did housework from dawn till dusk. A week does not seem long at all when the rest is work. The past was great, but this aspect thankfully has changed for most people.

Primary School

1962-1965

Moving to the junior school was far less traumatic than the start I had had at Infants. I suppose in my young mind I knew what to expect and it didn't seem a huge jump to make this time. I knew the kids and I actually knew the teacher. The school itself was the same distance from home as the infant school and all I had to do was walk down the path instead of up it.

I was taken to the school on the first day by my dad and dropped off at the gates. I was then allocated to Mrs Evans's class and shown into a new classroom right at the end of the corridor. There were a few more of us in this class than at the infant school. The desks were arranged in sets of two desks together and ran down in rows. There were maybe twenty kids in this class, and all of us were kids who had different types of learning difficulties. Mrs Evans's idea was to have each boy sitting next to a girl. This, I suspect, was a plan to ensure that the boys didn't mess about, but it didn't really work. We objected to this with a moan when we heard what the seating plan was going to be.

"What, sit with a girl? Are you joking?" we said.

Mrs Evans put us in our places. This was what was going to happen and if we didn't like it then that was tough. I was allocated a desk at the front with a girl called Marion. She was a redhead and was very shy and quietly spoken. It's strange because I don't remember her from Infants at all and I did wonder if we had some extra children in from another infant school. Behind me were Pat and Michael and together, as a bunch of four, we formed a bit of a gang together.

As a foursome we all got on really well. Marion was not a good reader at all and at one point Mrs Evans got her to read to me privately. I think Mrs Evans felt that my reading was good enough for me to at least go through the more simple books with her. She would read out the words in her very soft voice with her finger moving along the words slowly. It was slow progress but she got there in the end. I do look back with fondness on this activity and I hope that at least Marion found the help useful. Although Marion was not considered a girlfriend in any way, I did have a liking for her. We had something in common, which was a love for science fiction. One TV programme we looked forward to each week and talked about constantly was the TV puppet series *Space Patrol*. The adventures of Captain Larry Dart and his crew Slim and Husky were something we shared. She announced one term that her family would be moving to the coast (I think) and so she would be leaving school in Hemel for good. I was quite upset by this at the time and found her a real loss when she finally left us.

We would be at junior school for four years, which would take us up to age eleven years – the point where we would transfer to senior school. There was a split in the four years where in the first two years the kids had a separate playground area from the kids in the last two years. This seemed to be quite a good idea, as it stopped some of the older kids bullying the younger intake.

The headmaster of Belswains School at this time was a Mr Sully, a short stout man with a round face and bottom bottle glasses. He had a definite presence and no kid would ever give him cheek. We did learn very early on that Mr Sully had a cane and he would certainly use it if he needed to. A cane was used as a punishment and a deterrent. The cane was used across a boy's bottom. The expression was "Six of the best" … in other words six whips of the cane across your backside. In the time I was there I would say that he maybe used that cane once or twice. The actual fear of the cane was huge and definitely a deterrent. It may seem cruel these days to think that boys and sometimes girls were beaten for being naughty, but this was only done in exceptional cases. The value in having such a system in place for punishment was dramatic to say the least, as – really – kids just did as they were told. Usually a harsh voice from a teacher was enough to stop you and if you persisted then you would have to go to the front of the class and face the wall. Anything further meant Mr Sully was involved and you really didn't want to go there.

I stayed in Mrs Even's class for three years, moving room once to a better room near the third and fourth years' playground.

Mrs Evans seemed to be a good teacher although there was always some speculation as to her teaching credentials. There was a shortage of teachers at that time and I think Mr Sully found it difficult to employ good teaching staff.

We did far more in this school than we had done in the infant school. There was certainly more creativity here and we went on a variety of trips to different places – places that sometimes seemed to be at the ends of the earth. Some were relatively nearby like a trip to London Zoo, Madame Tussauds, Windsor Castle, and the Ovaltine Farm near Abbots Langley. All of these trips involved getting on a coach and driving to the destination. The coaches then were rattly old things that vibrated you as you sat on a seat that had that itchiest material you could ever imagine. As we all had short trousers on our legs would be a red mess by the end of the trip.

One or two of the boys would be physically sick on the trip out and there would be this nice smell of sick on the coach to remind you of your breakfast and its need to pay a visit to the real world once more. It seemed that trips out took ages to arrive at any destination. Once there we had a great time and our little satchels would be packed with a lunch that our mothers would have made for us, all wrapped up in greaseproof paper. A trip out was a great joy and really a day off school, but Mrs Evans always had some educational slant on the visit and we generally had to take some notes or colour in something.

The best trips out involved a train, and in the four years I was there we had a trip to Liverpool and a trip to Southampton Docks. Both these involved getting on a special train that was organised by the school to take us from Apsley to our destination. A train trip was a huge treat, and the excitement of being on a train was the best ever. I can remember being taken to Apsley station by my dad and then joining all the boys and girls on the platform. There was massive excitement, and I can only define the scene as like something out of *Harry Potter*. A huge steam train would arrive and we all got into coaches and found seats next to our pals. There was a massive noise with all the excitement, and the teachers and helpers on the train had a difficult time trying to control it all. Steam trains were exciting things to travel on. We all had tables, too, in blocks of four seats to do any work during the trip.

I'm so please that in later life I visited Mrs Evans in her eighties and took copies of the pictures she took on visits out. She had a good 35mm camera and liked to take slide films. She gave me this precious box of slides to get copies of the images taken all that time ago. It really was astonishing to see images of times past. To me these are priceless.

Another trip we had out was to the watercress beds down at Boxmoor in Hemel Hempstead. The trip entailed us walking from the school along the towpath of the canal to where we would be allowed to dip fishing nets in the water and see what we could find. We were warned in no uncertain terms that we should be careful near the edge of the hard standing where we would fish from. We had jam jars and those small fishing nets on bamboo poles. We took it in turns to pull out all sorts of monstrous things from the cress beds and put them into jars for inspection later. If you have never gone fishing with a net and jam jar you frankly have never lived.

There were small bridges across the streams we were fishing on. These had no handrails but had just basically a plank across from one side to another. I wanted to get across to the other side but standing on the bridge was one of the odd numbers children from my road. He would not budge, and as I tried to skirt around him he actually pushed me into the cress beds. There was a loud kersplosh as I hit the mix of lush green carpet and water. I can hear Mrs Evans's voice now. Talk about a telling-off … but, really, I had done nothing. The odd numbers kid just grinned. He knew full well what he had done. They dragged me out of the water. It was not deep – and just as well, as I could not swim.

"What now?" said Mrs Evans. "We need to get this boy dried. He is sopping wet."

I was indeed wet. I was dripping from head to toe and although it was a warm summer's day I needed to get out of those wet clothes fast. I'm not sure how the suggestion came about, but one of the boys in the group – a Polish boy, also named Richard – had his games kit on under his clothes. Now I have always wondered why he would have this kit on because we were not scheduled for a games lesson that day, but he had all this extra clothing on.

Richard was told to strip off and take the top and shorts off, and I was told to strip off and put all this sports gear on. Yes, I had to strip naked behind Mrs Evans and I could see all the girls trying to catch a glimpse of my bum. There were giggles and sniggers. I was not happy at all. For the rest of the day I stayed in these clothes until mine had dried out on a line that was made in school. I was the talk of the school, and looking different to everyone else meant I was teased all day. It was a memorably horrible day for me and I will never forget it.

Before I went home that day I went into the changing rooms and changed back out of Richard's kit into my own (now dry) clothes. I went home and said nothing of my adventure that day to my parents. I think they must have found out, though, in the end – or suspected, as my mum commented a day or two later that my clothes seemed kind of wrinkled, as if they had got wet in some way.

"Ducky, why are your shorts all creased? Have you been sitting somewhere funny?"

"Yes, Mum, I suppose I have," was the answer back.

Mrs Evans taught everything, and as well as reading, writing, and arithmetic we also had a lot of nature and geography. We generally learned about the Commonwealth countries and as Mrs Evans came from Canada that was one area we looked at in detail. Another was Australia, and we did have a trip to Australia House in London at one time. She would also from time to time read us stories from books and we also did some art on occasions. The class was a happy one, generally, and I felt that I might have been one of Mrs Evans's favourites at the time. Later on in life when I did catch up with her to talk over things she made a comment to me about how smartly I was dressed compared to a lot of the other boys. This – of course – was down to my dad who, no matter what the situation was concerning money, insisted that you had to look smart and your shoes always had to be polished.

One of the new things we were taught by Mrs Evans was to write using joined-up writing. Now I'm sure that every child has to perform this at some point in their education, but ours was the old-school way. First off we were given lined paper that had four lines across for writing these special joined-up letters. Two lines were close together and you would write your small letters in between these lines. The other two outer lines guided you to where the loops of some letters might reach, like a g or an f or the capital letters. You were given an ink pen to write with. These pens were basically a wooden stick with a metal nib on the end of it. At the back of the nib was a little reservoir pocket that held a small amount of ink. You dipped your ink pen into a big bottle of ink until the jacket was full. Then you could maybe write a couple of pages of work before your hand would go up and it would be,

"Miss, my pen's empty." Later, when we had established our writing better, we were told to buy our own ink pen. These would usually be the new ink cartridge-style pens that held a capsule of ink in a plastic throw-away reservoir. Under no circumstances were you allowed to use a biro. These were forbidden by children to use: only the teachers could use these for marking books and the register. Now because we were using real ink in our pens the stuff got everywhere. All the desks you sat at in those days were covered in ink splodges along with names written and carved into the wood. It was a tradition in those days to mark your desk somewhere with your name. There was no way a teacher would detect this because it was lost in among all the other etchings from previous years.

The Dreaded Games

One thing that I objected to so much at primary school was the afternoon each week when we had to participate in the dreaded games lesson. I would call it an hour of pure hell. The winter was the worst, as we were sent out in all weathers.

Football was the main game. We changed into our kit and then were sent outside on to the open grass playing field that connected both schools. A teacher in charge would then pick two captains to select the teams. Each captain would then take alternate turns to pick from the shivering huddle of boys on the pitch. One by one kids were chosen and each one walked away until all that was left was me alongside the classic tubby boy, and then a smaller boy than me who looked like he could die any minute of malnutrition and then a boy who looked like Stan Laurel with an excess of ear wax coming out of his ears. Then it was a toss-up as to which team would have either set of the four most unwanted players.

It was not as if I couldn't kick a ball. I could. All this selection thing was about those who could play football didn't actually want the smaller – or indeed fatter or waxier – boy to enter the play. By cutting us out of any of the action meant they could have a faster, better-paced game. You might think that the teachers would have levelled out all this bias – but no: the teachers really could not care less. Tubby and I always ended up on the same team and Waxy and his dying friend on the other. We were always ordered to play left back and right back. In this position we were told that we stood there on the spot near the goal and if the ball came towards us we should run away ... so much for defensive football, then.

You might know how young kids play football at that age. They don't pass the ball to their own team players. What they do is move in a huddled mass around the field chasing the ball. So this was the scene: a mass of kids running about the field after a very heavy leather ball and at each end of the field two sets of freezing, blue, cold defence players who never ever touched the ball in all the games we played.

The goalie had some action, of course, but his game was not that great either. I used to look at tubby and say to him,

"What do you reckon, John? Do you reckon it's half past yet?"

He would answer, and about a minute later I would repeat the question. We stood out there on our spots as blue as you could imagine skin could get. We danced from one foot to another like some strange pair of human metronome.

"Is it half past yet, John, do you reckon?"

"No idea," said John. "I can't feel my feet now. I want to go home."

I would spy the infant school pupils leaving for home in the distance. That meant fifteen minutes left for us to play this bloody awful game – or was it stand and shiver?

"Not long now, John. It's nearly over, mate. Try and make it through."

This wasn't football. This was like men climbing Mount Everest or attempting to reach the South Pole each week.

"Hold on, John, I'm just going outside. I maybe some time..."

Finally the whistle blew and we went in. I think what really got to me standing out there in the freezing cold was that from where I was standing with John I could see my house quite clearly. I could see my bedroom windows and almost feel the warmth and security inside. I was so close to home, yet in a total hostile and stupidly-managed situation. I hated Thursdays with a vengeance. I could put up with most of what went on at school but sports afternoon was something that turned my stomach over. To this day I can't watch it or play it or have any interest in it. To me school did a lot of harm regarding sport, and the teachers were totally to blame.

While on the subject of the cold it's interesting to note that all the boys wore short trousers all year round, with long socks in winter and shorter ones in summer. Our knees were often dirty and grazed from kneeling or banging into things. My knees had countless scars over the years. It was only at the age of eight that I was allowed to wear jeans at the weekends. Otherwise it was shorts all the time no matter how cold it was outside, and that included snow.

In the winter months it was the dreaded football and the cold. Then in the summer in some respects it got worse. When I started school I could not swim. While there I never managed to swim and now, even in later life, I still can't swim. So what went wrong?

During the third year of primary school you had to go swimming at Churchill's Swimming Baths near Cotterells. Churchill's was an open-air swimming baths open to the general public and available for school use on weekdays. The order of the day was that a certain morning in the week would be allotted to our school and a coach would turn up to drive us the short distance to the pool. To say I hated this was an understatement. The whole idea of water and jumping in and going under was something that would freak me out by just thinking about it. I would rather be standing in a cold field than right back than on that bloody coach.

Some kids could actually already swim but most could not. Lessons started off with flotation aids in front of us and for us to doggy-paddle from a distance out back to the side. The issue here was that there was no qualified instructor doing all this teaching to swim. Oh, no. This was all down to the teachers to perform this obviously simple and non-dangerous task. Teachers, I might add, who were of course very ready to jump in if there was any hint of danger. I'm sure the twinset and pearls were all part of the lifesaving kit in those days.

We had to jump in off the side in the three-foot end of the pool. Now this does not sound much as an adult but if you're only four feet tall it's a bloody big deal. I managed to do this, as it happens, a few times – and I think I was almost getting that confidence to go that bit further when something took place which affected me deeply. I was on the edge waiting to go in. I was feeling confident and I was watching the others drop in one by one. I was just getting ready to go when one of the teachers pushed me in.

I went in OK – not legs first, as was hoped, but more on my side – and my head went under and stayed under for what seemed ages. I suspect it was only seconds, but it felt like I would drown for sure. I must have found my footing as I surfaced and coughed up water. No one asked me if I was OK. Had someone made a mistake here? I suspect they had and then thought better of it, because at that point the lesson was stopped. The net result of all this was that I would be frightened of water for life. I hated Churchill's with a real hatred: hated its name and what it stood for. After that I think I may have even been excused going for swimming lessons as some kids seemed to still go and others didn't. I was one who didn't. I know who the teacher was on that day and I hated her too.

Jumping ahead slightly … when at senior school we had to go to Churchill's again. Again I was terrified. I was about twelve years old now, and still unable to swim. The group who could not swim at this age was much smaller now, as most could. They tried hard but I could not do it. This then fizzled out as I suspect the school just gave up on the ones who could not swim, expecting them to drown in later life.

While at this point in life – and when at Churchill's, aged twelve – we kids were all expected to change in the communal changing room. This was a large room and it was made available, it seems, to the kids from all the schools in the area. I was used to changing into my sports kit as this was done at school quite often. Changing at Churchill's was different. You had to get naked at some point and it sort of felt odd to show your body off in front of your schoolmates. Kids look, for sure, and make comments sometimes too. You were given the smallest of towels to dry with in those days too: no larger than a flannel, really.

At one particular time in these changing rooms we were all getting changed. There were no teachers about here. No supervision of course. There were two or three other older kids in there as well, drying off after a swim. I would guess these to be about thirteen or fourteen years old: we were maybe eleven or twelve. One of them stood in the middle of the changing rooms and said to all the congregation,

"Do all of you want to watch me wank?" The kids stopped drying and chattering. There was silence as heads twisted and faces looked puzzled.

I had no idea what any of this was about. Some of my school chums did, it would seem, and the puzzlement gave way to smirks and grins on faces around me.

"Go on, then," shouted someone from the far corner. "Let's see yer do it, then".

"This has to be something bad," I thought.

It just felt like it could be bad from how the congregation acted. You just know at that age when something is maybe just outside the parameters you're supposed to know about. Clearly wanking was not a subject teachers taught, clearly it was not something Mum and Dad talked about and, clearly – unlike the 100 yards swimming test – you weren't going to get a certificate in it.

A small group assembled around the lad, who was now pulling his privates about with some ungainly hand movements. He was totally naked and not bothered at all about the audience assembled.

"Oooh," went the congregation as he picked up speed. I watched in horror from a slight distance, craning my neck to try and understand what this was all about.

"Is he having a pee?" I thought. "What is this all about? What the hell is he doing with his willy?"

"Aaarrr," went the congregation as the lad spurted all over the changing room floor. There were blobs all over the place and some of the lads even crouched down to take a better look at the substance that had left the boy at speed.

"There you go," said the lad, with a grin on his face. "Simple, innit?"

The group went back to changing and drying again and lots of murmurs went on after that, and still went on during the ride back in the coach. There were some that said they were trying that tonight at home.

That was my sex education completed, then.

British Bulldog

The junior school had the same break times as we had had at Infants: one in the morning and one in the afternoon. Again we were expected to be outside in all weathers. The playgrounds had the bonus of a water fountain but this was mainly used to squirt people when it was working, and that was not often. The playground was a hard surface with a netball and a six-a-side football pitch marked out on it. One of the favourite games to play in the playground was British Bulldog. This was a bit of a rough game and although I didn't like it much we were kind of expected to take it on.

A group of players would be at one end of the playground. There would be one bulldog chosen at will in the middle to start with. The first bulldog was likely to be someone who was big and sporty. The object was to get from one end of the playground to the opposite end without being captured by the bulldog. You all had to go at once when the command was given. Usually the bulldog had his eye on one particular person to capture – maybe the weakest. It was a case of dodge and evade. Once you were caught the bulldog had to get you on to the ground, so it was not just a matter of tag: this was rough stuff and sometimes you might get hurled to the ground. Then, if caught like this, you too became a bulldog along with your captor. In order to win the objective was to be the last one standing. I can assure you that there was many a boy who went home from school with a ripped coat or blazer after playing this one.

Recorders

Instruments were introduced to us while we were at primary school. We were given the opportunity to purchase a recorder to play. Oh … I so wanted one of these and I persuaded my mum and dad to stump up the money to buy one of the smaller ones. They were a wooden affair in two bits with some wax string wound around one half to form a sort of seal. What I didn't appreciate then was that my inability to read and write well would also hinder my reading of music. In addition to all this, no one explained that there would be recorder lessons and playing to audiences.

If I had known all this then I would never have insisted on owning one. But it was too late. I was in the recorder section.

Mrs Sucliff was a stern young music teacher and she wore those glasses which looked like bats' wings from the front. They were slightly turned up where the side bars were attached. These glasses made her look even sterner than she actually was. In actual fact she was quite an attractive young lady but to us kids she was the Devil in disguise. Mrs Sucliff really put us through our paces and there were tunes to learn and that meant practice at home. Luckily my mum knew music and could help with the notes. She taught me the EGBDF and FACE way of working out what the notes were on the funny music paper.

But I still had trouble. I still could not easily read music and I suspect that my dyslexia didn't help any of this. I could remember parrot-fashion a simple tune but what we were expected to perform needed to be read from music sheets. The day arrived where we were expected to play in assembly, and this would be a whole hymn. There was no way I was going to be able to do this: it was too long to remember. I used to team up with a boy called Alan who always wore hand-knitted green cardigans. He could play, and he played well too. Maybe I could use him in some way to get through this ordeal.

The day came and I was as nervous as hell. The recorder players marched into the hall first and we sat on seats facing what was soon to become the assembled whole school. I sat next to Alan and in front of us stood a traditional music stand with the music for 'All Things Bright and Beautiful' detailed in quavers and other symbols that meant nothing to me. I was in deep trouble here, but I did have a cunning plan (if I could pull it off).

The classes started to file in and I sat and watched them as they did this and then sat down cross-legged on the floor in front of us. I looked down the line of my group of musical players. Alan and I (the only boys) were on the end. Then there were two or three more music stands with descant recorder players on them, followed by the bigger recorders and then the bass ones right at the end. I always envied the bass recorder players as their recorders were long and had nice shiny metal paddles (a bit like a clarinet) for covering the furthest holes. Of course, even if I had had such a beautiful instrument it would have still been useless in my hands.

All the children were now sitting down and some teachers lined the sides of the room on chairs, constantly inspecting the mass on the floor for mischief-makers. Mr Sully came in and climbed the short staircase that took him up on to the stage above us. He stood at his lectern.

Mr Sully would be speaking for a while, and then it would be our turn. I sat and looked around. The kids on the floor were a distraction: some looked at Mr Sully and some looked at us. My mouth went dry. I felt sick.

"Not long now," I thought as I looked at Alan's green knitted cardigan and the nice bobble buttons on it. "Nice, I thought. Why can't I have one with buttons like that?"

"All stand," came the voice behind us, and there was much scuffling and screeching of chairs as the congregation in front of us stood.

"This is better," I thought. "They are all standing now – and we, the players, are less of a centre of attention."

Mrs Sucliff was on the piano and nodded to us all to place our recorders in our mouths. We all did, and all the players placed their fingers on the right holes for the first note. My eyes went right, looking at Alan's finger positions, and I immediately copied them.

"If nothing else the first note will be the right one," I thought.

"Plooong," went the piano with a single note, to emphasise that the next note would be the one we started on. They blew and I blew the first note correctly.

"All things bright and beautiful, all creatures great and small," the whole school sang, and the recorders played in tune too. It all sounded magnificent.

"All things wise and wonderful…"

The players' fingers were moving over their instruments – and mine were, too, in a kind of deftness you would imagine could only come from a practised professional player.

"The Lord God made them all."

"Wow, that's the first verse over," I thought. "And I seem to be getting away with it."

The next verse started and we repeated what we had already played. I made sure that most of the recorder was shielded from the audience by the music stand. This meant slightly stooping to reduce my size slightly. Nobody actually noticed the sound coming out of my recorder, because actually there was no sound. My fingers were moving over the holes but no breath was being pushed down the mouthpiece. Nobody noticed that my fingers were constantly over the wrong notes. As Eric Morecambe would later say,

"I was playing all the right notes, but not necessarily in the right order." They may have observed my practised breathing where I took my mouth momentarily off the mouthpiece to gasp in more air at the end of a line. But no note – not one squeak – came out of the end of mine. I had mimed the whole hymn.

"The Lord God maaade themmm alll…"

"… and finish … and the school will applaud … and bow slightly to the school and sit down," Mrs Sucliff instructed us. I smiled at the applause.

"No … no. It was nothing, really," I thought inside with a grin on my face. Of course, it was nothing at all. I had pulled it off.

I laugh now at all this, but it was terrifying at the time. If I had been found out God knows what would have happened. I hated the recorder. I hated the practice sessions. I hated the playing to people. I needed a way out but I was so scared of Mrs Sucliff that I felt I could never go to her and say,

"Hey ... you know what, Mrs S? I can't play a bloody note. I'm shit at this recorder thing and I don't like your glasses. They give me nightmares."

Oh, no, I would not be talking to her. But I needed to do something – and soon, too, before someone suggested I do a solo. I talked to Mum and Dad about it all and they understood and could see the anguish on my face. They wrote a note:

Dear Mrs Sucliff,

Our son won't be coming to recorder lessons any more ... blah blah blah.

Your sincerely,

Mr and Mrs Blackshire.

It was put in an envelope and given to me to give to her.

Well do you know what? I didn't even have the guts to give the note to her. I feared that if I went to her with the note she would read it in front of me and then look down with her steely eyes and then lasers or something would come out of those bats' wing glasses. No, I slid it under her door while she was taking a class. That was that. No more miming, and no more looking at Alan's bobbly cardigan. I was free.

Playground Antics

The playground scene at junior school was slightly different to the one at Infants. We still had the same time outside but the play was different. Most of the boys were preoccupied with playing war. War was a big deal then, and most of the films on TV were depicting escapades from the Second World War. We would play the British against the Germans. You ran around and you shot your opponents by sticking one arm out as if you had a rifle or sub-machine gun and you made a noise to denote your gun had gone off. You then shouted something like,

"I got you, you filthy rotten Hun. You're dead…" or, "You're not taking your shots, you Nazi bastard."

You were supposed to roll to the ground if you were shot and stay dead until someone released you. The game was frantic and usually culminated in some argument over who had won the war. The Germans always lost, of course. That's always the case in anything we do, even today.

The train activities from the infant school where kids hung on to the backs of the one in front's jumper to form a train had largely been developed further. It was not to be trains now. No: we were in the space age, and the order of the day was something from a Gerry Anderson programme like *Fireball XL5* … so two of you would join up by one clutching on to the back of another's coat and charging off on some space adventure as Colonel Steve Zodiac and Robert the robot.

When the *Doctor Who* series screened the Daleks all hell broke loose in the playground. No longer were we soldiers of war shooting Germans but we were Daleks from the planet Skaro blasting the Thals to bits. Still with our arms stretched out to form a gun or a plunger, we would run about shouting,

"Exterrrminate," at every opportunity. This got so out of hand that Daleks were barred from the playground for a time.

Some other activities in the playground revolved around swapping bubblegum cards, which seemed to be very popular. It started off with black-and-white pictures of the Beatles being sold in little packets of four cards along with a strip of foul-tasting pink bubblegum. The cards depicted the Beatles in various poses and there were sixty in all to collect in the first series. It became so popular that Topps (the producers) made several more series of cards. As kids in the playground we would be constantly swapping cards to get the whole set.

Following on from this was another set of cards from the TV series *The Man from U.N.C.L.E.*. Again it was the same format, with cards and bubblegum in a sealed wrapper, and you really wanted to get the whole set if you could. Another set that we loved and what caused a bit of contention in the school was the American Civil War trading card set. These cards depicted scenes from the American war between the blues and the greys in very graphic detail.

In fact some of the cards were so horrific that it instigated a news item on the evening BBC news. One of the cards depicting men on spikes was entitled "Painful death". There were questions asked as to whether children should be allowed to see these scenes, as nearly all the cards had some form of bloodshed. In the pack of cards along with the awful pink bubblegum was a Confederate banknote. There were seventeen different notes in nine denominations in all, and these in themselves caused a whole new collection fever. Kids were walking around school with bundles of these notes and using them like real money – either to swap, or to buy sweets from other kids. I think in the end the school had to ban the cards and the money because of public outcry.

These fads, of course, come and go with the wind. Each term there would be something new. Teachers were ever vigilant as to what that new craze might bring to the school.

Mr Sully and his Music

Mr Sully was a great headmaster. That was a given. You might hate him as a boy or love him, but you had to admit that he ran the school with a sharpness and sturdiness like a captain might run a tight ship. He was not a big man by any means. He was short and rotund, with short podgy fingers that my dad said were like chipolata sausages. In fact my dad always wondered how Mr Sully could play the piano with fingers like that but he did – and very well he played it, too.

Sully was a great believer in teaching music to the school and he took it upon himself to do this himself. In assembly he would take over the proceedings and lecture us on certain musicians from the past. Handel, Bach, Beethoven … they all came rolling out for discussion and then he would play us a passage from something over the speakers.

I liked this part, and it seems to have stayed with me somewhat. Certain music I hear now takes me back to that hall where Sully's music was played. Before the music started he would ask us to move our fingers in the air in time to the beat. A march would be a two beat and we would have to move our fingers up and down in a one, two, one, two motion. A waltz would be a three beat: one, two, three – and the shape to make was a triangle in the air. Lastly would be a four beat, which had a complicated series of events to follow. This was not a simple shape – and it was definitely not a square, as you might expect. It was more of an upturned T shape.

Yes, Mr Sully was a great man and it was a pleasure to have known him.

The Last Day at Primary.

It came to pass that the final day arrived at primary school. We all knew which schools we would be going to after the summer holidays. There had been a selection process, and I think as part of that I had sat what was called the Eleven Plus exam. I was not going to be grammar school material at all. I knew that, and my parents knew it too. My dad had to fill out a form concerning schools selected for me to go to. The form asked for three grammar schools and three secondary modern schools and you listed these in order of preference. To ensure that I went to Bennetts End secondary modern my father only wrote down one option instead of three. The one school they didn't want me to go to was Corner Hall, a school very fondly known as the Prison on the Hill.

The last day of school was a day of reversal. We were told we could do what we liked as long as we were quiet. In mid afternoon there would be a special assembly, which had been moved from the customary morning slot. This would be the last event in school, and after this we would leave for good. We marched into the hall while some very grand music by Bach was playing – that very well-known stirring choral music which is played at royal weddings and suchlike. Whenever I hear this music today I always get one of those pangs, as it takes me back to this last final day at this school.

We sat and listened to the wise words of Mr Sully one final time as he told the ones who were leaving how we were destined for more wonderful things in life and how the senior school would be a different type of education to what we had experienced.

"New adventures," he said. "New possibilities and new friendships."

He was not wrong, of course. We did listen but in our minds the excitement of the summer holiday and seven weeks off was bubbling away to almost bursting point.

We marched out of the hall to yet again the same music as we had entered to. There wasn't much left to do but to go home. There was no big party, no shaking of hands, or anything. We just left. I walked out along the path that took you to the school gates with a friend, Richard K. I had made a few friends in primary school: David, John, Terry, and Richard, to name only a few. Richard and I spoke and chatted as we walked. The conversation was mainly about what would happen to us next at secondary and what it would be like. We had no idea. At the gates I turned right up the path and Richard walked straight on. I never saw Richard again, just like I didn't see many of the others, either. Our paths had crossed at primary school but the lines were now veering off in completely different directions. All but one of my friends would be going to Corner Hall, and that would be the end of that. I walked home in part elated, as it was now the school holidays, and in part a little sad that I was moving on. I knew that secondary school would be different, but how different could it really be? After all, Infants to Juniors was really a piece of cake. Surely this would be the same. Unfortunately, it wasn't. The new school would be a huge leap with totally new challenges to overcome, and my comfort zone would be stretched once more.

The Dawn of a Modern Age

It is difficult to say how important television was back in the fifties and sixties. It still is very important, of course, but having lived through its evolution I can only wonder at its impact back then in those early years.

To own a new TV back in the 1950s meant that you had to maybe pay something between £50 and £80. This would have been a huge amount of money then. An average man's wage a year was about £400 at that time. So a TV set would have cost more than a month's salary.

I can remember that we always had a TV set although I understand that as a baby we maybe didn't, and we may have gone next door occasionally to watch Auntie Joyce and Uncle Keith's TV set.

Our first TV back then was a Bush black-and-white TV. It would have had a screen size of about fifteen inches and was almost square. It didn't have a variable tuner as it only could receive the one BBC channel. This set had been bought before the ITV company had started transmission around 1955.

On the front of the TV below the screen were two large knobs, one on either side of a flip-down panel in the middle. There was an on and off switch one side and on the other was the volume control. The Bakelite flap in the middle hid a number of smaller control knobs. These controllers – about eight in all– were not to be touched by younger hands. Oh, no. It was forbidden for me to move these at all, and only adults could make adjustments here. There were names under the knobs like horizontal hold, vertical hold, and line linearity. These were complicated-sounding things to the young eye – but nonetheless, later in life I would know exactly what these terms meant.

The television was only switched on in the evenings and this was the only time any programmes were screened. Daytime TV had not been invented and if you were to switch on your TV in the daytime all you got was a test card and music, or maybe nothing – just the sound of static.

When you switched the TV on each night it was really hit-and-miss. You would click the on/off knob and then wait. No picture would appear for at least half a minute or sometimes longer. You would hear the line time base transformer inside the set whine as the power increased to drive the mighty cathode ray tube, the screen. It was this sound that gave you the clue that the TV set might in fact work that evening. A murky picture would start to appear which might roll over several times before settling down. You just hoped that the picture would be stable for the whole of the evening. If it wasn't then Dad had to open the flap at the front and jiggle with various controls until some stability resulted. There was always a smell from the back of a set – a sort of warm, sickly smell as the electrical components tried to do their job.

At least twice a year the set would break down and there was no willing it back to life, even with the controls under the flap. Hans Peters would arrive to fix the problem. Hans ran a TV repair shop in Hemel. He was one of the many German prisoners of war who after the war decided not to go back to Germany. He was a whizz at electronics and usually fixed it on the first visit out.

When Hans opened up the back of the set I always wanted to see inside. I was mesmerised by all that was in there. Waxy components and glass bulbs that lit up. It all looked like an Aladdin's cave to me. Invariably the issue was a valve, and Hans would replace this and leave the faulty glass object on top of the TV as proof of replacement. I loved it when the TV guy was coming, as I was interested in electronic components and all the wires that went with them.

In retrospect and looking back to those days I'm amazed this box of tricks worked at all. In later life I would become – like Hans – a TV engineer, and I would service TV sets from the 1970s in the future. The TV sets in the fifties were crude to say the least. Components had hardly any tolerance: some were made from wax and actually dripped inside the sets. There were no circuit boards at this stage: components were tagged to each other by solder on what were called tag boards. It always looked like a tangled mess. Cathode ray tubes (the screens) only lasted a few years and then became too expensive to replace. They would become what were called poisoned and the image on the set would almost be a negative to what you normally saw. We knew no better then and although I paint a picture of unreliability in actual fact to us it was all hi-tech and what today we would call leading-edge stuff.

Watching TV shows on a 405-line TV set as a family was magic: it was pure entertainment in your home for the very first time. It mattered not what was on the TV, as you just watched anything. You watched the magic that was TV in its infancy.

My interest for electrical things was sparked from that point, and I just loved playing with wire and bulbs and batteries. I could not get enough of it. If my dad had to rewire a plug I would be there to help. He would let me wire things and then check them over afterwards.

In those days electrical goods went wrong quite often and the man of the house was expected, to a degree, to fix simple things. Appliances then had mains leads as they do today but this then was called flex. Flex consisted of the normal copper cables with some rubber around to insulate them and then on the outer layer of the flex was a fabric covering like a long woven jacket. If ever you wanted to cut these wires and make new bare-wire contacts for something then my dad would carefully use an old razor blade to cut into the flex. He always had a small screwdriver to hand with a Bakelite handle and referred to this as the electrical screwdriver, which was only to be used on electrical goods.

There was always something to open up and fix. Sometimes the vacuum cleaner would need new brushes and I would be there to help. Or maybe the Christmas tree lights needed testing with a battery before we strung them out over the tree. I would be there to do this too.

The other item in the house that amused me was the wireless radio. Wireless was then a lovely term used to describe a radio set. These items then were mains-powered, as they used valves inside for amplification. Transistors – which would later replace thermionic valves – had not yet been invented. Like with the TV the wireless took a little while to warm up, but it always seemed to work and didn't really ever go wrong.

Along the top of the wireless under a clear Perspex window was a long list of radio stations running from left to right. You might be able to pick up these stations as you turned the tuner dial. These were stations not only in the UK but overseas as well. Some had magical, exotic names that I had never heard of before. You turned the dial on the front and an illuminated strip of plastic inside slowly moved across the band of station names. You would carefully turn the tuner knob: once you heard either some music or voices you stopped, sometimes going back and forth to find the right position to listen to. You had to be careful sometimes to get what you wanted, as some stations were on top of each other in frequency. You heard all sorts of languages, especially at night, when it seemed that the sky wave effect was more pronounced. Radio could be heard from the far-flung corners of the globe, although fading in and out was always an issue.

Radio was a big deal and nearly always on in the daytime for my mum to listen to. Programmes such as *The Archers* were a firm favourite along with *Workers' Playtime* and the *Billy Cotton Band Show*. Two of my mum's favourites were *Mrs Dale's Diary* with the melodic harp music at the beginning and *Woman's Hour* when women's issues would be discussed in the afternoon. Sometimes when *Woman's Hour* was on I was told to go out of the room as ladies things were to be discussed in that episode. There were also programmes for kids such as *Listen with Mother* with a story once a day and *Children's Favourites* at the weekends when they played music for kids.

'Little White Bull' by Tommy Steele was one I can recollect, and the great Danny Kaye had a few too which were favourites: 'The Emperor's New Clothes' is one example. As TV was not available in the daytime the wireless was a good substitute: it was good company for the housewives at home and the young children too.

My brother used to have the Eagle comic annuals then. These were red-coloured books with comic strips and articles about all sorts of derring-do from the day. Of course the most famous strip of the day in the *Eagle* was *Dan Dare, Pilot of the Future*. I loved these red annuals as there was always something in there to look at: not only the comic strips but also useful educational stuff too. In one of these books was a complete guide on how to make what was called a crystal set. A crystal set was in fact a wireless, but nothing like the one we would be listening to in the living room. No: a crystal set was basically a coil of wire, a diode crystal, and a tuner. That was it. No battery: no power needed. You did, however, need a set of headphones to listen to it with as there was no amplification here. My dad managed to get some old used headphones from the BBC on one of his customer visits there. Rob made the rest out of wood and hardboard and bits of wire he could scrounge.

The finished article was a block of wood and some sides made out of hardboard. In the middle was a large cardboard tube about four inches high to which copper cable had been neatly wound to form a coil. Other than that there was little else. The crystal or diode was a simple semiconductor component no bigger than a grain of rice. The tuner and the knob for it had been taken from an old scrapped radio. The headphones had bare wires on the end and you pushed these wires into little brass tubes on the side of the set. To hold the wires in place you used some matchsticks to retain the wires in the holes. This was about as hi-tech as you would get in the late fifties. No phono jack socket here, folks.

It was amazing to hear the faint reception through the phones. Mind you, it needed a good aerial input to get reception – but you could pick up one or two stations on this very simple device. My dad had this thought that if we used the telephone wires which ran to the house as a sort of aerial we could pick up far more than using our own TV aerial. We went upstairs into Rob's bedroom. My dad had this idea that if he threw a wire over the telephone cables just outside Rob's bedroom window then that would work well. Dad got as far as throwing the cable and hitting the wires outside before we heard a loud crack... My dad said some words I had not heard before and he dropped the cable on the floor. There were, I believe, about fifty volts running through the telephone line so we abandoned that idea and went back to a safer option.

I was about thirteen when I had the money saved up to buy myself a transistor radio. My mum already had a portable radio in the kitchen now and my brother had one too. My mum had the blue/grey Bush one you always now see in TV plays. The wireless in the living room was virtually redundant now. Things had moved on and tiny silicon transistors were now replacing the power-thirsty valves of the past. This meant that radios (although not televisions) could be portable, and we had a new word for our new radios: the tranny. In fact the tiny transistor used in these portable devices was exclusively responsible for pop culture taking off in the sixties.

When I was ten in 1964 a ship way out off the coast of Felixstowe started broadcasting popular music, or pop as we now know it today. The name of the station on this ship was Radio Caroline and its transmissions were seen to be illegal. This was called pirate radio. To us kids this rebellious situation of pop music being played almost 24/7 was dead cool and anti-establishment.

The BBC's Home and Light Services (as they were called in those days) only played pop music on a Saturday and Sunday afternoon. The rest of the time it was all the old fuddy-duddy music from before the war, and during it too. The BBC had not got their act together. They were not considered cool in any way. Now that kids and teens could buy a portable transistor radio, music could be listened to anywhere and at any time. It was like the mobile phone revolution of the 1980s and 1990s. Young people demanded that more pop music be played on the radio, and gradually and begrudgingly the BBC complied. It was not until 1967, some three years after Caroline had started transmitting, that Radio 1 started and the kids got pop music with better reception every day.

I knew the shop in Bennetts End sold transistor radios so I went up there with my dad to check them out. I could only afford the cheaper two-transistor radio: some had six transistors in for better amplification and fidelity. The make I purchased was a Benkson one made in China, as almost everything was at that time. It was a small box a little bigger than a packet of cigarettes. It was cream in colour with a gold speaker grille on the front. Two side wheels were the only adjustments: one to switch on and off and to change the volume and the other to move the tuning dial. On the back was a switch to change between long wave and medium wave. There was also a jack plug in the top for the essential earplug.

The tranny came with a brown leather case which stated it was leather, but what sort of leather? This was the question. The case smelled really bad, and I always wondered what Chinese animal this case had come from. There was no stereo then, so a simple earpiece was all that was needed to listen privately. This meant that I could go under my bedcovers with a torch and listen to all sorts of things at night, and no one would be able to hear my radio. This was fantastic, and a huge leap from what we had had only a few years previously. Technology was thundering along at an alarming speed. Transistors had replaced valves, and even the individual transistors would be short-lived as semiconductor technology and miniaturisation progressed.

The Goggle Box

It's worth a chapter on TV and the shows that were on at the time I was growing up. TV was a big thing, as already mentioned. Unfortunately our early TV set didn't have ITV, and for the first three or four years I was at a huge disadvantage regarding watching TV programmes as I only had one channel.

Baz and most people in the street had two channels, and would talk about things I could only dream about watching. We did eventually have to buy another TV set when I turned nine. The new TV had a push button set-up for switching channels and was the most modern of its time. It also had at the top the provision for another set of buttons for BBC2 and the new 625-line transmission that was about to start. These new sets were known as dual-standard TVs. They bridged the gap between the old murky 405-line system and the new and improved 625-line. Although we had a super-duper TV set now, guess what? It would still be another eight years before my family would have BBC 2.

There was not that much on TV for young people in the early days and that's another frustration for me as the other channel, ITV, would have at least given me some more options.

Children's Hour consisted of a time slot of programmes in the week from five o'clock till the six o'clock news started. Two programmes would normally be aired in this time. Programmes then were live unless a show from America was shown. Programmes like *Blue Peter* were screened live the same as *Crackerjack* on a Friday. American serials such as *The Lone Ranger* and the *Whirlybirds* were popular and usually had a film-like quality to them. All these of course were in black-and-white – or monochrome, as we know it today.

Most of the other time outside of *Children's Hour* I would have to watch adult programmes as those were basically the only other shows that were on. At the weekend there might be something along the lines of a variety show when singing, comedians, and other acts would perform on stage. *Sunday Night at the Palladium* was a firm favourite then for family entertainment.

Another time when we all would be watching was on a Sunday afternoon with what was called the Sunday matinee. This would be a film of some sort, which would be rated for family viewing. In those days there was a huge number of Wild West shows with cowboys and Indians fighting some battle somewhere, or World War II films based on some action that had taken place only a few years back. Sometimes the film would be a bit sloppy for us kids, like *Brief Encounter* (which I understand is a classic, but if you're seven years old it's not going to cut any mustard). I had to sit through all this, no matter what. Some films – the action ones – were great but some were really depressing. There was not much else to do on wet Sunday afternoons so TV was really the only option.

Of course whatever was shown, be it a film or a serial during a child's waking hours, it was never going to be anything really exciting. I really thought there was something missing from the schedule of programmes – and, of course, I was right – but then I didn't realise until it happened.

Although science fiction had been around for quite some time in books and comics it was only in the fifties that films started to appear in that particular genre. There was certainly no science fiction on the TV – although that's not quite correct as *The Quatermass Experiment* had been shown late at night, and I understand that ITV had screened something called *Target Luna*. For me as a child there was nothing.

On Saturday 23 November at 17:16:20 GMT some eighty seconds after the scheduled program time of 5:15pm. The first ever episode of *Doctor Who* was screened. It was the show I had been awaiting for but had no idea what it would be about. I just knew this was something different. On the first week of the scheduled transmission of the show there had been a power cut in certain areas and also the death of President Kennedy had been overshadowing things. Therefore on the following Saturday the BBC decided to show the first and then the second episode back to back.

In those days, like a lot of shows, the whole thing was acted out live but then filmed. It's a good job they filmed and retained all this. I think the only reason they did this was to sell the programme on to other countries. In those days the BBC and ITV didn't really see any value in retaining programmes for repeats.

I was mesmerised by the Doctor and his stories. This was a fantastic programme for kids and was talked about in the school playground the very next school day. The first story was a four-part weekly serial set in prehistoric times. It was great but then the second story emerged, and we know what happened next. History was made.

The family were at my Auntie Elsie and Uncle John's house – their white house in Horsham. We were staying there for a long weekend. They had a wonderful house set into the woods and it was always good to go and see Uncle John. He was such a character. Of course by this time I was into *Doctor Who* and it was Saturday and I was not going to be missing the next episode. Auntie Elsie understood and I sat down with my mum to watch what was, of course, the episode that would make *Doctor Who* what it is today.

We sat and watched the Doctor and his companions try and fathom out what the new planet that they had landed upon was all about. It looked dead, and there was a strange city in the fog.

"What was all this about?" I thought. No one knew what was coming in those days. There were no leaks of pictures in advance. No one said at the beginning of the programme what was going to be happening. You didn't know. You just watched and took it in. At the end of this episode Barbara faces the camera and the image on the screen is a round iris coming towards her with a stick and plunger towards the bottom. She screams and holds her hand to her face. The credits roll.

"What the hell was that, Mum?" I screamed.

"Oh, ducky, I don't know."

"But did you see it? Did you see that stick thing? What was that?"

"Oh, ducky, it was probably the microphone from the studio. It probably got in the picture, ducky."

Well … Mum was of course wrong, as we now know that the Daleks had made their appearance. From that point on everything changed in the UK. Everything went nuts.

The next week and subsequent weeks confirmed that the plunger had not been the cameraman's mike boom. It was in fact a creature from the planet Skaro.

Doctor Who and in particular the Daleks went huge after this story. From four million viewers to some ten million during the Dalek story. There were models, badges, and books … you name it. The merchandise started to flow out of the shops. For my following birthday I was give the first ever *Dalek Annual*, something I prized for years ... in fact, something I sought after later on in life.

I would not miss any episode of *Doctor Who*. In fact visits to relatives and even holidays had to be structured around whether there would be a television available for *Doctor Who*. I didn't miss one episode ever until I had to go to work, and that meant not getting back in time for the show on a Saturday.

I was fanatical about it, and I even wrote my first story on paper with no aid whatsoever. It's funny what you will do when you're driven. I had problems writing but I wanted to write down this story of the Daleks on paper. That way I could relive it if I wanted to. My mum and dad were so impressed with what I had written that the pages were sent to school for my teacher Mrs Evans to see. I got a gold star for the writing and was so thrilled.

There is one piece of information I now know about *Doctor Who* which I didn't know then. Some overwhelming disappointment struck as I can't emphasise more what a fan of *Doctor Who* I was. I lived and breathed the early Doctor (William Hartnell). What I didn't realise then that William Russell, the actor playing the Doctor's companion Ian Chesterton, lived less than a mile away from me. Yes, he lived in Hemel – and within walking distance – and I never knew. I went bonkers when I found this out. By then of course he had moved away.

Doctor Who was sandwiched between the Saturday afternoon sports programme *Grandstand* with David Coleman and the teenagers' pop programme *Juke Box Jury* with David Jacobs. If *Grandstand* overran with some sporting event like a football match going into extra time then *Doctor Who* would be cancelled. I would be furious when this happened. Why stupid *Juke Box Jury* couldn't be cancelled instead was beyond me. *Doctor Who* ran for weeks and weeks and the only time these actors got a rest was during the summer holidays, when they would get six or seven weeks off. Otherwise it was on every Saturday.

My love for science fiction expanded after this, and I would always be checking the *Radio Times* for any possible film or play that might give me that fix of sci-fi.

When we eventually got a TV set that would receive ITV as well as BBC I immediately got hooked into the Gerry Anderson series of futuristic TV shows. At the time we got the set the series *Fireball XL5* was being shown and I thought this was a wonderful series. I had already missed the *Supercar* stories (as Baz would often remind me) at the time when we could only get BBC in the Blackshire household. He would say in the street, knowing full well I could not watch it,

"Did you see *Supercar* yesterday? It was the best episode yet."

Thanks, Baz.

Another programme from this time was *Space Patrol*, yet another puppet series. I suspect that puppet series were cheaper to produce than having real actors on board. More money could then be spent on special effects. One of my all-time favourite lines from *Space Patrol* in one episode is when the spaceship is approaching the planet Uranus and Husky says to Captain Larry Dart,

"Captain, I can see a light coming from Uranus (chuckle, chuckle)," followed by, "Shall we go and explore Uranus, Captain?"

Even as kids we knew this was funny. Today it's even more so.

Gerry Anderson continued with his puppet supermarionation series with *Stingray* and then maybe the most important of all *Thunderbirds*. Each series was set in the future and each had its own set of new characters. *Stingray*'s Troy Tempest was modelled on the actor James Garner and the boys in *Thunderbirds* are all named after astronauts from the 1960s. It was pure genius how Gerry Anderson had captured a market here in television, and it would go on for some years too.

As you can tell, TV was as important then as it is today – maybe more so, in a way, as it was new. Before TV there was not much else to do in the evening. I'm so glad I was born right at the beginnings of television's inception into the lives of people in the UK, and to witness not only the changes in TV programmes but also in technology too. In my lifetime we have come a very long way from those greasy waxy radio components to micro circuitry.

A Traditional Christmas

Christmas needs a special chapter all of its own. It's a special time for children, and I'm sure we all have our own individual memories of childhood over the festive season. Christmas was different back in the fifties and sixties, but that's not to say that today's is any better or worse. It was just different then, and maybe the readers should make their mind up about how it was compared to how it is now.

Christmas, of course, is always special to kids – and for each generation that comes along there is always their Christmas and their special memories that they can take forward with them and share with their own children later on. That's the way it is, and I can only hope that although Christmas changes year on year and decade on decade the sentiment of Christmas will always remain the same.

For us kids Christmas was a two-week break from school, and it started around a week before the twenty-fifth. We got excited well before, of course, and as is usual for kids at Christmas the lists of what was wanted from Father Christmas were a constant discussion point.

Just having two weeks off from school was fantastic – and much needed, too. A week before the day my dad would bring home a four to five-foot Christmas tree. This would have been carried from the shops by hand – quite a way to carry such a thing. It would have some roots on it and would need to be put into a bucket of soil. This was done and then the whole thing was brought inside to be dressed. The tree nearly always sat in the hallway in such a way that the top of the tree could rise through the space surrounding the stairs. In this way we could have a taller tree than the ceiling allowed. Once the tree was so tall I could almost touch it from the upstairs landing by leaning over the banister.

The lights would go on first, and these were a set of twelve largish coloured bulbs. The bulbs would be tested first by connecting them to a touch battery and seeing if they glowed. We always needed spares as during the break a few of these would go, for sure.

Woolworths was always the shop for stocking up on these replacements.

After the lights were on then the balls and ornaments would go on the tree, followed by my dad's favourite decoration: lametta. The tree always looked fantastic and there would be a grand switching-on ceremony in which we all hoped the lights would come on and no bulb would blow right away.

The ceilings then had to be decorated. We always used rolls of crêpe paper in different colours. These were hung from side to side and from corner to corner of the rooms. Again, lametta was draped over the paper chains to add some gold and silver colours to the whole effect. Mostly these decorations were the same as the year before. There was no real money to go spending on new items. We had to make do with what we had and be inventive about where things were placed.

Mum would make a Christmas cake a few weeks before and then one night in the last week she would ice the cake and add on some of those silvery edible balls. I would be there watching the icing and hoping for some of that sugary mix to be going spare. My nan would have made us a Christmas pudding to her own recipe. All sorts of other traditional foods would be baked and cooked in preparation. Drink would be purchased and my dad always favoured the Party Seven kegs of beer. This was basically a large can of beer holding seven pints. A selection of drink would be displayed on the sideboard ready for guests. Although my parents were not big drinkers they always liked a drink, and at Christmas it was a good excuse to top up on bottles.

Other things that would be bought in preparation included a box of Eat Me dates: a long sticky box of sweetened dates which you had to prise out using a wooden or plastic long fork. There was also a box of Chinese figs, which were a sugary-covered lozenge of jelly-type jam in the shape of a teardrop. But the box that fascinated me was a round wooden box of Turkish delight. Everything was wrapped up specially for Christmas but the Turkish delight in its wooden box was like something else. Mum always insisted that we had a small box of Black Magic chocolates that never lasted long, and the marzipan one was always left at the end of the holidays. Again, all these things were treats and would never be bought at any time other than Christmas. We didn't sit and scoff all of this down in one or two sittings, either. Things were made and bought to last us, and were savoured over the period.

One of the pre-Christmas treats I can remember on the run-up to Christmas was that we could treat ourselves to a copy of the *Radio Times* and a copy of the *TV Times* over the Christmas period. This might not sound like a treat today, but it really was then. There was never the money to buy items like these magazines that were sold every week, that told you about what was coming up on the TV and radio. Through the year a newspaper told us what was on, or we had to guess. Looking through the pages and deciding what I would like to watch was fantastic as a child. There were always special things on over the period which would never have been seen before by the general public. This was the 1950s and the 1960s, remember, and films and TV programmes were not available unless you saw them at the cinema or viewed them on TV. Therefore the blockbuster films that were on were new to TV audiences. I looked through the *TV Times* one year and checked out Christmas Day and saw starting at eight in the morning not one, not two, but three Gerry Anderson stories: *Supercar*, *Fireball XL5*, and *Stingray*, all one after another. What a Christmas day this was going to be.

Of course, planning what you wanted to watch had its issues. You could not record anything then. Either you watched it or you missed it and if you missed it then it probably would not be on TV again for a very long time. Christmas was all about entertaining and while family were around the TV was always off. We made our own entertainment.

The workforce at that time only had Christmas Day, Boxing Day, and New Year's Day off work. That's it: just those days as holiday from work. The next day after Boxing Day everyone would be back at work – that included Dad and Granddad too, unless of course the season fell right and it was a weekend. No one really felt hard done by then: it was just how it was and was accepted. My parents made the most of those two days off and enjoyed themselves as much as they could do.

Excitement was uncontrollable as soon as we got to Christmas Eve. I would be sent to bed early in my younger days and allowed up a little later when I got older. There was always a pillowcase beside my bed – well, nearly always. One year I had it in my head that maybe I didn't actually want Father Christmas in my bedroom. So one year the pillowcase was left by the tree downstairs instead. It only happened once, as I soon realised that the excitement of waking up with a little sack of goodies far outweighed the issue of a white-bearded man in my bedroom while I slept.

Trying to get off to sleep was always a restless time but it always happens at some point, and before you know it you're waking up. Sometimes I woke too early, and a glimpse across at the pillowcase showed me instantly that the old gent had not been yet. Eventually of course you open your eyes and you just know it's Christmas Day. If someone could bottle that child's emotion they would make a fortune I'm sure. It is pure magic. I would glance down. The sack was full. He had been.

You might think that there would be the temptation to start whipping paper off things right away, but no: I was a good kid and very patient. In fact I wanted this moment to last as long as I could. I would lie there wide awake, waiting for the telltale signs that Mum or Dad were stirring. It would have been pitch-black outside and there was no telling what time it was. There was no clock in my room. No, I had to wait until I was told I could get up... Anyway ... to actually get up at this point would have been silly, as it was so cold in the house.

There was no central heating at number 18 then. If you wanted to be warm then you had a few options. Either you put loads of clothes on or you went downstairs and built a fire in the grate and lit it. Or in later times you plugged in a two-bar electric fire. That's all you could do. To say it was cold in the mornings was an understatement. Sometimes it was so cold inside the house and in my bedroom that frost appeared on the inside of the windows. Sometimes the frost was so thick on the windows that you couldn't see out at all until either the sun came up or some heating went on in the house. Frost on the windows was amazing, and sometimes strange swirly patterns were evident as if made overnight by Jack Frost himself.

Lying in bed with the thick covers over me on Christmas morning was as exciting as ever it could possibly get. I was warm in there and snuggled down under the covers, wondering what was in the sack. Dad would have gone down to make some tea and bring it back up and I knew this was the start of the opening-up process that would follow. Before he went down to the kitchen Dad would have switched on the two-kilowatt electric fire in their bedroom to warm the room up. While this was happening tea would be made and then brought up. No tea bags then, of course. Tea was made in a pot and one had to wait to brew before pouring. It was then some ten or fifteen minutes before I heard Dad's footsteps coming back up. He would be loaded with a tea tray. By then the heater would have done its job.

A face would poke its head around my bedroom door. Dad would be smiling and I would be smiling back. The excitement now was almost unbearable.

"Do you want to come in, son?" Dad would say, grinning from ear to ear. "You'd better bring that with you," he would say, pointing to the sack on the floor.

I didn't need telling twice, I can tell you. I ran the cold gauntlet from my room to theirs in a flash, towing the heavy white pillowcase with me. When I was really young I would have to drag it rather than lift it.

Inside Mum and Dad's bedroom the fire was pushing out a generous two kilowatts of much-needed warmth. Electric fires were used sparingly, as they used up oodles of money in no time at all. But this was Christmas and we were entitled to a bit of heat to unwrap our presents. My brother would have been woken up as well and usually showed his face in the bedroom.

The emphasis would be on me unwrapping my presents. Although Mum and Dad had a gift or two to unwrap I never really took much notice of what they had got themselves. I emptied my sack on the bed and five or six parcels would roll out on to the eiderdown. There would be something from my three aunties and uncles, something from Rob, and something from Mum and Dad. My nan and granddad's present might also be in the sack, but sometimes they brought it with them when they came up later in the morning. Not a huge amount there, but to me it was the best and most fantastic of times.

I always left Mum and Dad's present till last, savouring the delights of what they might have got me. Rob always got me something good, too, as he was earning some money. The smaller presents would maybe be something like a book or the *Beano Annual* or maybe an Airfix aeroplane kit to make up. These were simple things but they meant a lot. In those days you really didn't get very much in between Christmases so this was a big deal … five or six parcels of the unknown, and I would unwrap them as slowly as possible … make it last.

My dad had a budget of £5 to spend on me in those days for the main present. It was always something mega and I expect this holds true for any child. Some of the presents I got in those days are below.

One was a complete train set in OO gauge. I think on this Christmas that I was handed a small oblong box from Mum and Dad and was wondering how such a small box could be my main present. Of course it was only part of the present, and it was a lovely electric Hornby locomotive. I was then taken downstairs to see a full train layout impressively stretched out on the dining room table. There was a gasp from me as my eyes looked over the design of the tracks laid out on the board. My dad must have worked on this at night in secret to have it ready for me on the day. Other presents that year included a few more wagons and carriages for the train. I loved my train set and it stayed with me all though my childhood. It was moved upstairs into my bedroom and my dad made a special frame in there so the board could stay out permanently. It was therefore on display all the time. Some kids had Scalextrics car racing set-ups. You either were a car or a train kid in those days.

Another year I unwrapped a largish heavy box to find inside a lovely Mamod steam engine. Wow. What a surprise that was. This was an actual working steam engine with a boiler you filled with water and a meths burner you heated the boiler up with. The engine had a piston which drove a pulley wheel. The intention here was that you could make some sort of machine from your Meccano set and then drive this machine using the pulley on the steam engine. I could not wait to fire this monster up, and as soon as breakfast was over some newspaper was placed on top of the round coffee table and the engine fired up. It looked fantastic: it had a lovely shiny brass cylinder and pipes like a real engine. It hissed and spat before starting and you gave the fly wheel a spin. Then she was off and boy did she go. I was told not to place my fingers in certain places, not to overfill the boiler, and not to run it without any water. I stuck to the rules and loved running up this spluttering piece of machinery from a bygone age. Mum didn't like it much because it did make a bit of a mess and stink in the house – but, really, as we had a coal fire and my parents smoked the smell really was nothing to worry about. I made all sorts of contraptions, and luckily my brother had got me the gearwheel set so I could make all sorts using my Meccano.

I had a fascination for science in those days, and one of my early presents was a Hooke microscope kit. Robert Hooke used a microscope way back in the 1600s. This present was a reproduction of the microscope he used to study such things as slices of cork. Dad had to make the kit up as it was kind of complicated, but it was a wonderful bit of equipment that revealed wonders to the eye. I had to watch that my hair didn't burn when I looked into the eyepiece as the light source was a candle. Later on, around ten or eleven years old, I wanted a much better microscope and had a lovely Christmas present of a more traditional microscope which included slides of insect parts. I would go outside and find things to look at: insects and leaves from trees. I was fascinated and absorbed by the miniature world and what it looked like. Rob used to bring back vials of crystals from Nottingham University for me to look at. I was forever searching for things to place under the lens.

One other year I unwrapped a big box, and inside was an electrician's dream. The box said "Philips Electronic Engineer". It had a picture on the front of a boy constructing electrical circuits and behind him in the background were aircraft and fighter pilots and all the things that boys want to be.

"How exciting is this?" I thought. I never knew anything like this existed. All I had had up to now to play with was some old flex from the disused standard lamp and batteries and bulbs. I lifted the lid and then plonked it back down, as I was too frightened by what was inside. It was like an Aladdin's cave in this box. I quickly took the box downstairs and into the living room, where Rob was sleeping on the settee. Auntie Elsie was staying this Christmas and Rob had got the rough deal of sleeping on the sofa. He was half awake and seemed to be in an OK mood. I showed him the box and we opened it up again. There were all sorts in there: transistors, diodes, resistors and capacitors, wire, and loudspeakers. You name it and it was in there. Rob went through what things were and gave me a lecture about things that had to be treated with care and respect.

"Don't bend this too much and don't hold this like this," etc.. The instruction book showed me I could make all manner of things from types of radio to alarm systems and light detectors to even an electric organ. Wow. This was going to be so much fun. I played with this kit for months and months and it really did give me that grounding in electronics to use in a career later in life … but we will come to that later.

When I was about thirteen years old my present was a Polaroid Land Camera. The first of its kind in the UK, this camera took instant pictures on a film that only held eight plates. To see black-and-white prints develop in front of your very eyes was indeed magic. Everyone watched when a picture was taken. You had to pull out the print from the camera and tear it off and then wait. You had to time it right to then peel off a covering from the photo itself. Too early and you might be underexposed: too late and the image would be too dark. The print then had to have what was called some fixer applied using a sponge with a chemical on. How long you kept the cover on the picture was determined by the temperature. It was all a bit hit-and-miss but actually we got some good shots and I hope one or two maybe end up in this book.

My best present ever (of course) was the Johnny Seven, which I will talk about as part of the gun section later on. This present totally blew me away that year.

Now Christmas is of course to a child about presents and it might be argued that the presents are the highlight of the festive season. Way back then, when Christmas was in black-and-white, presents were not the only highlight by far. Don't get me wrong: those presents were important, but there were many treats in store during the two days we had. One thing that everyone looked forward to was the turkey. Now it has to be said that these days a turkey is quite common and is eaten at different times of the year by families. Poultry today is probably eaten several times a week by an average family. But back then in the fifties and sixties the only time anyone ever had a turkey – or even a chicken, for that matter – was at Christmas. Poultry was expensive and the average family could never afford such a luxury meat.

So maybe you can see how eager everyone was to tuck into that very rare meal: the roast turkey. It was literally a treat to behold. You savoured every mouthful because once gone then another year would have to pass before your lips would be smacking around that lovely meat again. If money was tight then a large chicken would be purchased. Again, this was such a luxury and equally valued.

The next day or two, if you were lucky to have a big bird, cold meat would be cut from the rest of the bird and divided up among us. Oh, how I do long sometimes to experience that situation again of eating something that was so restricted. I still love my turkey today, as I'm sure everyone does, but this was very special indeed.

Nan and Granddad would invariably come to us for the day, or if not we would go to them for Christmas Day. It depended on a lot of things, really, but turns were taken and it didn't matter where you were because the same Christmas cheer was always there in all the families' homes. Generally I would be playing with my main present all day, with only the break for the dinner holding up proceedings. I was allowed some alcohol at dinner: this might be a very small sherry or ginger wine. I always remember drinking these treats from small barrel-shaped glasses with a green sugar frosting around the middle. This was the only time these glasses were used, so I guess they were special and only for Christmas.

In the afternoon the adults would invariably fall asleep after the big meal and a few drinks. Nothing has changed there, I would think. I would have to entertain myself while a cacophony of snoring dominated the living room. It's a good job they did this as the evening was going to be another fun-packed time, and adults – as I have since found out – need a rest if they are to party into the night.

I hasten to add that at no time was the TV switched on apart from maybe the fifteen minutes for the Queen's speech. After this it was switched off. The Blackshires knew how to entertain themselves and we did this very well. In fact we still do.

The evening was a time to party with maybe more family turning up for fun and games. It might be at our house or my nan and granddad's or maybe at my Uncle Sid's. Uncle Sid was my mum's brother and the eldest out of the four Brandoms. Uncle Sid knew how to throw a party, especially from a kid's point of view. He wasn't a big drinker, having maybe only one pint of beer all night, but he had done his research and always came up with some fantastic games to play during the evening. One year there were so many of us that he hired out the upstairs room in the Oddfellows Arms in Apsley.

We played all sorts of things from paper games like consequences to bingo to card games like Chase the Ace. Again, some of the games we played would only be played at Christmas and were therefore a really special treat.

I can still hear my nan laughing, as she did to all that went on and the games we played. Her laugh was infectious and usually ended up with her having a coughing fit. Almost everyone smoked in those days and the air would be thick with cigarette smoke. Sometimes doors and windows had to be opened to let out all the smoke. It was non-stop and I must have consumed loads of second-hand smoke in those days.

One year when I was about nineteen I arrived home from a night out with the lads to the usual party going on at our house. By the time I got back it was in full swing, as it usually was. Generally on Christmas Day night all the pubs and clubs were closed, so on this occasion I had been around to a friend's house for a few hours and then come home to see what was going on. Nan and Granddad were there, and Rob and his new wife Agnes. They were having a whale of a time as my brother had brought around a guitar (which he played) and they were all taking it in turns to sing songs. Some were Beatles songs of the day, some were from Frank Sinatra – who was one of my dad's favourites – and also some were old songs from the First World War that my Granddad sang. I had the fortune and good sense during this evening to actually turn my tape recorder on and tape a good portion of the evening. The tape that resulted contains the only recorded voices of my dad and nan and granddad. To play this back now and hear them all is quite haunting in a way but it's priceless too, and I really do thank the Lord for having the inspiration to turn that machine on when I did. When people do leave this world all we have left are the memories of them. I have found over the years that to take pictures, record videos, etc. is so important. Today I record a bit of Christmas Day on video every year for this same reason.

The partying would go on till past twelve o'clock and taxis would be called to take people home or we would often just walk back.

On Boxing Day a similar party would take place at someone else's house – a repeat in a way of the Christmas Day one, but maybe ending a little earlier. After all, the men would need to be back at work the next day bright and early just like Bob Cratchit in *A Christmas Carol*.

Of course, for me as a schoolboy I had another week or so off and would not be going back to school until after New Year's Day.

Yes, Christmas was special. OK ... it was a time of the year when adults could just relax for a few days and eat things that were real treats and just have a damn good time.

Spud Gun to Airgun

I am dedicating this section to a subject that is very close to my heart. It always has been, and I guess it always will be. I still shoot some kind of gun to this very day so it does require a lengthy explanation. It will be of interest to guys, for sure, especially those who had an air rifle around the late 1960s. If you don't like guns then maybe miss the chapter out, but it's part of me and the story needs to be told. Oh … and there are some fun bits in here that will, I'm sure, amuse the reader.

I have no idea what it was that initially set off this passion for all things that fire something. I have a distinct feeling that it might have been all those films shown on TV: there were an awful lot of westerns and war films on at the time. When we were at school playing in the playground nearly all we did was play war.

My early recollections of a gun and the first gun I had was something called a spud gun. It was blue and made by the company Lone Star. The idea was to take a potato and dig the thin barrel end into the spud to block the barrel with a wad of spud. You then had to pull the trigger, which was in fact a pump action to apply pressure inside the gun itself. The result was a pop and the spud bit would fly out about fifteen feet – that's if you were lucky. More than likely the spud would just plop out about two yards away. I loved this gun. It was great, as you could set up things like playing cards and shoot them down in the garden. God knows how many potatoes I got through. I would go in the kitchen and ask Mum,

"Can I have another spud, Mum?" She would say to me,

"Yes, ducky, but make it last this time. Your father won't be happy if he has to go down the garden and dig some more up."

I was about six when I got my spud gun, and this started me off on this obsession with all things gun-related.

Some time later, when our gang was in full swing in the street, one of the guys had got himself a little derringer pistol. It was small much smaller than the spud gun and called the "Gambler cap firing

Spud Gun". The gang member showed us how it worked. It was an intricate bit of kit. He showed us that a chamber slid out from the side and inside this chamber was a metal slug. At one end of the slug was the design, just like on the spud gun. You dug into a spud and pull out, a wad was now situated in the end of this metal slug. At the other end of the slug was a round flat disc part. You tore off a paper gunpowder cap and placed on its surface. So with a bit of spud in one end and a cap in the other you loaded the slug back into the pistol and closed the chamber back up. You then pulled back the hammer on the gun until it clicked, and then you were ready to fire. On pulling the trigger the hammer would hit the cap sitting on the slug. The gun would go off with a crack and the spud would go flying out of the end. This action was utilising the physics of how a real gun works. The gas produced from the cap was propelling the spud.

Wow. I looked at this gun in wonder. I was in love with it. Pete said,

"What happens if you load more than one cap into it?"

"Don't know," said our friend.

"Try it," I said.

So he loaded more spud in and pulled out the ribbon of gun caps.

"Try three," I said. "Fold them up and make 'em flat."

So he did and cocked the gun and fired. Bang. The spud went OK and hit one of the cars over the road, splatting up the window in a mess of potato.

"Quick, run," said Pete. We ran into the bushes at the end of the road, panting away.

"God, did you see that?" I said.

We were all wide-eyed and inspecting the little derringer.

"Where did you get it?" we said.

"Up at the post office up at Bennetts End," was the response.

"Right," I thought. "That's mine."

Mum had her orders, and the next week I had my own little derringer ready to cause mayhem in the street by the next weekend. It was a fun gun, although slow to load up. You would maybe get it all set up and then keep it loaded in your pocket ready for use. Usually the target would be one of the odd numbers kids. They would run a mile when the pistol came out. We had experimented with all sorts of stuff to insert instead of the spud projectile. One favourite was elderberries when they were in season. These little juicy berries could be pushed into the spud compartment bit and fired with good results. They didn't really hurt anyone – but God, did that juice stain well. There was many an odd numbers kid running around with elderberry splat stains on their clothing. Even after a wash the stain would not come out. Some parents were not happy with us over that little design change, I can tell you.

I wanted guns and I always asked for them for birthdays and Christmas and in between times too. I owned the odd western style cap gun. I had a few plunger-type spud guns, one of which would fire caps too. I experimented with caps as well. I found that if I put some oil from one of the cans in the shed on some caps they would then go off with a phut rather than a bang. I thought this cool, and wanted to mimic the gun Napoleon Solo used in the TV series *The Man from U.N.C.L.E.*. His gun had a small silencer on the front and used to make this phut sound when he shot a THRUSH agent.

I took my spud gun and attached to the end of it the cylindrical gold cap from one of my mum's used lipsticks. And there you have it: A P38 special. OK, OK … so it had a golden lipstick silencer. To me it was a *Man from U.N.C.L.E.* gun and that was that. It sounded like it too, and I pointed it at some of the odd numbers kids in the road and made this phut sound while wisps of stinky, oily smoke wafted out from under the hammer as the oil burned with the powder. They were not impressed. They did not run.

Another type that came out was a military assault rifle which had a magazine that you filled with plastic bullets. These then fired out when you pulled the trigger. No good for using in the road of course but OK indoors to kill playing cards. I dressed up this gun again as a *Man from U.N.C.L.E.*-themed rifle. I was fascinated with the rifle that THRUSH agents (the enemy in the series) used. It had sort of an infrared lamp on the top of it so THRUSH agents could see people in the dark.

"What could I use?" I wondered. Well, I had some electrical bits and I found a pink lampshade in my toy chest.

"That will do," I thought and I strapped this shade to the top of the gun. To make it even more *Man from U.N.C.L.E.* I cut out the name U.N.C.L.E. from the *Man from U.N.C.L.E.* bubblegum wrappers and Sellotaped these to the gun. These labels were in pink, but I didn't care. I had what I considered to be the real THRUSH gun, and it was the business too. I think the poor dog got hit a few times down the hall as he was considered to be a *Man from U.N.C.L.E.* spy. It didn't hurt him, as the plastic bullets hardly had any velocity and they bounced off his thick hair. It would annoy him, though, and he would just walk off and try and find another position on the floor to snooze out of range of the THRUSH agent. He used to give me that knowing pissed-off look quite a bit around that time.

I was about ten or eleven and was asked what I wanted for Christmas one year. Guess what my reply was? There were no TV adverts on TV for kids then, really, so I had no idea what I wanted or what was even available. I wanted a gun and I wanted a good one: something special. Well, Christmas Eve arrived and I had no idea what I might be getting. I was excited, as always. Christmas Eve is an exciting time for most kids privileged enough to have some toys. I went to bed early, as usual. I had trouble getting to sleep. I lay awake for what seemed hours but I suspect it wasn't. I suspect I was out like a light within half an hour of going to bed. I may have woken up at some point in the night. I would have immediately looked across to where a pillowcase had been placed by my mum. This would be filled during the night by that mystifying person we all believe in.

A pillowcase does not hold much. It's quite a big bag to a kid, but in reality it's quite small. All my presents for Christmas always fitted inside this little sack in those days. I awoke and looked. It was empty, and my head hit the pillow again. I was out like a light again, for how long I have no idea. I awoke again. It was dark. I knew it was still dark outside but then it was winter and there would not be no daylight until at least eight o'clock. I rolled over and looked over to where the pillowcase would be.

Oh my God... The vision that hit me was one of surprise, excitement, and almost panic. The pillowcase was now on the floor and bulging with goodies. But it had no chance of containing everything within its confines. Out of the top of the case rose this huge long obelisk-shaped parcel, the like of which I had never seen before. It was huge and stretched out of the pillowcase and leant against the wall.

"It's Christmas Day," I thought. "It's come already." My eyes returned back to the huge package. "What the hell is that?" I wondered.

Oh, yes, there was a gun inside that huge box: a gun of mega proportions and the best present I think I ever had as a kid. I had never seen the likes of it before, and it was truly an awesome bit of kit. The gun was called a Johnny Seven and had the letters O.M.A. stamped on the side of it. I worked out later that O.M.A. stood for One Man Army. Johnny Seven was a Topper toy gun. It had, as the name hints, seven actions that it could perform. It had a multitude of rockets that it could fire including a grenade launcher, an anti-tank rocket and an armour-piercing shell. It had a fully repeating magazine rifle that shot bullets. It had a tommy gun effect sound. It also had a detachable cap pistol that formed part of the rifle, but you could take it out and use on its own. It also had a collapsible bipod. The whole thing was massive, and I could hardly carry the thing. To say I was pleased is an understatement.

The gun was used all though Christmas by all the family taking it in turns to shoot down the hall at any target we could think of. The gun fired plastic bullets at quite a rate and you could easy knock over targets at – say – five yards. After Christmas Mum and Dad devised some Dalek targets to shoot at. These were made from matchboxes painted in Dalek colours which then had matchsticks inserted to give them some reality. OK ... a matchbox is oblong and a Dalek round, but it didn't matter. If you fired the anti-tank rocket at a group of Daleks down the hall you might take out four or five at a time. It was fantastic.

I have no idea what happened to my Jonny Seven. In recent years I have seen these guns sell on eBay for around £700. They are sought after and are quite rare now. I would guess my dad would have paid about £5 at the time. I sometimes wonder if I will end up buying one at some point just to fire down my hall again.

After the age of eleven there were no more guns in my life for some time. I was neither child enough to have toy guns nor grown-up enough to have a real one. As I entered my teens my interest turned towards something a little more grown-up.

Something that renewed my interest was a trip to my auntie's house in Norwich. My family used to go there now and again to stay with Auntie Elsie and Uncle John. Elsie was one of my mum's sisters and Uncle John was a charismatic artist who was principal at the art college in Norwich. In fact Uncle John was quite a famous guy in the art world and knew a number of notable artists of the time. I understand he knew Lucian Freud who would visit from time to time. He had a good job, for sure, and this was evident in the size of the house they had. Their house had its own parapets on the roof and you could go and walk around the edge like you would in a castle. The house had several floors and a huge winding staircase which led up to the first floor where Auntie and Uncle lived. The ground floor was let out to some notable TV personality.

We were staying there and looking after the house while Auntie and Uncle were on holiday. This meant we had unrestricted use of this castle-like dwelling. This was a far cry from the council house I lived in. It had huge rooms with lofty ceilings. There were antiques in every room and in every corner, from furniture to ceramics to paintings. It was chock-a-block and looked like an antique dealer's sale room. I loved looking at all the old things in this house but my favourite was always the grandfather clock which stood in the main living room. Its dials were impressive and what used to fascinate me were the sun and moon and season dials depicted in lovely pictures which would slowly move over time.

One of the rooms I discovered and went into was my cousin Richard's room. He was about five years older than me and was also away at this time. This room was full of interesting artefacts. There was a lovely brass microscope on one of the tables next to his bed. He seemed to have everything in there. But one other thing that caught my eye was propped up against the wall by his bed.

"Wow," I thought. "A gun."

I picked it up and looked it over. It was heavy, with a wooden stock and black metal internals. On the top were some markings of a lady holding a bow and some arrows. The word Diana was also stamped just under the figure and some letters and numbers that said MOD 28. There were some tins of ammo on a shelf. I got them down and examined the tins. I opened two tins up and saw that the slugs inside were different sizes: number 1 and number 2 bore. I took a slug from one of the tins and put them back. He wouldn't miss one, would he? Later that day I said to my dad that there was an airgun in Richards's room and asked if we could we have a go.

"I don't see why not," he said. So that afternoon the sash window in the main room was pulled up on its rollers and the garden below was exposed. The gun was brought down with the tins of slugs.

"OK, son, you can have first go," said my dad, handing me the rifle and then showing me how to cock the gun ready to accept a slug. I did as was told and then I reached down into the tins. I thought about it for a second and then picked up a number 1 bore pellet. My thoughts were that this smaller projectile would not kick as much as the bigger two bore. Of course as I put the tiny slug into the breech it just ran down the barrel and out of the end on to the carpet.

"Oh," I thought.

"No," Dad said. "This gun is a .22 calibre. It will only take the bigger slug."

So it was that I then loaded the more fearsome bigger slug into the breech, closed up the rifle and took aim at some garden pegs down below in the garden. It was not, of course, as bad as I had imagined. There was some recoil but nothing too bad, and we had several goes until Mum called us over for tea.

After that day I could not get airguns out of my head. I saw airguns everywhere: in adverts in papers and in the *Exchange and Mart* which my brother had on and off. I wanted one. I wanted one so badly, but I knew there was an age restriction on airguns and I could not have one until I was fourteen.

Time passed, as it always does, and I had eventually got to the age of fourteen and was in my third year at Bennetts End secondary modern school. I had some new mates in this year and they already had their own air rifles. They used to say to me,

"Why don't you come up to the dump with us on a Saturday morning, Rich? You can have a go at shooting some cans and light bulbs." I was taken with this idea and thought I would make the suggestion to Baz when I next saw him. Baz was at the grammar school and I only really had contact with him when walking to school in the week and again over the weekends.

Baz and I had some useful catapults: metal ones with strong elastic. Although we fired stones out of these we also liked to buy a bag of marbles. Marbles were perfectly round and flew really straight. A packet of twenty or so marbles would only cost six old pence, so by spending a shilling you got a whole afternoon's worth of ammo. I said to Baz about what my mates at school had said.

"Maybe we can go up there on Saturday morning, Baz, and take our cats up there too."

"OK," he said. "It could be some fun."

This, then, started my long association with air rifles that I still have today … and you can read about the adventures we had in those early years later.

Secondary Modern School

1965-1971

The summer holiday between the finishing of primary and the starting of senior school was a strange one. At the start I was quite relaxed but midway through a kind of anxiety took over me. Usually the depression of going back to school starts to take place when the last week of the summer holidays winds down. This was different. This felt odd and different. I was certainly nervous about going to this new school in Bennetts End.

First Year

I had heard stories of what it would be like, but nothing made much sense. We all know how kids talk. Some boasted about what their older brother had said it was like: how there would be bullies and teachers wearing gowns and whipping the cane at kids to make them work. I had no real notion in my head as to what it could be like. All I knew was that it would be so much different to what I had known before. There would be no nice Mrs Evans: no Mr Sully with his chipolata fingers.

I was taken to see the new school, of course, on an open evening. My dad made sure I knew the walk to school too, as I would be walking about a mile each way – and that would include coming home to lunch as well. I would walk four miles in a day. The night came then, as it always does. I hit the pillow in my bed knowing that the next day would be some God-awful nightmare day of newness and uncertainty.

I don't think parents quite know what to do in situations like this. Maybe they don't understand the worry that goes on in a child's head when such a huge change takes place to their routine. I was tossing and turning all night. That was apparent to me because my dad came into my bedroom at some point and asked if I wanted to sleep in their bed. It might seem strange to think of a young boy of eleven still needing to have that close contact with his mum and dad in their

157

bed, but I needed it that night. I needed the comfort and the warmth for sure.

I could tell through the curtains of my parents' bedroom that dawn had indeed broken. They were lit up, and I knew that the time must be about seven o'clock and that Mum and Dad would be getting up soon. Oh, the dread of it all. I was sick to the stomach. I'm not sure what I ate for breakfast but I got myself ready in a new school uniform with a new blazer and school badge. I had insisted with my parents that I would be wearing short trousers to this new school. What a poor decision that was: one I would regret. Dad said he would walk me to the school on the first day to the gates and that would be it. I would be on my own after that.

The morning was a sunny, warm one.

"At least the sun is out," I thought as I walked towards the school entrance. The sun always makes things look that much better, and in retrospect I'm so glad the weather was kind on that day.

I marched into the playground where a large number of kids were running around and mostly talking in groups. This was different, for sure. This was totally different. I didn't know most of the kids here from Adam. The catchment area for attending Bennetts End secondary modern was quite large and the children starting at this school on this day would have come from maybe four different schools around the area, maybe even more. I spotted a few mates from primary school and went over to talk to them. There was excitement in the air, and also a degree or wonderment and dread. You come from a school where you're the oldest in that school and you know the tricks and you feel in control, and then you're put in this position: a new school, new rules, new teachers, and you're the youngest, the smallest ... and you're in short trousers.

The school was huge in comparison to primary school. It was a sprawl of buildings: different ones, and so many entrances too.

"Where do we go?" I thought.

A whistle was blown.

"All new first years come here immediately," was the cry a teacher made. It was made clear that the first years should assemble in groups relating to the schools they had come from.

"Line up. Line up. No pushing. Stand in a line and wait for your name to be called," were the commands shouted out. Names were called out for the particular form classes, and when your name was called you would stand in another line with the form teacher at the head. Lots of names were called and classes made and, when completed, they walked off to their new form classroom. Eventually my name was called:

"Blackshire."

I moved over into line with some other kids. The form teacher was a Mr Bingham and he eventually marched his group of boys and girls off to where his classroom was. We had an annexe – a hut-type classroom that had obviously been built to expand the school's capacity. Each annexe had two classrooms with a reception area in the middle for hats, coats, and bags, etc.. As we marched off to the classroom I looked around at my future classmates. I knew none of them. In fact I was the only boy from my primary school in this class. The rest were total strangers.

A wave of anxiety drifted again over me.

"Oh, hell. Where is this going?" I thought.

In fact when I looked back at this situation it was very apparent that a high percentage of kids from my class in primary school had gone to Corner Hall, the school known as the Prison on the Hill. I still feel this was a lucky escape, and the Prison didn't sound like a very nice place at all. But here at Bennetts End I really was thin on the ground for mates.

We marched into our new form classroom and sat at desks. The desks were paired up as they were at primary school and I sat down, and a largish boy whom I had never seen before sat next to me.

"Mind if I sit next to you, mate?", said the boy.

"No, not at all," I replied, feeling at least that I wasn't sitting on my own.

"My name's Graham but everyone calls me Podge," said the rather overweight boy.

"Hi, Podge," I said. "My name's Rich. I don't know anyone in this class."

Podge told me the school he had come from and who he knew from his primary school.

"We can be mates," said Podge with a smile on his face.

"Maybe this won't be so bad after all," I thought.

Mr Bingham was a really nice kind teacher and the first male teacher for me. Bingham taught geography as his main subject and he would be taking us for that subject at a later date. He was approaching middle age, and looked the typical teacher in his sports jacket with corduroy patches on the elbows. He was gentle in the way he spoke, but persuasive too. He hardly ever had to raise his voice to us which, I guess, is an indicator of a good teacher. The girls loved Mr Bingham and he did tend to favour the girls when taking class. He used to think that us boys were just useless dirty yobs who didn't really have any interest in geography at all. Of course the girls were that much more mature than us boys and they tended to be favoured by the teaching staff because of their maturity. I suspect that a few of the girls had a bit of a crush on Bingham. You could just tell by the way the girls looked at him. Even today, some fifty years on, if I talk about Bingham to my old girlfriends from school they will be quite protective of him.

Bingham said quite a lot about the school and how it functioned, but one thing he said to us stuck in our minds. He said to us kids that it was exciting for all of us kids to think that we would be all alive to see and live in the next millennium. What a forward-thinking man Mr Bingham was. He really did strike some wonderment into us on that first day. This was, it seemed to me, a new type of teacher from what I had experienced before. Yes … this was my first male teacher, and it struck me at this time how different that was.

The first thing Mr Bingham had us do was to construct a timetable. This was all very new to all of us. In primary school you had one teacher and one classroom and that was basically it. What they were inferring here was that you would be moving around the school to different classrooms with different teachers. The timetable was split up, with two periods in the morning before a break time and then two more periods before lunch. In the afternoon there were three periods with a break in the middle. So there were seven periods a day, and some of these would be double periods where you stayed in the class for – say – double English or double Chemistry. This all felt strange and uncomfortable at the time. To boot, there were classes with subjects that we had never been taught in primary school. We would be having woodwork and metalwork, physics, and the dreaded French… In fact the last lesson for that starting day was going to be a French lesson. Creating the timetable seemed to take a long time, as the class was split up at times for different subjects. The girls, for a start, wouldn't be doing woodwork or metalwork. They would have needlework and domestic science. In those days girls would be groomed for being good housewives, not hands that worked in industry.

The timetable was an important thing, it seemed. You needed to have it to hand all the time and know where you were going. This school was large and had several levels of floors in the main block.

I had messed up completely, it would seem. As I sat in that classroom on the first day and looked around at the boys, all of them apart from one had long trousers on. It was me and the little kid at the back of the class with buck teeth who they would soon be calling Squirrel. When break time came I could then see better how much I stood out against the whole school. Maybe four of us in all – out of over 100 first years – had short trousers on. Now you might think that as soon as I got home I might plead with my parents to go out and buy some long kecks, but you would be wrong. I was one stubborn kid and I was going to see this out to the bitter end.

Needless to say, in the coming weeks, months, and terms I would on occasion be bullied just on the basis of having shorties on. Don't get me wrong: it wasn't actually that bad with the kids taking the mick. No: the issue was actually with the Welsh teacher Mr PJ. He was a big burly Welshman with a thick beard. He taught English, art, and also games. It was he that came up with the name Black Bottom. He used it in class to refer to me and found it quite funny to intimidate me in a way that the rest of the class could also join in with. I never knew, really, if actually he might have been trying to do me a favour in forcing me to wear long pants. Whatever his motive was it hurt all the same.

The first year intake was made up of five classes. These classes were identified in order of ability, thus: 1A1, 1A2, 1A3, 1B1, and 1B2. I had been placed in 1A3, right smack in the middle of the abilities list. This actually made me a lot happier than I had been in my last school, because the less able kids were in those 1B classes and I had not been placed there. Someone saw a spark in me, it seemed.

The 1A1 class had all the kids who had just missed out on grammar school. They were expected to do well, still, and could go on to the sixth form and take O and A levels eventually. Classes 1A2 and 1A3 was a bit of a mixed bag of abilities, and basically we would be expected to take what were then called CSE exams. We would, more than likely, end up as tradesmen or in low-key office administration jobs. The guys in the B forms might also take CSEs if they pulled their weight, but more than likely they might leave school at the end of the fourth form with what was called a school diploma. This diploma just signified to potential employers that the child had been to school. There was no exam here. These guys were destined for factory and manual work.

You can see that, using class streaming, our working life was being mapped out there and then. We as kids were none the wiser: we just lived day to day, trying to survive. I had no idea what I wanted to do when I left school but I knew that doing well was something that was required.

That first year was a strange one and (in part) a lonely one, as Podge soon got fed up with his shorts-wearing classmate and moved desks to sit with someone else. I was then relegated to the back of the class and sat on my own with an empty desk next to me. I would be sitting with other boys for some of the lessons but mostly I would be on my own. I was becoming a little withdrawn and isolated. Break times were the only times when I really had much interaction with kids – my old friends from primary school, who all seemed to be in those B classes. At one point I wished they had moved me into the B classes as I certainly would have known more people, but it was not to be.

I stuck it out and muddled through. I liked some lessons, and I started to excel at maths and the sciences. I was getting top marks and getting into the top three of the class in these subjects. What let me down was English. I was hopeless, and low down the ranking within my class. I didn't know it then, of course, that I was dyslexic. I'm not even sure that the word had been invented then. God knows what name Mr PJ would have awarded me with my shorts on and being dyslexic.

Games was still an issue, and I still had to deal with the sports side of things – and football, on occasions. But the school was more flexible than primary school and tended to get all the kids involved. We had an indoor gym for a start, so there was indoor cricket and basketball too. I actually liked the basketball and started to enjoy a bit of sport for once.

Mr Nesbitt was a Scottish games teacher. He smoked like a chimney and he was quite strict with us kids but I actually liked the guy and respected him. He always organised some fun games and tried to keep it fair with how the teams were made up. The one games teacher you just didn't want to teacher you was Basher. Basher was a relatively new young teacher and this was probably his first post. OK, so kids would get the slipper from Nesbitt – say – if you forgot your kit or you did something wrong, but Basher was on another level. This guy looked for excuses to beat kids, and when he did it you could see he enjoyed it a little too much for our liking. He hit kids hard on the arse in front of the class and took great delight in threatening that more would be given out if us kids didn't comply with his orders. We saw a number of slippers get smashed to bits on kids' backsides in the changing rooms by him. It's strange how out of all the teachers and subjects taught in the school it was really only the games teachers who used corporal punishment.

One new aspect to the dreaded double games was the introduction to us all of what was called cross-country running. Simply put, this was a great scam by the games teachers because what it entailed was us kids walking around some country lanes while the teachers sat back in the warm having a fag.

OK … so on the first outing Mr Nesbit took us around the course, which was maybe about two miles of woodland running. Then it was on to Bunkers Lane up to a point where you cut across a field, and then down Chambersbury Lane to the school. If you did that route today you would be run over and killed, for sure. But when we ran this – sorry, walked this – there were no cars about.

For us it was a bit of a soft option, as we only ever ran it once or twice. If we walked it then it took us the whole games lesson and we would not then have to play football. It was also a way for some of the kids to have a fag. Doing this in winter was not always fun, to be honest. It was often cold and raining but we did it all the same, and it didn't seem to do us any harm.

If you have ever seen the film *Kes* about a northern school and a boy who has a kestrel as a pet you would know about the shower scenes in that film. Whenever I see that film it reminds me of how school was in those days. It was quite brutal in a way, and hard-hitting. One aspect I didn't like about games day was that after the games we played we were told to strip off and wash in the communal shower. Yes: it was exactly like a scene out of *Kes* with boys running around nude and whipping bums with the pocket handkerchief-sized towels they gave us. The changing rooms would be full of steam as the hot jets were turned on and we were told to get in there and wash. To this day I can never remember there being any soap. Was there? If you didn't get in then you were slippered. It was as simple as that and so you just got on with it.

As the first year came to an end we were told within our form classes that there were to be some adjustments. It seemed that the school had been scrutinising us and evaluating our position in the ranks. Some kids would be leaving our class and moving up to higher ones. Some would be coming down into ours. This would all start from the start of the next term. Some of the girls in our form had done so well that they were being moved right up to 1A1. But who might be coming down? Indeed, who might enter the new 2A3? It might be someone I knew.

Second Year

The second year started with a better start than the first one. For a start I had long trousers at last, and finally looked like a grown-up boy. I think Mr PJ made a comment to the effect that I was no longer Black Bottom but more Long Bottom. Whatever this joker meant it was all short-lived and I now looked no different to the rest of the class, finally.

As the classes had shifted pupils about we had some new people in our class. One extra was a chap called Steven who was totally new to the school. The other was a tall guy called Fred. I knew this guy from primary school. He had been moved down to our class for underperforming. Fred made a beeline for me (to sit next to me). I was overjoyed, as I had gone from no class pals to now having three. This was going to be a far better year for me, and along with another new starter the three of us were going to have so much fun together. That's what I thought and that's what I hoped, but sadly I was wrong.

Fred was volatile, for sure. He was one of those kids who would go out their way to disrupt the class as much as they could. He was in my opinion on the edge sometimes, almost acting in a totally irrational way. He was a clever guy in how he manipulated the new guy and me. He would play one of us off against the other, taking it in turns to befriend one of us more than the other and then almost intimidate the other one. Then he would switch it around and do the same, only using the one who had been chosen to be the one he befriended. It was a strange relationship, for sure, and in retrospect I have no idea why the new guy and I didn't just tell the Fred to piss off. We didn't. We were being controlled, and it went on all through that second year. Fred upset the French lady teacher so much and disrupted the class so badly that she had to leave the school. We believe she had a nervous breakdown or some other illness connected with stress.

To this day I don't understand what was driving Fred at that time. He was a maniac. On one occasion he was sitting next to me in class and said he could read my fortune by looking at the lines in the palm of my hand. I then showed him my upturned hand on the desk and he held my hand there while he stabbed me in the palm with a pencil. Yes, the pencil went in OK – and my hand bled a bit from the small wound. He found it most funny, of course, and gave out one of his manic laughs. If I look at my hand today I can still see the small indent made by Fred. It's a nice reminder of how school could be.

I didn't do as well in the second year as I did in the first. Can anyone guess why? I had a whole year of disruption, and it seemed like I had no way of resolving it. I was so controlled by all this that I never mentioned any of this manipulation and mental torture to my parents.

Fred even asked me to come around his house on Saturday mornings for a play. That was not too bad, to be honest, but it was all part of him controlling me. In the end I just didn't go and felt a lot better for it. Making that decision to break away from him was in part a way of recovering my mental health.

I have subsequently talked to other school friends about situations at school in those early days, and it seems that I was not alone. Many have said that there had been someone who befriended them that then either went on to bully them or controlled them in some way. The problem with school was that there was no escape from it, and teachers just didn't want to hear or do anything about these kinds of issues.

Hopping from lesson to lesson with a bag full of the correct books for each lesson, the school day always seemed long to me. We had been told right from day one that all our exercise books had to be covered. This always seemed quite strange to me. In fact when I went home and said to my dad that the books needed to be covered he had no idea what that meant. In the end my dad used some old wallpaper left on an odd roll from under the stairs to cover them. It worked well and I had the best-looking books in the class, even if they did match the paper in the living room.

The day started with assembly, where the then headmaster would give out any news and we would sing some hymns and take prayers. The headmaster then was a Mr Fowler, a middle-aged and middle-girthed gentleman with slicked-back greying hair and dark thick-rimmed glasses. He seemed a fair man and always had the respect of the kids. He would if pushed use his cane to dish out six of the best on the bottoms of naughty boys – but these were few and far between, and certainly not as many as speculated by kids before we started this school.

He always wore his university gown. This always gave teachers and the head a frightening look. They actually looked a bit like Dracula as they drifted down the corridor. If you have seen any of the *Harry Potter* films then think of Snape and you won't be far from the vision we had: black gowns flapping away with lots of chalk dust on them. Some even wore the mortar board hats to complete the look of total authority and menace.

The deputy head was a totally different man altogether: a Mr Dane. Now Dane wore a smart suit all the time and was very tall and slender. In fact the resemblance to John Cleese playing Basil Fawlty was at times unmistakable. But Dane was nothing like Fawlty in how he took charge. He was very cool and calculating: a man you really did stand to attention to when he entered a room. I never knew him teach a subject but he did stand in sometimes when teachers were ill.

One story that always intrigues me about Dane was told to me by one of my school friends, Tina. She had apparently done something so terrible at school that she needed some punishment. Knowing Tina well I know this misdemeanour would have been something really small indeed, like dropping a pencil on the floor or maybe talking when told not to. Mr Dane dished out the punishment and was very clear and precise on what he wanted from her. She should write a story that night about a pig, and along with the story there should be illustrations too.

One might consider this to be a slightly over-the-top punishment for such a small wrongdoing, but old Dane had a purpose in all this. You see, Dane kept all the stories in a box. Yes, that's right. He had many an illustrated story from the different kids that he had used the same punishment on. These stories were taken home, and Mr Dane used these illustrated stories to send his young daughter off to her slumbers by reading them to her as bedtime stories ... a little bit different, then, to 100 lines or Basher's slipper.

One of the new things introduced to me was metalwork and woodwork. There were purpose-built machine shops with drills and lathes, and even a furnace for manufacturing all sorts of things. What a far cry this was from the junior school, where each classroom was basically the same.

Our woodwork teacher was a Mr Goodwin, a tall stick-like man who rode this pushbike to work every day. He was a strict man, and had very strict rules that we all had to adhere to. Let's face it, a woodwork or metalwork shop has a lot of pointy sharp things that boys could easily do the wrong thing with in the wrong hands. He had to run a tight ship, for sure, because us boys and pointy things were made for much mischief.

At that time you had to wear a white apron in the machine shops but no eye protection at all. I quite liked woodwork and metalwork. We made a wooden toy car and lovely wooden bowls on the lathes. You had to be so careful with sharp chisels and anything, really, that might inflict pain. Kids would throw things when Mr Goodwin wasn't watching, but he kind of had eyes in the back of his head and always knew. Mr Goodwin would demonstrate in stages what was needed to complete the project we were undertaking, and he would announce this demonstration by the following phrase,

"Now gather round, everybody, and listen to me gently."

To this day I have no idea if he was being serious or trying to make a joke because he never changed his expression.

"Can you really listen gently," we all thought? In the playground we would take Mr Goodwin off by strutting about making ourselves as tall and stiff as we could.

"Now, boys, listen to me gently," we would say, like some sketch out of *Monty Python*.

In metalwork we made a metal shovel. I took mine home and it would be used on the open fire to shovel out the old clinkers in the morning, and we made a fire rake that also had the purpose of helping with the cleaning out of coke boilers and coal fires. What we made was used and useful, which was great. We actually learned that what you produced would have a purpose, and you felt you had a skill at the end of it.

As the second year was coming to a close I was getting a bit fed up, to be honest. Fred was as mad as a hatter, and I was not enjoying his company or his antics at all. Three guys took it upon themselves to start talking to me: Barrie, Clive, and Terry. We kind of formed a little group at break times and this took me away from Fred's clutches. Barrie and Clive were both big enough to deal with any potential bullies or control freaks, that was for sure. One day they warned Fred off when he came over to try and take me back to his control centre. Clive came up to me at the end of term and said to me,

"Next term, Rich – when we move into the new form class – I want you to sit next to me, OK? Barrie is going to sit next to Terry."

"Oh," I said. "That's fantastic. We can all be together, then."

"Yes," said Clive, "And you can help me with my maths too, as you're really smart."

He then said,

"I don't want you going anywhere near that Fred guy again, and if he so much as makes a move on you next year let us know and we will deal with it."

This was a huge turning point for me. This was the beginning of the third year, and a time when it really all started to come together for me. Finally I had some real mates who cared what happened and I expected that we were going to have some fun, too.

The Old Dump

1968

The dump was a strange place indeed. It was situated towards the lower end of Shendish in Apsley, about a mile walk from home.

Shendish today is better known as Shendish Manor hotel and golf course. Back then the area was just farm land with cows grazing on lush pastures.

You walked to Apsley, crossed the main road, and then walked up by the side of St Mary's Church over the railway bridge and then into the fields. The dump was the dumping ground for the paper company known as John Dickinson's. It amassed so much rubbish in a day that it warranted its own dumping ground, where it could burn off any combustibles. When we say rubbish here it was not like the general rubbish, as in food or wastepaper bins. No: this was industrial rubbish, inflammables, packing cases and allsorts.

Shendish was mainly farmland but this dump existed in the middle of it, surrounded by trees and a fence to keep cattle out. A dirt road track fed into the dump so that a dumper truck could access and feed a smouldering heap several times a day. It was a bit of a coincidence that one of the drivers of the dump truck actually lived in our road. This would be a constant concern to us over the time we went there, as in part what we got up to was at times a little naughty.

Baz and I had been to the dump once before, just to take a gander at what was there. We knew where it was, and so we crossed the field by first ducking under some barbed wire and then walking up the slope towards the tree line of the dump. We got to the perimeter and crossed over another set of barbed wire fencing to enter the dumping area itself. The dump consisted of a flat top which a truck could drive on to, and then it dropped away like a small cliff of maybe twenty feet in height. The cliff face was not sheer but fell away in a gradual slope of unburnt rubbish. This slope was piled high with all manner of items from the factory. When we got there rubbish was already burning, with some boxes and general rubbish combustibles. The dump always smouldered away, even on a Sunday when no rubbish was dumped. I had been warned by my school chums to keep an ear open for the sound of the dump truck coming, as we would get a good telling-off if caught out.

Beware the dump truck they said. Don't get caught!

We made our way up the slope to the top flat surface, where the ground was clear and open. It was just a round hard surface. Trees surrounded us in a circle apart from where the track road led into the dump. The track was quite long, and so if any truck came down it would be obvious to see and hear. We made note of this and I said to Baz,

"We really need to keep one eye and one ear on that track. If we hear anything then we run. OK, Baz?"

Baz acknowledged this and said

"Sure. It will be OK."

Baz and I found some tin cans and set them up on a bank to shoot with our catapults. Tins were in abundance here: mostly old paint tins, but there was every variety here. You never had to search far for anything to shoot at here: it was filled with all manner of objects. There was a nice earth mound over to one side and we set up our targets to shoot.

We fired a few marbles off and dented a few cans. It was fun to have a range where we could just fire and not worry where the shots were going if we missed. We were having so much fun, but all of a sudden the silence was disrupted. I heard a noise.

"Not the truck … it can't be the truck, surely," I thought.

"What's that, Baz?" I said. "Did you hear that?"

Some twigs cracking from the boundary of the dump behind us made us jump. I heard the characteristic swat noise of an airgun pellet as it came from above, hissed beside us, and hit one of the tins we had set up. It was then followed by a much slower and heaver .22 slug that buzzed like an angry bee as it flew past us. You can clearly tell the difference in velocity between the two main calibre's of air guns.

171

We both looked around and, sure enough, there were some familiar faces coming into the dump area with big grins on their faces.

"Watcha, Rich," said Clive, who sat next to me in class. Clive was followed in by Barrie and Terry from my form and two other guys behind them whom I didn't know. Baz had never met these guys before now, and I was hoping we would all get on well. Baz, after all, was from the grammar school and secondary modern kids didn't take to well to the posh ones at grammar: that's how they saw it.

It didn't take long, though, before we were all sharing in on what we had. Barrie had an old post-war Diana Mod 23, Clive had a Mod 28, and Terry had nothing and was sharing the other guys' rifles. The other two guys, who were a year or so older than us, were Harry and Steve. Harry had a post-war BSA Meteor .22 and Steve had another old Diana. Clearly, Harry had the better rifle out of all of them. The Diana's worked OK and would hit the cans six times out of ten, but it was the Meteor that smashed them to bits. Baz and I were allowed to have goes of the various guns and in exchange we let them have some marbles and the cats to try out.

Barrie had a rummage around the dump. He seemed to be expert at this, clinging to the side of the dump cliff face and searching out stuff. In the middle of the smouldering abyss he found some long rods of fluorescent tubes. He knew what he wanted, and after five minutes he had an array of light tubes and some big light bulbs from the factory. He also found some jam jars. We set these up on the same bank where the tins had been and stood back a decent distance.

We took it in turns to shoot and explode the tubes and bulbs. Some would pop and others would really go bang. Once or twice someone with the cat would hit smack on target, and the larger marble projectile would take something out completely. We jumped for joy when the glass shattered in a cloud of dust. We were really enjoying ourselves and so wrapped up in what we were doing. Here we were, all new-found pals bonding well and enjoying one of the best Saturdays I had had for a long time. So engrossed were we that none of us heard the murmur in the distance.

The rumble had probably been there for some time, but in our excitement we had blotted out every sound around us. Our chatter and screams of delight were masking another noise. We were like some naughty school class gone AWOL. Then it happened. One ear picked up a sound that was not of our making.

Terry shouted out clearly and loudly in one long scream,

"Dumper… Runnn…"

It took a second to sink in as our eyes lifted from what we were doing. We looked over to Terry, and then to the opening of the dump. Horrified, we saw this monster trundling towards us. It was terrifying, to say the least. We had all watched these World War II films on TV where some lone soldiers would be out somewhere in the desert and then they would hear this squeaking noise. The sounds of a panzer tank and its characteristic squeaking tracks would promote fear into the bravest Tommy's heart. This was the noise that met our ears. This was no truck. In our minds this was a German panzer, for sure, squeaking and trundling towards us. It was slow-moving but if it caught us it would consume us all … it was a thing of nightmares.

"Runnn," Terry shouted again. You could say that we didn't need telling twice – but clearly we certainly did, as we were almost stuck to the spot by fright.

"Runnn," said Barrie. We ran, OK. We ran like the wind all in different directions. We had no plan and no thought-out route of escape, so we just ran in different directions to seek out some cover. Baz and I jumped down into the dump and back up the other side, to a point where there was cover in the thick bushes and an eye-level view of the top of the dump. Barrie and Terry had gone off to the side and towards where the truck was coming from. They then jumped into a thick clump of bushes to the side of the dump entrance. They would be really near that dump truck when it arrived, but they would be OK as long as they kept their heads down.

The others were over the other side from us and down in the dip of the dump. Again there was cover here, but they would not be able to see the dumper truck from where they were. They could, however, see us and we made some arm movements to inform them to keep down. Baz and I sat low on the ground as we saw this swaying dinosaur lurch into the dump arena. It turned sharply and backed up towards the edge of the dump. It looked like something out of *Mad Max* (although that movie had not yet been made).

One guy jumped out the turret of the tank – or was it a cab? We were confused. This was exciting and scary at the same time. Had the dumper guys actually seen us? We could hear the men talking now. One had a fag in his mouth and a cloth cap on. Both were dressed in blue dirty stained overalls. Were they talking about us? The back of the truck was let down with a loud clang and then the truck moved up closer to the edge of the cliff. The man with the fag was shouting out instructions. We could not hear but I guess it was,

"Back a bit… Back a bit."

Fag man then raised his hand and the tank-like truck lurched to a halt. It then raised up its back portion until its contents spewed down the sides of the cliff face of the dump. Some more chatter went on between the two guys and then the driver got out and walked off over towards the bushes where Terry and Barrie were lying low.

"God," I said to Baz. "They've been rumbled. They've been seen for sure."

"Shit," said Baz. "We're in a whole lot of trouble now if they see those guns."

The guy was now really close to Terry and Barrie. He looked around as if he might have been looking for someone just a foot or two from the bush they were hiding in.

"He's looking for 'em, Baz," I whispered. "The bloody guy knows they are there. It must be… We are finished."

The guy then fumbled around with his overalls and reached inside. Baz responded to this with,

"What's he doing now? Oh, man … he isn't, is he?"

Fag man then started to pee into the bushes. The guy was actually urinating into the bush where Barrie and Terry were lying low. Baz and I looked at each other and grinned.

"They are not going to be happy, are they?" I said.

Meanwhile the other guy had lit some paper and thrown it down to the dumped cargo. It burst into flames. It was quite obvious that what they had dumped was inflammable. It went off like a cannon.

Pee man came back, adjusting his overalls and tackle as workmen do: stretching their pants inside to ensure that things fitted nicely.

The guys then jumped back in the truck and off it went, lumbering along at its speedy five miles per hour back up the dump track.

"Phew," I said. "That was a close shave."

That was too much excitement for one day, and we regrouped back on top of the flat area.

"Did you bloody see that?" said Terry, running towards us. "That bloody dump guy pissed on me. I've got bloody splashes of piss on my bloody jeans."

Then someone stated that maybe pissing on Terry was perhaps a good idea, anyway, and maybe we should all try it. Terry suddenly shut up at this suggestion and we all laughed together as he realised it was a joke.

Barrie told us that we would probably be OK now, as on Saturday they only make one or two dumps – and they definitely don't work Saturday afternoons.

Although we knew that the dumper would not be back we still had an ear out for anything that might sound like a motor, and we definitely jumped once or twice during the day when we heard a sound coming from over the back of the line of trees.

We continued to shoot stuff for a while longer until it got to midday, and I said to Baz,

"We had better go home for dinner."

Dinner in those days was a large meal you had at midday, and you didn't miss this meal.

"We are definitely coming back, though, aren't we Baz?" I said.

"Yep. We sure are," said Baz.

We raced home, ate our dinners, and were back up there within an hour and a half. The weather had changed. The morning had been a nice warm sunny day but now there was mist coming in and the air felt damp. Baz and I were alone up there for a while until we heard our new-found shooting friends over in one of the fields. Sometimes you can hear an air rifle from quite a distance.

The original band regrouped, and we decided to set light to a few things in the dump. Barrie had this great idea that we could build a fire and then place a huge empty oil drum on it, and it should expand

and make quite a bang. Sounds silly, sounds dangerous … and yes, it is. That oil drum sat on that fire for ages and it creaked and moaned for about an hour before the top few off into the air maybe 100 feet up, followed by a column of thick rings of black smoke. There were grins from Barrie as he turned to us and said,

"Told you it would be good."

We were patting Barrie on the back for being so clever and nearly killing us all when there was a smack against one of the trees near us. We all looked around at each other.

"Who's missing?" said Clive?

"Nope, we are all here," I said.

"So where the fuck did that come from, then?" said Terry. We looked around. Who was shooting at us?

Two characters arrived around the parameter of the dump above us now: one male and one female. The male was carrying a gun. They were both older than us, maybe four or five years older. The female was obviously the girlfriend, and was tagging along with her boyfriend that afternoon. She had a tight heavy sweater on and ski pants. He was a tall chap with dark wavy hair slightly slicked back in a Teddy boy style. We didn't feel threatened at all. After all there were more of us, and this guy was outnumbered, outgunned.

He strolled out on to the dump top where we were and walked over to us with a smile. He had in his hands a much bigger airgun than I had seen to date. It was a monster of a gun in comparison to the old Diana's that my mates had.

"What's that you got there, mate?" chirped Barrie.

"A BSA Air Sporter," said The Bloke. He then went about cocking the gun by pulling a lever out from under the mid section of the stock. After this he turned a tap on top of the gun and loaded a slug into a hole in the top. Returning the tap back to where it had been he then shouldered the gun and took aim at one of our tins. There was quite a clout as the gun went off, and instantly the tin was in the air. We could tell this gun was very powerful: there was no lapse of time in between him firing and the tin jumping.

"Wow," said Clive. "That's a fine gun you've got there, mate."

"A BSA Air Sporter," he said once again. "One of the best guns you can get."

We looked at this masterpiece with envy. There was no way we would ever have such a gun like this. It was almost a privilege to just look at it close up. One or two of the guys had a go with The Bloke's gun. It was a bit big for us, really, but the bigger of the stocky guys managed it. Me being small, I didn't even want to try.

We plinked away all afternoon, The Bloke joining in our fun, until it began to get a bit too foggy to see much. It was time for Baz and me to leave. We said our goodbyes and left down one of the slopes to meet the field that would take us down back towards the church in Apsley. We had had a fantastic day: one of the best days ever, as kids. As we walked down the field we heard a few shots go over our heads. You can hear airgun pellets coming. It's like a buzz as they pass: a bit like a loud bee. I said to Baz,

"The silly buggers are trying to get us to run."

"They're trying to get us scared, I bet," said Baz.

"Well, I'm not running," I said. "They wouldn't shoot us, would they?" I asked.

"'Course not," said Baz.

A smacking sound and a yell from Baz confirmed my worst fear.

"They fucking shot me," said Baz, holding his leg and jumping around the field like some demented animal. I could now hear the cheers from the dump as our new chums had accomplished their task. I almost wanted to say,

"That was a good shot, Baz," but I'm not sure he would have appreciated it. The shot had been taken from over 100 yards away and, secretly, I was impressed. There were no further shots and Baz was OK: he had just a bit of broken skin on his leg. I found out later that it was The Bloke who had shot Baz with his powerful .22. It sure made a bruise.

"What the fuck am I going to tell my mum has happened here?" he said.

"Maybe you could say you've been bitten by an insect," I said, trying to reassure him.

"Oh, sure. You know my mum. An insect. What fucking insect bites like that?"

I had to agree that the excuse was lame. It was not going to be easy, but I think Baz just made sure that his leg was not on show for a week or so. The bloke turned up many times after this, usually on his own, and was always known as The Bloke. We never knew his name for real. He lived around Apsley somewhere and he was a complete mystery but he had three rifles, and each of them was top-notch.

Photographs from the Past

☆☆☆☆☆☆☆☆
☆ **Belswains** ☆
☆ **Junior School.** ☆
☆ **I'm second** ☆
☆ **from right, the** ☆
☆ **small lad. Circ** ☆
☆ **1962.** ☆
☆☆☆☆☆☆☆☆

☆☆☆☆☆☆☆
☆ **The dreaded** ☆
☆ **water cress** ☆
☆ **beds. Just** ☆
☆ **before I was** ☆
☆ **pushed in.** ☆
☆☆☆☆☆☆☆

☆☆☆☆☆☆☆☆☆☆☆
☆ **Some of the teachers** ☆
☆ **from the Junior** ☆
☆ **School. Mr Sully sits at** ☆
☆ **the back. Mr Dawson** ☆
☆ **makes a joke. 1960s.** ☆
☆☆☆☆☆☆☆☆☆☆☆

☆☆☆☆☆☆☆☆☆☆☆
☆ A rare school trip ☆
☆ from Apsley Station. ☆
☆ Parents and ☆
☆ teachers await the ☆
☆ train. Circ 1964. ☆
☆☆☆☆☆☆☆☆☆☆☆

☆☆☆☆☆☆☆☆☆
☆ On the platform. ☆
☆ The train arrives ☆
☆ for our school ☆
☆ trip to ☆
☆ Southampton. ☆
☆ Circ 1964 ☆
☆ ☆
☆☆☆☆☆☆☆☆☆

☆☆☆☆☆☆☆☆☆☆☆☆☆
☆ The motley crew from ☆
☆ Belswains out to London ☆
☆ and on the Cutty Sark. Circ. ☆
☆ 1963/4. (curtesy of Jim) ☆
☆ ☆
☆☆☆☆☆☆☆☆☆☆☆☆☆

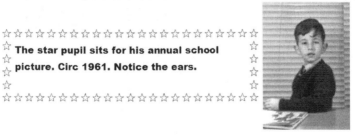

☆☆☆☆☆☆☆☆☆☆☆☆☆
☆ My first Polaroid with my ☆
☆ xmas present from Mum ☆
☆ and Dad. Baz taking Ricky ☆
☆ for a sledge ride. Circ 1966. ☆
☆ ☆
☆☆☆☆☆☆☆☆☆☆☆☆☆☆

☆☆☆☆☆☆☆☆☆☆
☆ Showing off my ☆
☆ hand me down ☆
☆ bike on the garden ☆
☆ path of number 18. ☆
☆ Circ 1966. ☆
☆☆☆☆☆☆☆☆☆☆

☆☆☆☆☆☆☆☆☆☆☆☆☆☆☆☆
☆ My lovely scooter in the back- ☆
☆ ground. Check those turn ups out ☆
☆ and the snake belt. Circ 1964. ☆
☆ ☆
☆☆☆☆☆☆☆☆☆☆☆☆☆☆☆☆

☆☆☆☆☆☆☆☆☆☆
☆ On holiday with ☆
☆ Rob and Mum. Circ ☆
☆ 1958. ☆
☆ ☆
☆ ☆
☆ ☆
☆☆☆☆☆☆☆☆☆☆

☆ ☆ ☆ ☆ ☆ ☆ ☆ ☆ ☆
☆ **Holiday picture** ☆
☆ **with Mum and** ☆
☆ **Dad. Circ 1961.** ☆
☆ ☆
☆ ☆
☆ ☆ ☆ ☆ ☆ ☆ ☆ ☆ ☆

☆ ☆ ☆ ☆ ☆ ☆ ☆ ☆ ☆ ☆
☆ **Sharing my ice** ☆
☆ **cream with Rob.** ☆
☆ **Circ 1957.** ☆
☆ ☆
☆ ☆
☆ ☆ ☆ ☆ ☆ ☆ ☆ ☆ ☆ ☆

☆ ☆ ☆ ☆ ☆ ☆ ☆ ☆ ☆ ☆ ☆ ☆ ☆ ☆ ☆ ☆
☆ **A very young couple. Mum and Dad** ☆
☆ **during the WW2.** ☆
☆ ☆ ☆ ☆ ☆ ☆ ☆ ☆ ☆ ☆ ☆ ☆ ☆ ☆ ☆ ☆

☆ ☆ ☆ ☆ ☆ ☆ ☆ ☆ ☆ ☆ ☆ ☆ ☆ ☆ ☆
☆ **Lovely professional photograph of** ☆
☆ **Nan and Granddad. After the 1st** ☆
☆ **World War.** ☆
☆ ☆
☆ ☆ ☆ ☆ ☆ ☆ ☆ ☆ ☆ ☆ ☆ ☆ ☆ ☆ ☆

☆☆☆☆☆☆☆☆☆
☆ **You just had to** ☆
☆ **have a white** ☆
☆ **suit back in the** ☆
☆ **seventies. Circ** ☆
☆ **1975.** ☆
☆☆☆☆☆☆☆☆☆

☆☆☆☆☆☆☆☆☆☆
☆ **Getting ready for a** ☆
☆ **night out with my** ☆
☆ **robot dog shirt on.** ☆
☆ **Circ 1976** ☆
☆☆☆☆☆☆☆☆☆☆

☆☆☆☆☆☆☆☆☆☆☆
☆ **Les and me downing a** ☆
☆ **half pint at Puckpool.** ☆
☆ **Looking a little odd.** ☆
☆ **Circ 1974** ☆
☆☆☆☆☆☆☆☆☆☆☆

☆☆☆☆☆☆☆☆☆
☆ **The Top Rank** ☆
☆ **Watford closes.** ☆
☆☆☆☆☆☆☆☆☆

TOP RANK CLOSURE
Top Rank ceased to operate Public Dance Sessions from April 1, 1974. Consequently Thursday's Bubbles, Saturday Mornings Children's Dance and Saturday Night Out are now Cancelled.

☆☆☆☆☆☆☆☆☆
☆ **Caz and me and** ☆
☆ **the crew out at** ☆
☆ **the Friday disco,** ☆
☆ **Kings Langley** ☆
☆ **Services club. Circ** ☆
☆ **1975.** ☆
☆☆☆☆☆☆☆☆☆

☆☆☆☆☆☆☆☆☆☆☆
☆ **Dodds Disco KLSC.** ☆
☆ **Circ 1975** ☆
☆☆☆☆☆☆☆☆☆☆☆

☆☆☆☆☆☆☆☆☆☆
☆ **Vic (Checky Boy)** ☆
☆ **and me on a day out** ☆
☆ **to Clacton. Circ.** ☆
☆ **1977.** ☆
☆☆☆☆☆☆☆☆☆☆

☆☆☆☆☆☆☆☆☆☆☆☆
☆ **Bill dons Baz's lucky** ☆
☆ **Mistletoe hat for a laugh at** ☆
☆ **the Cali. Circ 1975** ☆
☆ ☆
☆☆☆☆☆☆☆☆☆☆☆☆

☆ ☆ ☆ ☆ ☆ ☆ ☆ ☆
☆ **A day out at** ☆
☆ **Clacton with a** ☆
☆ **young lady.** ☆
☆ **Check those** ☆
☆ **flares out. Circ** ☆
☆ **1977** ☆
☆ ☆ ☆ ☆ ☆ ☆ ☆ ☆

☆ ☆
☆ **The collage guys just after taking their finals. Would you** ☆
☆ **trust these guys with your electronic equipment? My mate** ☆
☆ **Tony stands third from left. Circ 1974** ☆
☆ ☆

☆ ☆ ☆ ☆ ☆ ☆ ☆ ☆ ☆ ☆ ☆ ☆
☆ **A young lady models the** ☆
☆ **famous Moggy Minor. Circ** ☆
☆ **1974.** ☆
☆ ☆ ☆ ☆ ☆ ☆ ☆ ☆ ☆ ☆ ☆ ☆

188

☆ ☆

The class of '66' standing in the playground of what was Bennetts End Secondary Modern School. Later to become Longdean. Celibrating 60 years for both us and the school. With a new school being built on this site both these buildings and the old Apsley Grammar school are to be demolished in 2016.

☆ ☆

☆ ☆

Some of my old school chums celebrating 60 years in 2015 at Shendish Manor.

☆ ☆

Secondary Modern Third Year

The third year was a good start for me. I had my new friends and they would be a permanent fixture with me through the third, fourth, and fifth years. Mr Brown was to be our form master for the third year. Again, he was a typical-looking teacher type in his dress, sporting a dark full beard and having a longish face. Mr Brown reminded me a bit of Jesus in his looks in many ways – which was quite ironic, really, as he taught religious education (or RE, as we called it then).

You could not help but like Mr Brown, as he was a teacher with many stories and tales to tell. His only weakness was that you could steer him off the main lesson subject and on to something much more lively if you so wanted to. Mr Brown liked to preach his views and – of course – being a deeply religious guy, he really loved the emphasis on how sinful the world was and why we should be so careful in life of sin and its terrible pitfalls. We loved the subject of sin with Mr Brown. We loved hearing about why we should be fearful of unreal gods and talismans, how we should not play with ourselves at night, and how we should be married first before even thinking about kissing. It was all exciting stuff to hear, and always far better than the boring lesson old Brown thought he was going to lecture on.

Mr Brown occupied one of the annexes, like the one we had been accustomed to during the first year. We kind of felt at home here. In the room was a huge oil burner that would heat the classroom in the winter. Although it had a mesh cage around it to stop little hands getting in we always managed to push things on to the boiler to let off a bit of a stink. Brown was never amused when he picked up any unsavoury smell emanating from the old stove. He might have been a religious man, but boy could he let rip if he was angry. What is it they call it? The wrath of God?

I had the protection of my new mates now: Clive, Barrie, and Terry. Fred was no longer an issue now, and the bullying stopped.

Fred had teamed up in a twosome with the kid who was the new boy, which of course was great for me. I kind of felt sorry for the new boy. I knew the pain of being controlled.

Although I was a small chap I never really got bullied to the extent that some of the other kids did. I put this down to quick thinking and just being plain savvy. I'm not being big-headed here at all, but I think that some of the aspects of why kids get bullied are basically down to not reading situations in the first place. How I saw it was this: bullies were fundamentally stupid, anyway. They were thickos who had nothing better to do than vent their own frustrations out on others who would not or could not fight back.

In my book these egotistical thugs were easy to outwit. All you had to do was make sure you were not where they were: easy. So if you were – say – walking to school or walking back home and you saw a group of the aforementioned arseholes of society in front of you then you basically didn't keep walking towards them. You turned around and changed direction. Yes, you might indeed be walking out of your way – and even back to where you came from – but that's got to be better than being punched, kicked, or abused. I did this many a time and I got really good at detecting a potential hot spot from a distance. My super brain (as I saw it) had already recalculated a new route to take, like some satnav system for avoiding bullies.

Another situation was in the playgrounds and the corridors of the school. Again, if you saw trouble in a certain place you could just dodge it and keep out of the way … oh … the times I saw some of the smaller kids walk right into the lion's den, with appalling results. Once a bully sees you as a potential plaything then you will appear on their radar, for sure. So you make sure you're never there in the first place. I was like a ghost at times, slipping past the observation towers that were these mindless boneheads.

There is always that hierarchy in schools, like a pecking order. The bully types are at the top and then the lesser types. It then leads down to the really smaller weedy guys at the bottom, and anyone who would be classified these days as special needs. I was sitting somewhere in the middle of all this now, with my mates as some protection. But even once or twice I saw Clive and Barrie get a bit of abuse, and you kind of realised that protection was only as good as the level you were batting at.

The class I never wanted to be in was Upper 22 (or U22), the next one up from where I was in the second year. I was then in U23. This U22 class seemed to be top-heavy with bullies, and in fact there was one individual in this class who made many kids' lives sheer hell. Of course he had a group of mates who could all handle themselves, but I guess they were also a bit frightened of this one guy. It's a game of fear to an extent. After all, Hitler managed to stay alive and was never overthrown by any of his henchmen. No, that class was a complete no-no and I suppose in some respects I was pleased I never did well enough to move up to that form.

My good friend Jim was a bright boy whom I had known since Juniors. He was in the U22 form and generally cut off from me for most lessons. I didn't know it then that Jim's father was of Indian descent: looking at Jim, you would never have guessed that he was from a mixed-race background. His mother was from the East End and they had moved out from London after the war, as did a lot of families. Jim was in a lesson once where the teacher asked each kid in turn to talk about their parents and where they had come from. All Jim said was that his dad came from India, but then someone else chimed up in the class and added that his dad was dark-skinned. Well … that was it from that point on, and Jim's world started to fall apart as the bullies took this information on and used it to their advantage.

At that time in the UK there was a certain cultural change going on which fuelled racial hatred. Indeed the media was not helping by showing such TV programmes as *Till Death Us Do Part* with the bigot Alf Garnett and the comedy programme which followed called *Love Thy Neighbour*. I think there was even one comedy with Spike Milligan in called *Curry and Chips* which was taken off the air in the end. It all seemed that as far as the media was concerned it was good fun to poke fun at black and Asian communities. This helped to promote a divide between white and black people in the UK during the late sixties and into the seventies. Even the skinhead movement of the time was linked with something called Paki-bashing.

Jim too has many stories relating to having to take protracted routes home to miss the bullies, and even once or twice having to hide in the boiler room at school. Fortunately for Jim and the rest of us things got much better once the idiots had left school in the fourth and fifth years. Even in our late fifties Jim and I still talk about these bullies from that time and how awful they were. When you have been bullied it never really leaves you, and the bitterness never goes away. You wonder what sort of adults these kids turned into.

We were sitting in the form room annexe one morning waiting for the registration to be called by Mr Brown. Most of the class was already sitting down waiting and there was, as usual, loads of chat and merriment going on – bits of paper being thrown, and general boyish behaviour. In strolls Terry – a bit later than normal but still not late enough to get marked down, as old Brown had not come in yet. Now this would not have attracted any attention whatsoever but for the fact that one of Terry's hands was stuck firmly to the side of his head.

"What's up, Tell?" said Clive as he observed the strange appearance before him.

"Nuffin'," said Terry as he plonked himself down next to Barrie in front of us.

"Oh, come on, Tell. What are you holding your head for, you twat?" was the reply back from Clive.

"I said that nuffin' is wrong," said Terry. But by this time he was grinning, with one of those shameful grins you have when something is definitely up. Clive reached across to pull the hand away and Terry recoiled to deflect the attack. Chairs squeaked and others turned around.

Now the whole class was aware of the new Terry look, with one hand seemingly permanently attached to his head. A number of boys now came over.

"Hold him down," someone said. Terry was attacked in not a nasty way but a way that was nonetheless going to compromise his situation. The hand was removed and a gasp –"Oooh" – filled the air as all observed the side of Terry's head.

Terry had about an inch thick or so of hair on his head, apart from a nice neat strip of bare skin that appeared from the bottom of his neck up to halfway up his bonce. The appearance was so unexpected that the gang of boys holding Terry just moved backwards away from him with open mouths. It was like they had discovered some alien.

"Unclean," someone shouted.

"What the hell have you done to your head, Terry...?" said Barrie, as he tried to stifle the laughter by sticking his fist in his mouth.

"Terry, you twathead," said another from outside our camp of friends. There were also a few girls giggling over in the far corner also with their hands to their mouths, like girls do when shocked.

Terry explained.

"Well ... you see ... me mum bought this new comb thing that you can use to cut your hair with. It's like a comb but has a razor blade in it, and you sort of comb and it cuts your hair."

Now I had seen the adverts for the Ronco Hair Trimmer on TV. It had been on countless times on ITV and made haircutting look easy. I even thought it could be good for me.

"So what went wrong, then, Tell?" asked Clive.

"Well," he said, "I decided to have a go myself, but didn't realise that you had to comb in the down direction. I tried to go up, and it's just taken a lump of hair out..."

"You bloody twat," said Clive, as twat seemed to be the word of the day.

Now we heard the outer door go to the annexe and Mr Brown entered the room. He had already spied a certain commotion in the corner of the room – which was Terry and his new alien haircut. Instead of going straight to his desk for register he drifted over immediately to inspect the scene.

194

"What's all this, boy...?" he said to Terry. Terry's hand was now fixed back in position to cover the landing strip on his head. Terry had no option but to drop his hand and show Brown the damage.

In fairness to Brown, he acted on this in the best possible way. He sent Terry home immediately and instructed him to go to the hairdressers that day and have it sorted out. Terry came back in the next day as a skinhead, as really that was always going to be the only option available to him now. He might have had a bit of teasing for a day but it was the best solution for him, and we got used to him having no hair for a while. In fact, after that, Terry had short hair for as long as I can remember.

In my other chapters concerning shooting you will have observed that Barrie, Clive, and Terry formed my shooting pals, and it was this third year when all that started. We could not get enough of it, and were constantly talking in class about guns and hunting and what we might be doing next weekend. We formed a close friendship and bond that lasted until we parted and went our different ways.

Shooting Tails

Baz came around one weekend, and he had brought along a couple of catalogues his mum used to sell from to get some pin money. One was Kays and the other was Grattan's catalogue. Catalogues then were a way in which you could buy more expensive items and then pay them off on a weekly basis. You could have what you wanted sooner, but you ended up paying much more for the item you bought. In addition the quality was usually not that great, either. People had no credit cards in those days: they hadn't been invented. Cash was the order of the day, with working men and women being paid weekly. The only way to purchase without paying up front was to buy from a club book. It was big business back then, and many women ran these club books to supplement the household income because they got a small commission when they sold to others.

We thumbed through the pages, stopping on some of the pages where pictures of ladies in stockings and suspenders were depicted.

"Cor," said Baz. "Look at the legs on that one."

This was really the only naughtiness that boys could view in those days. Women's club book catalogues always had a deep fascination for boys. You learned stuff in those books that would be needed later on in life. I bet there were some well-thumbed pages in households throughout the sixties.

"Look," I said to Baz, as we eyed a page full of corsets. "I reckon those are wrist cutters," as I pointed to the tight elastic around one lady's thighs.

"You what?" said Baz, trying not to laugh. "What's a wrist cutter, then?

"I dunno, Baz," I said. "I just heard me dad call 'em that."

It took me many a year after this to understand what a wrist cutter was, but I did in the end.

"Come on, Baz," I said. "We're not looking for that sort of thing today. Get on to the later pages."

"OK, OK," said Baz, with a smirk on his face.

We flipped through the pages. These catalogues were very thick, with hundreds of pages selling everything you might want. When we got to the pages where the fishing tackle was detailed we then knew that the next page would be airguns.

"There you go," said Baz. "Airguns."

We looked over the pictures with envy, looking and taking even more in than on the previous pages of ladies' corsets.

"What do you reckon, Baz," I said. "Do you reckon you can talk your old lady into one of these?"

"Sure, I can," he said. So we flipped through and decided on what might be achievable to buy on the never-never. Sure to his word, Baz did persuade his mum to get an air rifle. He would be paying it off from his paper round money for years.

After three weeks the gun arrived. Baz brought it around straight away to my house. There was no case or anything: he just walked down the road to my house with it and a tin of slugs.

"What is it?" I said, looking at this short rifle with a light wooden stock.

"It's a Relum Jelly," he said trying to pull a more-than-serious face.

"A what?" I said.

"It's Czech," he said. "You know: foreign. It was cheap in the club book and it was the only one my mum would agree to." In actual fact the gun was from Hungary but all the same we called it a Czech gun because it sounded better.

Well ... an airgun is an airgun, and Baz had one and I didn't. Who was I to pass judgement? As far as we were concerned this was the best air rifle in the world ... and, hey – this was new, too – and not second-hand like the old Diana's we had used up at the dump.

We immediately took it down the bottom of my garden with a few tin cans. My garden was perfect for shooting as there was a back stop at the end (the communal garage). We set some targets up on a wooden board I found and plinked until we ran out of slugs, taking it in turns to have goes. My dad came down at one point.

"What have you got there, Baz?" said my dad.

My dad was just a more grown-up version of me, and he understood everything to do with guns.

"It's my new airgun, Reg," said Baz, using my dad's first name in a very informal way. My dad had a go and hit stuff and then gave us a lecture on safety.

To pass the final test that we were both responsible kids to have and own an airgun we had to go to Shendish with Baz's mum and dad and his sister and shoot at some targets in the woods. This was Baz's parents just making sure that where we might go was OK to do so. We passed the test and were told that we could next go all by ourselves. God, what a mistake that was.

Shendish would beckon us every weekend for some time. We wrapped Baz's gun up in an old hessian sack I found in the shed and we walked up to the dump. The only hot spot for us was crossing the road in Apsley. Although we were old enough to shoot an airgun we kind of felt worried about carrying a gun about … if the police were around and driving past in Apsley, two likely lads with a sack were going to get stopped for sure. I was always nervous crossing here and wanted to get that short stretch over and done with quickly. Once in the grounds of the old church you were fine.

We took Baz's gun up to the dump and had our own private shoot at the bottles and cans up there till we were met by my old schoolmates again. We messed about at the dump once more and we were all astonished by Barrie and his antics: once again he was clinging to the face of the dump and finding stuff to shoot at. He was performing one of these manoeuvres when he shouted out,

"Hey … come look at this, guys. Look what I found."

We stood at the bottom of the cliff, our eyes turning towards Barrie where he was clinging on in the smouldering mass. He began to throw down what looked like rings, and it was only when they landed near us that we realised what they were.

"Wow," we exclaimed. "Sellotape…" There were reels and reels of the stuff of different colours and different widths, all unburned and waiting to be found. There was enough here for all of us to have about ten reels each. We left them in a pile near the dump perimeter and came back for them when we left for home. Those reels of tape lasted years at home, and even when I finally left home at the age of twenty-five I still took some with me.

After Baz had shown off his new gun to the other guys and they had had a go with it to test it out Barrie suggested that we leave the dump and go over to the fields. Barrie said there was a coppice on the other side of the field adjoining the dump. He said that there were tall trees which had grey squirrels in them. We got excited. Bottles and tins were one thing, but shooting something live was going to exceed anything we had done before. We had become quite good at shooting stuff from the dump at ranges up to about thirty yards. We would even throw tins into the air to see if we could shoot them.

"How difficult could a squirrel be to shoot?" we thought.

We made our way across the field like a marauding bunch of guys with guns. We must have looked like something out of one of those western films. We were the guys from *The Magnificent Seven* and no squirrel was going to be left standing, that was for sure. The field was flat and had some cows roaming and grazing on the grassland. At odd places there were huge cowpats steaming away in the grass. This was freshly dropped cow poo, and some of them had the added bonus of cow pee in the centre: a little lake of brown liquid festering in the middle of a soft squishy pat surrounded by flies.

Clive thought it would be fun to wait for an opportune moment. Terry was just passing by one of these soggy cowpats.

"Hey, Tell," said Clive, ensuring that Terry came to a halt right by the pat. Terry stopped and turned as Clive fired into the piss-laden cow shit at point-blank range.

An airgun slug is small, but the energy it has at point-blank range is substantial. It hit the pat with a smack. Terry was covered.

"Hey, you bastards," said Terry. "I'm covered in shit and piss now. What did you do that for, you gits?"

We couldn't help but laugh at the sight that greeted our eyes. Clive said,

"It's lucky, Tell."

"What's fucking lucky about being covered in cow shit, then?" said Terry.

Barrie commented that maybe Terry might smell a bit better now and Clive concluded by informing Terry that it would help him get close to the squirrel, as he would now smell like one. We moved on, each of us now keeping a watchful eye on the grass for more cowpats. No one would be caught out a second time.

We could see our destination in the distance and, sure enough, there was activity here. We could see at least two or three flashes of grey darting about in the trees. Barrie said,

"Hold up, guys. We need to be careful here how we approach them."

Grey squirrels are not an indigenous species to the UK, and certainly not to Hemel Hempstead either. They came over to us in the late nineteenth century from North America, and loved it here so much that they decided to stay. Being a prolific breeder twice a year (with two to seven kittens) they have managed to push out our native red squirrel into just a few areas of the UK.

Many people find them cute, and love to watch their antics. They certainly do have a way with acrobatics, and can be fun to watch. However, they are vermin: they do carry disease, they do wreck our trees, and they can be very aggressive indeed. I would warn anyone with children to keep a distance from these animals, especially the adult ones. I have had one or two have a go at me before now. They also eat our small birds and destroy nests, eating the eggs they find. They are not a nice animal in any respect: Barrie named them tree rats from the start. This was a name that really did seem appropriate, once you dismissed the cute facade they exhibited.

Barrie suggested that we approach them from a line of bushes so no eyes would see our approach. Terry was still cleaning himself of cow shit and bovine urine as we climbed over a rusty metal fence into the coppice area. Barrie knew his stuff and told us exactly what we should do next. He wanted us to surround this group of trees from every point and angle: to get into position using stealth.

I'm not sure that we managed that too well because when we did get into position the treetops were now completely void of activity.

"OK," Barrie said. "Wait up, sit down, and just wait."

So we took up our positions and sat in wait for what we envisaged would be a re-enactment of the gunfight at the O.K. Corral.

Squirrels build two types of drey. They either make large nests of twigs and moss or they nest inside trees. In this case the tree rats were inside the trunk and holding up. The tree they were in had been bored through. Where the tree was clearly dying it was hollow inside, to an extent. Eventually this tree would fall apart or the forestry people would have to cut it down. The tree rats would then move on to a new home.

"Movement," Barrie hissed, pointing to a small hole up near the top of the main trunk. A nose was sticking out. Terry shouldered.

"No, you twat," said Clive. "Wait. Wait till the bugger comes out, for Christ's sake."

After a few minutes, more of the body came out as the rat became brave.

"Wait," Barrie hissed in a hushed tone. The rat was now fully out and clinging to the side of the tree, twitching its tail and sniffing the air.

"Now," said Barrie, and we all let rip with a hail of lead from every possible direction. Bits of dead bark from the tree went flying as the slugs hit high. The tree rat went back in its hole and I almost thought I saw one finger poke up at us as it did. We had missed. Five guns had fired and nothing had hit.

"Crap," said Clive. "How the hell did we miss that?"

Well it would take me another forty years to understand why five guns had all missed the target. When you point a gun at forty-five degrees up (or indeed down) your shot will go higher than expected. That's clearly what had happened here. That's science, and we knew none of it at that time.

"He won't be out now," I said. "That's it. We may as well go back to the dump to shoot some cans."

"Oh, no, we're not," said Barrie. "I have a plan. I'm not finished with this guy just yet…"

I have to admire Barrie, my old school chum. In all honesty I loved him to bits. I loved his ingenuity and his positive nature and passion. He was a kind soul, and I have to say that it was an honour to be his mate for those few years. Barrie was bright as far as hatching plans and solving things was concerned. I only hope I learned something from him in those wild days.

What Barrie did next was astonishing, to say the least. He took off his jacket and dropped all his gun stuff on the ground. He then searched about in the bushes for a length of branch and cut one out with his penknife which looked about right for his purpose.

"Right," he said. "I need some rag."

"OK," I said, handing him my handkerchief.

In those days almost everyone would have had a cloth handkerchief in their pocket. There were no paper tissues in those days. Mine had not been used – and Barrie was thankful for that, at least.

Barrie fixed the hanky to the end of the pole that he had cut down with some twine he had also found in the bushes. He then dug in his pocket and produced a bulb. This was not a light bulb, but a lighter fuel bulb. In those days cigarette lighters were powered by petrol and you could buy a bulb, which was a sealed plastic container that had just enough liquid fuel in it to fill a lighter. Barrie bit the top off the plastic nozzle and shot the petrol over my snot rag.

"I'm not going to get this back, then," I thought. We kind of now knew what Barrie had in mind.

"How are you going to get that up there, Barrie? The pole's not long enough," Terry erupted.

"Yes, I know, Terry," retorted Barrie. "Terry, it's long enough if one were to reach across from this other tree here with the stick," continued Barrie.

"Oh," said Terry. "That's bloody smart, Barrie. You're so damn clever at times. Are you going to climb up there, then?"

"Nope," said Barrie. "I'm not climbing up the tree at all."

"Nooo?" said Terry, in complete surprise and wonderment.

"No, I'm not … but you are, Terry… you're going up there"

"Shit," said Terry. "Why me? Why is it me who has to do these jobs?"

Barrie explained that as Terry didn't actually have a gun of his own – and as he was a better shot with his own gun – that he needed to be on the ground to shoot. He also explained that Terry was expendable. Terry didn't understand what that meant but thought it might mean brave. It was reaffirmed that Terry should be the one to climb the tree.

"Yes, and you smell like shit," Clive chimed in. "That's a good enough excuse."

Terry was given a box of matches and told to climb the tree. He duly did as he was told as he was an accommodating chap, and actually was a good climber. He was the perfect choice for this job: lean and mean. He would need to go up about twenty feet to reach across.

"Don't light the rag till we hand it to you up there, OK? said Barrie.

"OK, OK … I know," retorted Terry in a very apprehensive way. His voice was now a little shaky.

"I don't have a good feeling about this," said Terry. "Are you sure this will work, Barrie?"

"Sure it will," we all said in unison. "Get on with it."

Terry climbed up, and at the point where the pole was about to pass out of reaching distance from us we handed it to him. He was on a thick branch now, and parallel with the tree rat's nest hole in the opposite tree.

"OK … light the rag, Tell," said Barrie. We all loaded up. Baz was to take a shot this time, as I had had a go on the first try. Terry lit the hanky first time. The fuel on the rag ensured that it would burn well for a while before consuming the cloth.

"OK … stick it in the hole, Terry…"

Terry leant across with the stick in one hand. It was going to reach, for sure, but he needed to use almost all the length to get there.

"Push it in, Tell," said Clive. "Push it in…"

Terry did what was obvious and pushed the burning torch into the entry door to the tree rat's nest. The rag came off the stick but it was already in the tree and burning well. The hole was ablaze, in fact.

What happened next happened quickly. It was a blur, to be honest, and it wasn't what any of us expected at all. Animals don't like fire, it seemed. We learned that on this day. Terry learned it faster than the rest of us, though. Nope. Animals don't like fire, especially when fire is poked into their home.

There was a lot of noise coming from up above … agitated noises, for sure. Three squirrels flew out of a secondary hole (not the one the guns were trained on). Why we thought that these animals would stamp out the hanky and just march out of the same hole is beyond me now. Having jumped across several trees in a split second, two shot off into the distance. The third, however, jumped across to the tree near to us … the tree Terry was clinging to.

Terry panicked. I think someone said something like,

"They like you, Terry…"

Terry didn't so much climb back down the tree as he sort of screamed and fell at the same time. Terry had come face to face with the tree rat. I'm not sure to this day who was more surprised, to be honest: the tree rat coming face to face with a kid smelling of cow poo or Terry looking at the prospect of some very sharp teeth.

He made it down OK without anything broken and we laughed our heads off. We laughed so much that we forgot about the third tree rat, which was now miles away.

"What's so fucking funny, guys? said Terry as he adjusted his smelly clothing once again. We had to admit that we had not shot anything, but we had had so much fun trying.

"Back to the dump, then, lads – and let's shoot something we know we can hit, tin cans" I said.

My Own Gun At last
Up to now I had been shooting with Baz and shared the Jelly with him. We had gone through quite a few boxes of pellets and the gun was getting a bit weak. The cheapness of this Hungarian rifle was

showing through and we would need to do some maintenance on it very soon.

I wanted a gun for myself and I guess I had requested one, but I wasn't a kid who would have pestered my family for anything. I knew money was sometimes tight, and I for one didn't expect anything. I was hankering to buy my cousin's rifle, which I had seen on a visit to Norwich. I had asked several times if I could buy it, as this seemed to be an affordable way for my family to buy me a gun.

I was, then, greatly surprised when I returned home from school one day and mum and dad were in the kitchen as I entered the house through the back door. They had grins on their faces, and there was a large long box propped up against the wall.

"This is for you, son," said my dad. "You've done so well at school of late that we thought you might like this."

"Wow," I thought, not really knowing what it might be – but sort of guessing what it possibly could be. This was a long box. It could only hold something long. It was even longer than the Jonny Seven I had got one Christmas a few years back.

One wonders if it's possible to bottle that excitement you get sometimes: that really pure excitement when you get something to unwrap and you know what's inside. You can't wait, and you're so damn excited that you almost wet yourself. It takes something special to bring about that excitement, and this was one of those occasions.

I laid the box down on the floor. It had brown paper around it and I took this off to reveal a box with the words Birmingham Small Arms written across it in big black type. I lifted the lid and it slid up, making one of those farting noises that boxes always do when it's an exciting time.

Inside was a band new airgun. You can tell a new airgun: it just smells of newness. The oil and the blued metal just give a unique smell. The box had a polystyrene insert to hold the gun in position. There were some loose targets, a target holder, and a small thin tube of BSA Pylarm pellets. I lifted the gun out of its shell and admired its beauty. On the top was stamped the name BSA Meteor .177cal.

I was so surprised. I looked at my parents almost with tears in my eyes as if to say,

"What? For me?" I was truly grateful for this present, as I knew this was not a cheap purchase. I'm still astonished today by having had such a lovely gun when all my mates could really afford were old pre-war Dianas or club book guns. This was a gun that was another level above anything anyone else had. It was a quality piece built in Birmingham by BSA. It had a dark-stained glossy wooden stock. It had adjustable rear sights and a tunnel forend sight. Inside – although I didn't know it yet – the piston seal was not leather as with my pals' guns, but synthetic nylon. God, this was a beast. It pushed its .177 pellets out at over 700 feet per second, and when I tried it in the garden it had no trouble hitting anything at all.

My dad and I shot in the garden that afternoon. We used up all the targets supplied and then had to make some more. This gun was running fast and hot, and it took a while to realise how to handle such a powerful gun.

I was excited about taking the gun out. Next weekend I would be up at the dump with it to show all my mates. Baz came around later, and we had another plink in the garden. I think he was impressed, as the gun was a real beauty.

I found another old sack in the shed I could use to cover the gun while transporting it to Shendish. The sack was only just long enough, and I would probably have to be careful that the barrel didn't poke out of it as I walked the streets. In fact it wasn't long before a major mishap happened and the issue I was always worried about came to pass.

Baz and I were walking back from the dump and had crossed over the main road in Apsley. We had just turned the corner on to the footpath that would take us along over the canal bridge. As we had turned the corner I looked back and saw a police car driving up through the village. It's funny how you sort of know something is not right: it's like a sixth sense, and something had clearly made me look back.

"Police," I whispered to Baz. "Don't look back."

Baz didn't say anything.

"Hey, guys," said a policeman.

It was too late. We had been rumbled. I didn't need to look around again to know what the situation was here, but of course we had to now stop and turn around to face the two coppers beckoning us back at the entrance to the footpath. We walked back to the two men in blue. One was tall and the other was a short, stockier guy.

"Where you going?" one officer asked.

"Home," we both replied.

"Where have you been, then?"

We replied again, being totally honest.

"I see," said the stocky one.

"Are these yours?" the other asked.

"Yes," I said.

"Let's have a look, then, guys," the copper said.

We handed over our prize possessions. The coppers unwrapped them and had a quick look.

"OK, boys. Do you know what's wrong here, then?"

We both shook our heads in unison. We must have looked a right couple of green criminals (if in fact we were criminals) .

"These airguns ..." said the stocky one, "They need to be in proper covers."

"Oh," Baz said. "Yes, we know ... but we just got 'em."

Baz was telling a bit of a lie here, as we had had them a few weeks by then.

"I see," said the tall one. "Well, lads, we will let you off this time ... but if we see you again without a proper cover on you will be in trouble. Is that clear?"

"Yes, officer," we both replied as we rewrapped the sacks around our shooting irons.

"OK. Run along now, and stay out of trouble," said the officer.

"OK. Yes, sir," we both replied in unison again.

That was enough to put the bejesus up us both. Covers were obtained within a week. We didn't see any police after that, thank God, but crossing at Apsley always freaked me out.

My first visit to the dump with my new gun was an eventful one in many ways. We met the usual gang up at the top where the dump was. It was a fine autumn day and we all had coats on. Baz had this overlarge trench coat he used to wear which made him look like something out of the Russian army. His feet only just poking out the bottom of it made him look like he was all coat and nothing else.

We assembled on the top of the dump and had a plink at some freshly found objects from the discarded smouldering mass that constantly burned there. Then Barrie pipes up,

"Why don't we have a raid?"

"You what?" says Baz.

"A raid. You know: a war."

"How's that gonna work, then?" said Terry, still with no gun.

"Well," said Barrie. "We split up into two teams: three or four on each side. One lot go off into the fields: the other lot stay here. The lot in the fields try and take over the dump."

"How do we do that?" said Terry. "I mean, it sounds easy ... we just walk in and take the dump, don't we?"

"Not if you're getting fired at, it's not..." said Barrie.

We all looked at Barrie at this point as if to say,

"Are you mad?"

I think my book needs a warnings alert at this point. I can't resist stating here the phrase "Don't try this at home, folks". My readers will have the common sense to understand that what we did sometimes back in those days was just pure lunacy. Pointing any gun – whether loaded or unloaded – at anyone is just asking for trouble. Back then we just did stuff and managed to get through it without too much damage. But I don't condone anyone trying or doing anything like what's described here. It's stupid, to say the least, and highly dangerous.

Barrie decided that maybe Baz, me, and Harry should go off out into the fields while Barrie, Clive, Terry, and Steve would stay in the dump area. There were four of them and three of us, but Terry had no weapon and would have to take a turn of Barrie's gun.

"OK," we said, thinking, "This sounds fun." Barrie said,

"OK. Now don't aim for the head, OK? Aim low. We don't want anyone seriously hurt…"

When someone is about 100 or 150 yards from you and you look through open sights at them using an air rifle what you see is a speck – a pinhead in the distance. There is no head or body as such, just something in the distance that looks different to a tree. In all honesty this was madness, but we did it all the same because it sounded exciting.

We attacked the dump – Baz, Harry, and I moving up and hiding behind trees as we went. We approached closer and closer in, using the trees and bushes for cover. We could hear the sound of weak energy pellets hitting the trees near us. We were still over 150 yards away and the shots from inside the dump were only just reaching us. We could not see anyone, but their view of us in the field and in the light was a much easier prospect and target. I said to Baz and Harry,

"We need to split up here. We're an easy target, guys. We need to come at them from different directions and outflank them." I gave out some instructions. I would make my way to around the other side of the dump while they drew their fire.

As I left my fighting force of two I could see my plan might work out. I could hear the shots going over to Baz and Harry as I wandered wide and around to a new position. Once there I could see my targets clearly. Barrie was in a bush area and shooting crossways from me towards Baz and Harry. I could not quite make out Barrie's position in the bush so I aimed low so as to surprise him. The shot did not hit but it made him jump, for sure. I heard off to my left a yelp. I guessed that Terry, who was now coming further into the parameter of the dump, had been hit by either Baz or Harry. Terry was going to be an obvious target and I think that they had him pinned down behind a tree without a gun. He didn't know which way to go and was defenceless.

In the meantime Barrie had sighted me, and his Diana was punching shots out into the tree I was behind. He then made a huge mistake, followed by an even bigger one by me. I loaded up and shot low to where I had last seen him, but Barrie had moved his position and had gone much lower to the ground. He had gone into a kneeling position and my low shot had hit him square in the head…

Barrie let out a cry and I stopped shooting. He came out the bushes and I will never forget that moment. Blood was running down his face from a position on his cheek. He didn't sound too distressed, to be honest. The others came running over too. I ran up to Barrie.

"Are you OK mate?" I shouted. I was shaking all over. He nodded and said he was OK.

"Bloody hell," said one of the others as they all came running over. "Are you OK, Barrie?"

"Yep, I'm OK. It just hit me on the cheekbone. I'll be fine."

He was OK … but I realised that an inch or so higher and I would have caught his eye and then he would have lost his sight for sure.

Even though this happened, and it was very distressing, do you think that it put any of us off? Nope. Of course it didn't. It seemed that whenever you entered the Shendish area then you would be fair game to be shot at if your mates were there … the times we went up there and heard the whistle and buzz of a slug flying towards us from a distance …

One day Baz and I were up there on our own. We had been to the dump and got our guns sighted up and thought that we might go over the fields and take a look at those squirrels again. It was a damp day: thick fog had come down around us. One would call it a miserable day, and only idiots like us would be out in such weather. It was so thick that at times you might see a glimpse of a tree in the distance – and then, looking again, the tree was gone.

We had warmed ourselves up at the dump with a little fire we had got going off the main smouldering mass. Then went strolling across the fields to the coppice where we thought we might find some unsuspecting tree rats. We were wrapped up to the nines. I had my brown simmi coat on. This was a simulated fur-lined brown affair that we kids used to call a simmi because it was made of Bri-Nylon. Baz had his usual full-length trench coat on – and, from a distance, without his legs showing, probably looked like a huge Dalek crossing the field. I heard it first, but only momentarily. I had no way to react to it as it was fast.

Swat. God, that hurt. I looked down at my hand – the one holding the gun. The side of my wrist right on the bone had taken a .177. It really hurt but I was not in any danger. If you're shot it's much better to have at least some clothing to stop the impact first. This shot was on bare skin, and my bone had taken the full impact of a fast slug from what could only be one person. I knew exactly who had fired this because of the quickness of the shot. The Bloke was out there somewhere in the mist. He could see us but we could not see him.

"Run," said Baz . And we did, as hard as we could across the field, not knowing if in fact we were running towards the gun or away. Thwack. Another slug hit the ground close to where we were.

"We need some cover," I said. "Get to those trees as soon as you can." Run!

We ran on, and I had an idea where The Bloke was now from where the first slug had hit me and from the noise I had heard from the second coming in. He was off to our left, and as long as we kept running at a pace we should be OK. We made it to the trees where the squirrels were and set about analysing our position in relation to The Bloke.

"I can see him," I said. "He is way down the field and behind that large oak."

"OK," said Baz. "Let's outflank him. He is on his own. If we move quickly we can get him."

We did just that. Baz moved right and I moved left under the cover of each other's shots until either of us could get a clear shot. He had no protection and either Baz or me, I can't remember who, gave him a shot in the leg. He came out with his hands up.

"Fair cop," he said. "You got me fair and square."

We spent the rest of the afternoon in the murky mist trying to shoot squirrels before giving up and going home to a warm inviting fire at home.

Cold days or warm days it was always a fun day out.

Secondary Modern Fourth and Fifth Year

The fourth year was going to be a serious year for working. This was the start of the CSE two-year build-up to the main exams. Each student would now take as many as seven subjects and progress over two years to a final assessment, which would be made up of exams and project work. In some ways I always felt that the CSE was a much harder two-year stint than O levels were. The amount of background project work I had to do was far more than Baz had to do at grammar school for his O levels. All he had to do was pass a bloody exam after two years.

Mr Nesbit the PE and games teacher was our form master for the fourth year, and we had moved out of the annexe now and into a room that was in the main block of the school. Although Mr Nesbit might use the slipper on occasions I always found him a really nice easy going teacher. He was, of course, Scottish and would start every sentence with an "Ehhh" sound which all us kids would take the mickey out of.

"Ehhh, settle doon ney in yer seets whill I tak the ragister," he would say. He was always in tracksuit bottoms and baseball shoes, which seemed to be the universal uniform of games teachers. You might take him off in the playground and mimic his Scottish accent, but by Christ you would never ever attempt to take him off in earshot. He was a teacher you certainly respected enough not to do that.

I loved TD or technical drawing. We had our own drawing boards at home to do homework on, and in class we also had boards to use at our desks. Industry at that time required technical draughtsmen for all manner of design work. The UK made things in those days, and things needed to be drawn first before production started. This was an industry I really thought about getting into and it was a subject I knew about and could do well. Mr Goodwin the woodwork teacher took us for the fourth year, and in the final year the lovely Mr Boston was our TD teacher. Now Mr Boston was a war hero if ever there was one but at the time no one knew his secret. This guy was a navigator on aircraft during the war and he got shot down over Germany and captured. He was the only one of his aircraft crew who made it back to England alive.

Goodwin was good but really his forte was woodwork and I always got the impression that he didn't really like teaching this second subject. One day we were working at our boards at some isometric projection we had to draw from three separate images. Then all of a sudden Goodwin spotted something with his steely eye while it traversed the classroom like some Martian from *The War of the Worlds*. One wondered if a heat ray was coming, but it didn't. Far worse was about to happen as the near silence within that class was broken.

"What's that, boy…?"

We all looked up to see who he might be addressing. Goodwin really could command a class. He was like the sergeant major of all teachers. He projected this stern voice that just said,

"You had better take notice here or you could quite easily just die.

"You, boy… Stand up," he barked.

We had in the class at that time one Asian boy, Mohamed – or Mo to all of us. Mo stood up and the chair squeaked on the floor as it slid back. All eyes were on Mo now and our pencils and set squares were placed down on your desks. Mo showed what was in his hand. It was a magazine.

"Come here, boy," was Goodwin's next staccato order.

Mo walked over to the head of the class and handed Goodwin the magazine he had been reading. Goodwin's eyes flashed over the cover with mechanical precision and then looked back at Mo and then to the rest of the class.

"Sit down, boy," Goodwin commanded, still clutching Mo's mag in his hand. His face was red like an old furnace ready to explode. I actually thought I saw smoke coming out of his ears at one point as he scanned the mag again with what seemed like one eye while watching Mo with the other.

"Could he really do that?" I wondered. "Is this teacher real"?

"Nooow," came the start of what we all knew was going to be an important lecture.

Jim my old school mate used to call these words of wisdom from Goodwin a "Wally concert". We were in for a good one of these today, for sure. And so we all sat there rigid in our chairs ready for the curtain to swing open and the concert begin.

"Nooow listen to me gently," Goodwin started as we now realised that what was coming would be for the whole class and not just for Mo. The wise words of Goodwin were about to be heard loud and clear. I don't think any of us expected the response we got then as Goodwin spoke out about this misdemeanour. But, fair cop to the guy, he had the balls to deliver what he said to this class that day. Waving the dirty pornographic mag in front of us all he said,

"Nooow, all you boys," because actually it was all boys in that classroom. No girls did TD in those days. "All you boys take note. You can sit at home wanking to these magazines if you sooooooooooooooo wish." His eyes flittered on the word sooo.

"But I don't want you everrrrrrrrrrrrrrrrrrr bringing this sort of material into my class… Do you understand?" Is that perfectly clear!

"Yes, sir," was the weak reply from the class.

"IS IT…?" he repeated even louder.

"Yes, sir," was the more impressive answer back from the very stunned selection of boys, me included.

Yes, he had used the wank word – and yes, he had just held up a mag in front of the whole class demonstrating a brunette holding her legs wide open showing us all what she had had for breakfast. I think the shock of that alone just put an end to anything like that happening ever again. I just hoped he was never going to ask us to draw anything like that in TD.

Goodwin then chucked across the room the mag back to Mo. It flapped wildly in the air as it passed over us.

"Put it away, boy," was the instruction, and nothing else was said again. We all got on with our drawings with smirks on our faces.

The fourth year was a good time, and with my shooting buddies at school with me as well as at the weekends it was a joy to go to school. I would often walk the mile in the morning with Baz, as Apsley Grammar was next door to what we called Bennetts End Borstal. Baz would tell me about his class and his mates in school and I would tell him about mine, although of course Baz was fully aware of my schoolmates as he saw them at weekends too.

Baz would tell me about the teachers where he was and what they had to do. God, Baz had to do Latin, French, and German. I was so glad I didn't have to do all that stuff. Sometimes when it was a frosty morning and the spiders' webs in the bushes glistened with frost we would take a Y-shaped stick and collect the webs up. I have no idea why we did this as you never kept the sticky stick when you got to school, but it sort of seemed fun and made the walk a bit more interesting.

When the fifth year came around things changed no end. Firstly a few boys and girls left school for good and started work. These tended to be the less academic achievers and they really were destined for the factory floor in unskilled jobs. The rest of us would continue with our final year of CSEs and the final exams. But there was one huge difference for the fifth year. Bennetts End and Apsley Grammar were now to become a comprehensive school named Longdean. There was now a lower school for the first three years and an upper school for the fourth, fifth, and sixth years.

Barrie, Clive, Terry, and I found ourselves in a new classroom in the grammar school with a brand new teacher called Mrs Locus. She was new to both schools and was very well liked by us students. Although she had a rather large nose and some rude boys called her

Concorde, she was actually a very attractive young lady. We all loved her because she was just nice, and we were all getting just that little bit older and were able to appreciate a nice-looking female teacher.

"Yes, miss," we would say, all goggle-eyed.

The biggest change for us was the amalgamation with the students from the grammar school. There had always been a bit of friction between the two schools being so close together. In fact whenever the snow came and it was thick with the white stuff there would be the mother of all snowball fights outside between the buildings. Even teachers would join in. It was like one of the accepted things you did when it was winter in the snowfall.

Now we were all walking the corridors together and going into different classrooms that we had never been in before. One area I was amazed at was the metalwork room in what was Apsley Grammar. The machines in there were far superior to what we had had at Bennetts End, even though us lot in secondary modern would be more likely to be performing a job with this type of gear. They had some really cool stuff, and now we had use of it too.

I don't think the Apsley lot really liked all this sharing and us coming into their school as it was us that seemed to benefit here. What did they get out of it?

I took my exams and my results were as follows. I can tell you my grades too, as they are etched into my mind for the CSE exams I took.

Technical Drawing   1
Maths   2
Physics and Chemistry 2
Art   3
English   4
Metalwork   4
Geography   4

Not great, eh? However, I was surprised by my technical drawing O level. I was pleased with maths too. I was just happy I had passed English.

There was a certain sadness at the end of the fifth year, as my mates were all leaving school. I had decided to stay on for another year and go to the sixth form with a few others who wanted to improve their grades and take some more O levels. Barrie, Clive, and Terry (along with a whole multitude of others) left and there were just some bare bones left of the original five streams of the classes who had started out five years previously. Out of maybe 100 of us who started I would think only about fifteen of us would be staying on.

The Big Chap

There was a gang of us regulars who used to go shooting. However, on odd occasions others would come up too. Terry had a sister who used to come up, and it was not long before Barrie had claimed her as his girlfriend. Terry's sister was one of the lads, and she was a really good shot too. We had no problem with a girl in tow. It made life a bit more interesting. I think at one point Barrie carved a heart with his and her initials in it way up in one of the trees near the dump. I suspect it's still there to this day.

As Baz went to the grammar school he had his own set of school friends, whom he would talk about. None were really interested in airguns, and I suspect most were too academically minded to have that sort of distraction happening in their lives. There was, however, an exception to this rule: a most unusual one.

The big guy was a huge guy for his age. He outdid Baz on the large stakes – and that was going some, to be honest. But don't get me wrong. People were not fat then. They might be a large build but they were never fat. This guy was one of these. He was not fat at all. He was just well special, really: a powerful hulk. He was like a slightly smaller version of that wrestler Giant Haystacks who would be on ITV on a Saturday afternoon. Well … that's how he seemed to me, but then I was a small guy.

He was special and has a really special place in my life, as do plenty of others too. He was a year younger than all of us but was actually in the same year at school. This was to all intents and purposes a strange situation. This guy was so bright that the school moved him up a year. But if you met him then you might mistake him for something completely different. He looked the part OK. He was big and had this presence. He had long hair and was into motorbikes in a big way, not stupid mopeds like many of my friends were getting into. He liked rock and roll and considered himself to be what was termed then a hairy or a greaser.

He didn't live in Hemel: he lived further out. Baz had invited him over to meet us all and I had forewarned my secondary modern mates to give this new guy a chance. He had to get the train over to us. Although he had a motorbike he was too young to ride it on the road at that time. The train stopped at Apsley station and he got off it. He would have then hiked it up the bank from the station over the fence into Shendish. This must have looked a bit odd to anyone on that station platform, but then who's going to argue with a big guy holding a long bag that might have a gun in it? We were already in the field chatting when we saw the shape of him lumbering up the field towards us.

"Shit. He's fucking big," said Clive – who, again, was no small chap either.

He came marching up to us, his long shoulder-length hair waving in the wind and a big smile on his rosy red face. One thing about him was that his smile was as big as he was and if he beamed out then you could not help but smile back. Baz introduced him and we all sat about talking guns.

"What have you got in the bag?" I said.

"I'll get it out," he said. "I need to try this out,".

He undid the bag and pulled out the metal and wood that was inside. Well ... to say we were surprised was an understatement. All our eyes were out on stalks.

"Blooody 'ell," said Baz.

"Where the fuck did you get that?" said another of us.

"Found it," he said. He was sometimes a guy of few words, but I always got the feeling that he would milk a situation by using just a few words. He knew how to play the surprise card.

"You found it...?" said Baz. "Where?"

"I found it in the cut," he responded. The cut was a word used quite often then to refer to the canal. The cut referred to the fact that a cut had been made in the land to accommodate a water path.

"The fucking cut," someone said in exasperation.

He picked the gun up. It was a 410 shotgun.

"Bloody hell," said Baz. "Where did you say you got this?"

He recited the story that he was walking along the canal one day and he saw an object in the water. He said that it was poking out of the water a bit, so he reached in and pulled out this shotgun. He said it could not have been in long as it didn't need too much cleaning up.

My school friends at this point were – let's say – speechless. All of them stood there with their mouths wide open and their chins on the ground. Talk about my pals being upstaged. They had not come across anyone quite like him before, and this situation with shotgun was way, way out of what they could imagine someone of our age minus one year could have.

"Are we going to shoot this thing?" said Baz?

Yes he said,

"Well, I've been thinking. We don't really know how this gun is going to work. We might fire it and the whole thing might explode in my face."

We looked on in astonishment. He was right. It might seriously hurt someone.

"But," he continued, "I have thought that out. Here," and he reached in his pocket and pulled out a ball of string. "This is what we do: we tie it to a tree, load it up, and attach some string to the trigger. We'll go back a safe distance and pull."

It seemed like a good plan, to be honest. He had thought this through, for sure. We stuck it in a tree near us and made sure it was secure, with the barrel pointing downward. The gun was then loaded with its 410 cartridge and string was attached to the trigger and played out to a distance inside the dump of maybe thirty yards.

We all lay down on the ground as if some sort of World War II bomber was going to strafe us. He had the string and had to pull quite hard from that distance. The gun went off OK … BANG. We went over to the gun and checked it over. It seemed OK to us all, and He took it off the tree and had a look inside and down the barrel.

"Nope, it looks OK," he said. He loaded another cartridge in and this time he just aimed at some metal plate at the side of the dump. The pellets peppered it instantly and produced a loud clang as it hit.

Although He was Baz's friend at school he did became a great shooting companion of mine for a while. It would sometimes be just me and him out for a Sunday afternoon. A couple of times he even walked back home with me to my house. One Sunday it had been considerably wet out and we arrived home in a very wet and bedraggled state. My dad thought he was fantastic and always made a huge fuss of him. We sat by the living room coal fire warming up and getting dry. My dad brought down a pair of my brother's socks for him to put on.

"Don't worry about those" said my dad. "You bring them back when you like." He was invited to the traditional Sunday tinned salmon tea. It's kind of surreal now when I think back to all this … this big guy sitting with my family eating tinned salmon and brown Hovis bread with an illegal shotgun propped up against the door. My mum and dad never knew that bit.

Secondary Modern: The Lower Sixth

One thing one could say about the next year at Longdean in the lower sixth was,

"What a waste of time that was."

You could say that if you were cynical and if you didn't understand the value of this part of school. If you measured my time by what I achieved academically then you clearly might ask why I stayed on. I managed to obtain one more new CSE in something called engineering science and I managed an O level in technical drawing, which really I already had in CSE as a grade 1.

If the truth be known I needed this extra year. I needed it for all sorts of reasons, but I needed it mostly to grow up and have some fun and develop myself into something that might resemble an adult.

The lower sixth was like nothing else in school I had known before. We had a common room for a start, and the onus was put on the students to turn up on time and do the work. You had the responsibility and the teachers would not be chasing you up unless it was apparent you really were not pulling your weight. My form teacher was a Mr Rutt. Rutt was one of the old Apsley teachers, and ordinarily I would guess that for other years he would be seen as a bit of a tyrant. But he was good with us and I liked the man. He was educated and he was no bully. That to me made a huge difference, and he had my respect.

We had the usual timetable, of course, but some periods in our timetable were called free periods, which meant no lessons. Wow. We could actually sit in the common room and do what we pleased. However, the free periods were supposed to be for revision and extra studying. It's strange how none of us actually saw it like that. This all felt grown-up, and I would guess that this was all part of the learning process for us to transition into adults and work. Taking responsibility for your own time is all part of life and still is today.

It was an easy deal, to be honest. I had fewer subjects to do and most of the useless subjects, in my opinion, had been dropped. Games was still on the list of activities we had to do – but hey, no more standing in a cold field while some bullying teacher shouting at you while you turned blue. Nope. Games had options and, while some could go off and play football if they wished, we also had other new options which included tenpin bowling and … wait for it … shooting. Games had suddenly turned from *A Nightmare on Elm Street* to heaven.

A few of us chose shooting to start with, and on the first afternoon of this we had not realised that you had to make your own way to the range. A bit confused, three of us went to see Nesbit.

"Where is the coach, Mr Nesbit?" one of us said.

"Ehhh, laddy, there be no cooch," he replied.

"Oh," we responded.

"Come on," said Nesbit, and he piled us in his car and took us up to Wood Lane End where the .22 rim fire shooting was. That was how nice this guy was, and we respected him loads. What an easy afternoon that was. Twenty rounds at paper targets and then a walk home. That's what I call a proper games lesson: no going blue, no getting in a cold shower, no drying yourself with a pocket handkerchief, and no waxy-eared kid looking at your private parts with envy or disgust.

In some ways the tenpin bowling was even better. Hemel had a big bowling alley at the back of The Marlowes and the school had organised really cheap rates for us to go down there. It was really great, as we could take up several lanes and bowl away all afternoon, and have some fizzy pop to boot. Martin and Neil (the twins who could bowl well) would try and get a lightweight ball all the way down the alley without it touching the floor. We got told off quite a few times for messing about like that and putting dents in the nice shiny lane. What a far cry this was from those cold Thursday afternoons on a football pitch. Games was now enjoyable and fun, exactly how it should be.

In the lower sixth we had a few new teachers, and one of those was a chemistry teacher – a young lady whose name I can't remember for the life of me. She was new to the school. I had chosen chemistry to do as an O level and this class was rather small: only about six or seven of us in total. As a lot of classes from the old Bennetts End had been amalgamated it meant that most of our lessons had kids from a multitude of streams. Chaz was one character that I seemed to get hooked up with and we sat in chemistry together. Chaz was from that top stream, and I had never really taken much notice of him from one year to the next. But now we had some commonality. We sat together in chemistry and struck up a friendship that would last outside of school and into married life.

Our chemistry teacher was (it appeared) a dab hand at the card game bridge, and one evening she volunteered to come into the common room after school and we would learn the game of bridge from her. As I loved playing cards this was something I really needed to be involved with.

In bridge you have a partner, and Chaz and I teamed up to be a pair at one of the bridge tables. We had a bit of fun here and, actually, many of us continued to play even outside of school. Once a few of us had leant bridge we took it upon ourselves to go around each other's houses and play in the evenings with a few bottles of beer. It was a pleasant time, but the games tended to be a bit cutthroat at times and some partnerships did get frayed. Bridge is like any partnership game: it's only as good as the strongest link. I used to go around and play with Baz, mostly at some of the posher houses where the ex-grammar school kids lived. It was at one of these houses that I saw my very first colour TV set. We sat and played bridge but could not take our eyes from the colour TV image in the corner of the room. It was a huge step forward from black-and-white to colour, and we just sat mesmerised.

There was a really slack time towards the end of the lower sixth where no lessons were taking place and you just seemed to have endless free periods. The TV would be on in the common room with the cricket playing, and we would be sitting with a deck of cards playing all sorts of things. School was coming to an end. It had no real purpose now, and in your mind you kind of knew the end was near. I could have gone on and done yet another year but this would just have been delaying things. What was the point? There was no reason to stay: no academic reason, anyway. Most would be leaving now and those left would be the ones taking A levels for uni.

Pockets of people drifted off over the weeks before summer. You would come into school and find that another one had not bothered to come in any longer, and you realised that that was it: they were gone for good. Baz had gone. He decided to opt out and not continue. Even the big guy dropped out – the guy who was clever, yet a year younger than us. Some had just had enough and wanted to work and have money to spend.

So the final day came when I walked out of the gates for the last time, on my own and with no job. This was it. This was the last summer holiday ever and now I would be working. The prospect looked grim. I would now be working till I was sixty-five, and at that age sixty-five seems an eternity away.

A Lucky Escape

1969

Around about the time when we were shooting Baz came to me with a suggestion of how we could all make some money. He had heard that Gower's (the gun shop) which had now relocated to the old town was advertising for lads to come help out on a Sunday at the clay pigeon shoot.

"I'll have some of that," I told Baz. "How much are they paying?"

"A pound for all day," he replied.

Now a pound in money then was quite a bit … but, still, for a whole day's work on a Sunday it was still a bit on the side of slave labour.

"What have we got to do?" I asked Baz.

"Don't know, mate," he said. "Let's go and see."

So sure enough Baz, the big guy, and I got up the next Sunday and arrived at the back of the premises of Gower's. Here we were met by some of the staff and some others who would also be working the traps on this shotgun shoot. There were about six lads and we were all about the same age. We were taken by car up to Gaddesden Row, where a shoot took place every Sunday.

We were shown what we had to do. Around the field were little huts like sheds. Inside was a mechanical device that would send a clay pigeon (a disc made of clay) out of the hut at high speed. The shooters would then attempt to hit the disc while it was in flight. Each hut was a different discipline for shooting. Some huts sent the bird or clay towards the shooter and some away. One hut was situated high, way up in an old oak tree in what looked like a tree house. I looked at this one with dread: no way was I going to climb up there to that one.

When in the huts you armed the trap (as it's called) with a clay disc. Then from the outside someone could press a button and release the clay. You had to be damn quick to load the clay up, as

227

you didn't want your hands anywhere near the arm of the trap when it went off – and you didn't know quite when it was going to go off, either. I'm not sure this would have been allowed today. It was clearly a health and safety issue.

We liked this work. It was enjoyable and we got paid and we got some food too. It was hard work, and by the end of the day you had had enough. Your arms ached with the continued cocking of the trap with its huge powerful spring.

One week we were nearing the end of the afternoon. It would not be long now before we would be finishing. Someone shouted over,

"We need one more in the trap in the field."

I was nearest and made a move to go over to the field when one of the other lads stepped in.

"I'll take this one mate," he said. "I've been doing this one all day and I quite like it. I'll finish it off."

"OK, mate," I said, and in a way I was not bothered. I was tired and wanted to get my pay and go.

The trap in the field launched clays low and towards the shooter. The shooter typically sighted his gun on the roof of the hut and then shouted the command "Pull" to instruct the release of the clay. He would then track the clay with his sight as it rose and flew towards him. It was nothing too difficult, really, and it was a popular trap as it was quite easy.

I was helping to clear up some of the old clay boxes when I heard the scream. That sort of scream made you realise that something was up big time. I could only guess that someone had got themselves hurt in one of the traps. It would have been easy, and if it was late on and you were tired it would be easy to forget to get your fingers out of the way of the swinging arm.

This, however, was not the case. We all ran towards where a big crowd was surrounding the lad who had entered the trap not five minutes ago. He was on the ground on the grass and his head was bleeding quite a bit.

The shooter had let his shot off while still lining up with the small wooden hut: the opening from where the clay flies out is directly in line with the shooter. Some of the shot from the gun had entered the hut and hit the lad in the face. Luckily no shot had hit the lad's eyes, else he would have been blinded for sure.

The accident shook us all up and we went home feeling quite down about the whole affair. I of course had had a lucky escape. I was to be the one in that hut and it would have been me taking that shot if I had done. With me being quite short, who knows where the shot would have gone? To this day I still feel a pang in my gut when I think about this episode.

Needless to say the hut was changed and made safe for the next week's shoot, and the lad who had been shot even turned up. We didn't do this work for much longer after this incident. We were fed up with it, and the whole thing felt unsafe.

Shooting to the End

I had my BSA rifle, for sure, but it didn't stop there. By chance Baz and I had decided one Sunday to go for a walk along the cut or the canal in expectation, I suspect, of getting up to some mischief along the way. The canal was easily accessible for us as it was basically a short walk down to Belswains Lane and then along a footpath until you met an access path on to the Grand Union Canal.

The towpath (as it was called) ran on either one side or the other of the canal. You would use either the bridges or locks to hop from one side to the other. In those days the canal was certainly used, and Hemel had a big industrial presence situated along the part we walked. John Dickinson's was an extensive large paper mill which stretched along a fair way. Then after that another mill – Nash Mills – extended further. Barges were still being used to bring coal to the mill. It was a frequent event to see the coal barges come along the canal, and we used to help open the lock gates for them. Barge people were usually a friendly bunch and were grateful for any help to send them on their way.

We walked along a bit and on odd occasions we would stop and throw a few stones into the canal, maybe to hit certain items floating by or to skim across the surface. Up ahead of us on this day were three boys, two of whom had air pistols.

"I know who that is," I said to Baz.

"Yes … it's John from the primary school, isn't it?" said Baz.

John had been a guy we had both known at the junior school, and we had parted company when we all went our different ways to various secondary or grammar schools. We caught up with the guys ahead. John had a very old Webley Senior pistol and one of the others had an old Mod 2 Diana gat gun. After checking things out with them, and with John stating that he wanted to sell the gun, I agreed a thirty-bob deal. The collection didn't stop there, either. I got a real taste for it. I found out that in the local *Hemel Hempstead Gazette* known locally as the *Gazette* newspaper and the *Hemel*

Hempstead Evening Post-Echo would have adverts selling second-hand airguns by private advertisers in the area.

The *Evening Post-Echo* was a British newspaper published in Hemel Hempstead and launched in 1967. It was launched initially as two papers, the *Evening Post* and *Evening Echo*.

The *Hemel Hempstead Gazette* was first published in 1858 as *The Hemel Hempstead Gazette and West Herts Advertiser,* this was renamed in 1899 as *The Hertfordshire, Hemel Hempstead Gazette and West Herts Advertiser* and it was published under this title until 1973. From 1973 it was known simply as the *Hemel Hempstead Gazette*, and from 1991 as *The Gazette*.

I would then persuade my dad to take me to various houses locally to purchase these items. I would then work on these guns in the garden shed. Most of what I bought worked OK. Some guns really needed a good clean-up and service. I would strip the wooden stocks down sometimes and re-stain and varnish them. Or I would take the internals apart in the vice in the shed.

I would try and replace the main bits that could be replaced, namely the springs and the leather washers. There was a problem with getting the spare parts, and usually my only hope was to get the bus down into town and go to Gower's the gun shop at the end of The Marlowes. Gower's was a general shotgun shop but it did carry some airguns and spares. I would go into the shop: the guys who served knew me quite well. Whatever I asked for in there would result in a dirty old box being lifted out from under the counter and the shop assistant sifting through loose bits and packets. There was no organisation here, and it was always the same old box that was produced each time. I would usually have to take in a spring or washer to try and match the right size and get the nearest fit they could come up with. Many a time I would get home and have to then cut a spring down to a shorter one so it would fit.

I would then re-advertise the gun in the paper and make a small profit. In this way I did very well for myself and managed to briefly enjoy a variety of different guns.

In the end, and as I approached sixteen, I eventually had the money. Yes, I had saved up the huge sum (then) of £21. This was the right amount of money for going to Gower's and buying a brand new BSA Air Sporter, the gun that I had seen The Bloke use all those years back. I now had my own. It was to be one of the last airguns I would use and own for a long while, but I loved this gun. It was the best.

Baz and I were out doing the rounds through Shendish one hot summer's day when off from school in the holidays. We had turned up at the dump. There was no one around on this day ... no one from my school to have some fun with, as was usually the case. It was to be only Baz and me, then. We were shooting at cans in the dump when something caught Baz's eye.

"Ginger," said Baz.

"Where?" I said.

"Over there," said Baz. "Can't you see him?"

I looked over in the direction of where Baz was pointing. There were two dots in the distance and they must have been some 150 yards away. They were two kids: unmistakably, one had red hair and one had brown. There could only be one person in the whole of Hemel that matched this shape in the distance. I'm not sure if we figured it out then who the other person was, as they were a long way away from us.

It was Baz who had the great idea.

"Let's send 'em a warning shot," he exclaimed.

"Er ... OK," I said, thinking, "Well, why not? It's just a bit of fun."

We had grown a bit tired of the cans and this seemed like a better challenge: a moving target. It all sounded like a great idea at the time. They were miles away – some 150 yards – and walking parallel to where we were.

"OK," said Baz, loading a .177 into the not-so-powerful Jelly.

"You need to give that some elevation," I said. "They are miles away, Baz, and you want to make sure the shot goes over their heads too."

"OK," said Baz, and he aimed the gun literally at forty-five degrees in the direction of Ginger and his mate. Twang went the Jelly as it spat out a very low-velocity slug out of the end of the barrel.

It seemed quite a time to us while we stood there and watched for a reaction. Baz had already put the gun down before the effect was seen. I'm still not sure to this day what the odds were, and I'm convinced that hitting that target was probably less likely than winning the football pools (which my dad did relentlessly every week without ever winning). There is an expression that's said sometimes when referring to guns and targets: that you couldn't hit a barn door with that. Well, that would not be the case with Baz's gun. Not here anyway.

In the distance we saw two guys walking, and then we saw one guy stop walking while he watched a ginger-headed boy jump in the air. It was like something out of a *Beano* comic. You could almost imagine a speech bubble come out of the furious jumping ginger guy which would simply say,

"Yaaarooo."

We stood and watched. I then looked at Baz and Baz looked at me. Both our mouths were open.

"You hit him," I said.

"Now there's a thing," said Baz in a stunned tone.

We looked back and momentarily watched the cartoon strip play out, with lots of jumping and red faces that we could only imagine from the distance we were away.

The two red faces started running. Not away from us, as expected, but towards us. There was no straight path between us and them but we damn well knew they were running to catch us.

"Shit," said Baz.

"We'd better get out of here," I said. We ran back out of the dump and hid up behind some bushes. I'm not sure why we didn't run and run because we could have made an easy escape. Maybe we thought they would give up, but they didn't give up at all. When they arrived and found us they were not best pleased at all. Ginger had been shot in the tummy. Like some artillery shell, Baz's slug had flown in a perfect arc over a distance of 150 yards and landed on Ginger's gut.

They marched over to us.

"Who shot me?" asked Ginger.

Baz owned up. It was a hopeless cause. There was no need to lie to these two. Ginger swiped Baz's gun off him.

"Let's see how you like it," said Ginger, and he requested a slug from Baz. Baz duly gave him a lead pellet from the box of Beatall low cost and low quality skirted slugs sold by the cycle shop in Lawn Lane. Ginger then loaded up the Jelly and told Baz to start walking away. Ginger then shot him at the top of the leg in the groin, which must have hurt like billy-o. The gun was then thrown down on the ground.

"Let that be a lesson to you," said Ginger.

Baz was not happy at all but he made no attempt to retaliate. Once they were gone Baz dropped his trousers to take a look at the shot to the top of the inside of his leg. The pellet had grazed the inner part of his leg just below his private parts. The wound was bleeding, but nothing too bad. It would not need stitches.

"You're going to have a heck of a bruise there," I said.

"Yes, mate," said Baz. "It hurts like fuck at the moment."

"I have to say, though, Baz..." I said. "That was a bloody good shot you made there."

Baz had issues with his club book airgun after only a few months of use. The thing was cheap and it got all loose in its stock and rattled itself to bits on many an occasion. I tried really hard to fix this gun for him. One option I had was to actually take it into school to fix it in metalwork. I'm not sure these days that anyone would be able to do that. I was allowed to do this, and the teacher would help me do whatever was needed to the gun to get it working. Sadly Baz's gun became totally unusable in the end. It would just go off sometimes without pulling the trigger. He junked it in the end and got himself a slightly better Tornado – a slightly better underlever airgun from behind the Iron Curtain. This he managed to at least keep going for a bit longer. We tuned it up and made it a bit more powerful by putting an Airsporter spring in it. After that it barked like a wild dog whenever you shot it.

As time went on Baz came up shooting with me less and less. On one occasion when we were about to come back from the dump Baz noticed a tree we had passed many times. It was just by the dump, but in the field. It was one of those trees that had a sort of hollowed-out trunk. I think it was dying, as trees don't usually look like this (with their innards carved out).

"Let's light a fire in there," said Baz.

"Are you joking, Baz?" I responded, wondering what he was thinking about.

"No, it will be OK," he said. "Just set it alight inside and leave it. We'll see what it's like next time we come up."

"OK," I said handing him some matches. "Here you go, mate."

Well, Baz set light to it OK and it really burned inside quite easily. It was dry inside and it just caught easily, with flames licking out of the hole. We left it to burn and went on our way. I didn't think too much about all this until the next day. I had just left home and was walking to school and I looked back over my shoulder. I have no idea what made me do this. It was as if some invisible man had just tapped on my shoulder and said,

"Psst ... look over there."

From where we lived you could easily see over to the other side of the valley where Shendish is. The view was uninterrupted. What I saw made me gasp. The tree we had set light to was clearly not its usual upright shape. It was lying now in the field as flat as a pancake.

"God," I thought. "This is not good. That farmer is not going to be pleased at all." I quickened my pace and hurried to school to tell my mates.

I told Barrie about the tree being down when I got to the classroom.

"Oh," he said. "Do you know what? We might be able to use that."

"What do you mean?" I said to him.

"Well," said Barrie, "It's getting towards November the fifth. What do you reckon to us holding our own Bonfire Night at the dump?"

"Wow," I said, as the realisation of what he had said sank in. "That sounds bloody good to me," I said, "But where does the tree fit in?"

"Well," said Barrie, "If we take some branches off that tree now we can build our own massive fire inside the dump."

Barrie had a point, and it seemed like a good idea to me. At the next opportunity I had I talked to Baz and told him what we would do. Armed with all sorts of saws and a machete we went up to the dump the following weekend before Bonfire Night and set about taking branches off the fallen tree. We did well, as it happens, and it was not long before we had quite a pile of wood dragged over the fence line into the dump. It was while we were busy and not taking note that a tractor pulled up just by where we were. Without doubt this was the farmer. Oh, hell.

"What are you up to, guys?" said the farmer, with the typical farmer look on his face that was put on when he saw boys doing stuff on his land.

"Er … well, sir, we saw this downed tree from home and we thought that we would take some branches off the tree for a bonfire."

We waited for the response from the farmer. In our books this didn't look good, and I guessed we looked as guilty as hell.

"Good work, chaps," said the famer. "Take as much as you need. This tree has been in my way in this field for so long. I'm just pleased it's finally come down."

Phew. You could see the relief on our faces as we all realised that we had the go-ahead to use the wood. Of course, Baz lighting the fire in this instance had done the farmer a favour – which he never let us forget. I'm not sure that Baz realised this when he started the fire in the beginning, though.

On the night of November 5 I set about what I would need to get up to the dump. I packed a small shoulder bag I had with a few things: torch, bangers, food, and an air pistol (the essentials, mind you). Baz had to do something first before he could come up, so I said I would meet him up at the dump later. I set out and soon entered St Mary's Church and the path that led over the railway bridge. It was dark, of course, and where I was heading had no lights at all. The graveyard usually looked pleasant enough in the day but in the early evening November bleakness this place looked very unsettling.

I wished I had waited for Baz now. I made it through and over the train bridge. There were no lights at all now. It was completely dark in the pitch-black evening and my eyes needed to adjust to this before I could find the fence line into the fields. It was quite strange indeed to be out at night in the countryside in pitch-black darkness. I could just about make out the outline of the dump in the distance. I had at least a point of focus to aim for. I walked across the field at a steady pace, not really wanting to light a torch and attract attention. As I got near the dump I could make out some noise. Someone was already in there and shifting stuff about.

"Who's that?" I hissed in a low tone.

"Barrie," came back the reply. "I'm up here with Terry."

I made it over the dump's fence line and into the area where the fire was to be. What a magnificent sight. Barrie and Terry had arranged the branches and also added in some other material from the dump. There was usually a good load of wooden pallets lying about, and these had been collected and pushed in to form a good basic structure for the fire. Some inflammable paint tins were also in there, and I knew this was going to be one heck of a fire. It was more a beacon than a bonfire.

"Clive and the others will be up soon," said Barrie, as I responded with,

"Baz is following me. He will be here in a few minutes."

We moved a few more bits around and soon the others turned up. Baz was wearing his huge grey trench coat as usual. He looked like something out of some American Civil War film. He had long hair to his shoulders and the huge coat that nearly touched the ground. Mind you, it was cold that night … but in a few minutes it would feel like the centre of the sun.

"OK, let's do this," said Barrie.

"You light it, Barrie," I said. "It was your idea. You've done a lot of work on this."

"I brought the tree down," Baz added.

"Shut up, Baz," I remarked. "That was a fluke."

Barrie lit the fire and it went up like a rocket. It was totally out of control, of course, and lit up the whole area. There was no more blackness now. The whole of the dump and the surrounding fields were washed with the light from the blaze. I sometimes wonder what that must have looked like looking across the valley from back home.

We loved it, and piled more on as the wood burned through. Packing cases and pallets spat as they burned. As the night drifted on and the fire calmed down to embers we were all handed some spuds that Barrie had brought up. We shoved these into the ashes and turned them occasionally to even out the cooking. Cooked spuds on an open fire get a second mention in this book. It's one of the finest things you can ever eat.

We sat around the fire discussing this and that, trying to eat our hot spuds with our bare hands.

"I reckon this might be the best fire we have ever had up here," said Terry.

I had to agree it was but I added,

"And this has to be one of the best dump visits we have ever had too, guys."

They all agreed and we chatted some more, let some bangers off, teased Terry a bit, and then went home smelling of fire and spud. Our hands were filthy. When you have nights like that with friends the visions, smells, and conversations stay in your mind for a lifetime. They are true gems that can't be destroyed.

I'm not sure I saw my shooting pals much after this at all. Barrie became a butcher at the local shops and I have no idea what Clive and Terry did. I hope they have all had happy lives, as they were indeed very special to me for that short period in my life. Nothing stays the same: things change constantly, and now there were new people to meet and be friends with. Things were changing but looking up.

I continued shooting, or at least visiting Shendish at the weekends, into my late teens. In the end it was just me. All my pals had left me alone to my shooting antics. They had gone off on to other things. Girls were mainly the big driver here. Baz had a steady girlfriend and was not available at all. He was loved-up, for sure. The guys from school had left early and gone into jobs of different kinds. The contact was lost and *The Magnificent Seven* guys disbanded. Like Steve McQueen, I was the only one left.

I went up to the dump come rain or shine, hoping that someone might pop up at some point and rekindle all the excitement we had had. Nothing, of course, happened. I put it down to my maturity at the time. I was not ready for girls or drinking quite yet: that would be coming soon.

At some point I stopped going altogether, and it was one day while up at Shendish that I noticed the fields being marked out and some excavations taking place. I brought Baz up for one last look and we surveyed our empire, as it were, for one last time. We shared my gun this time, like we had shared his gun in the very beginning. We guessed what was happening to Shendish: it was going to be made into a golf course.

"This is the end, then," said Baz.

"Yep. Time to move on, then, and do something else," I said.

"Are you going to the George tonight?" said Baz. "You really should give it a try."

"Yes, OK," I said. "Come around later and I'll go down with you."

Don't Try This at Home

1968-1970

This chapter spans a few years of my childhood and covers a number of related subjects that were of interest to me in those formative years. However, I have to give the reader another warning. This chapter does detail a number of episodes and incidents which should never be attempted by anyone. To coin a phrase: don't try this at home is exactly what this chapter is about. So be warned, and don't attempt to copy in any way what's described here. We were reckless and stupid. It's a wonder I'm still in one bit.

I have already mentioned the fascination with fire from an early age, where we would light small fires in the bushes for our amusement. This really was just the start for me, and to an extent Baz and a few others. It gradually progressed through our childhood and into our teens.

In the days of the 1950s and 1960s it was quite common for a boy to receive something called a chemistry set as a present. Now I think (to a large degree today) that these so-called toys are much safer. My brother had one when he was a child and so did I then.

Along with a whole set of chemicals held in test tubes were instructions on performing certain experiments. Dad supervised me to begin with so that I understood how to use the methylated spirit burner to heat things up in test tubes. From then on I was allowed to do what I wanted. Never mind safety in the form of safety glasses or an apron. Oh, no. In those days as long as you had some old newspaper down on the table then you were considered to be as safe as houses. As long as the carpet was OK then burning skin or blinding yourself was never an issue. My parents' only concern was that I didn't do what my brother had done when he was a kid. He boiled a test tube of potassium permanganate which then exploded up the walls, resulting in a nice purple stained wall.

Because I had a chemistry set and because I had experimented I found myself wanting to do more … mainly with explosives.

Bangers and Flash

From a very early age I had some fireworks each year on November 5. In the fifties and sixties hardly anyone went to an organised display event, although they did exist. The way in which people celebrated Bonfire Night was in their own back gardens with their own fire and fireworks. For me this date – or, rather, night – was almost the most important night of the year, with only Christmas Eve topping it. To say I loved fireworks is an understatement. I was completely taken over by these little rods of black powder while they were on sale. I looked forward to winter because to me it was a series of exciting dates and things to look forward to. Bonfire Night was the first of these dates, of course.

Generally the format was that I would be given some money from parents, aunts and uncles, and grandparents to buy my own fireworks. Of course I could not buy these myself. I had to be accompanied, but I always knew what I wanted. In those days if you walked into the sweet shops at Bennetts End during late October you would be faced with huge counters of displays of fireworks. Sweet counters were converted to show off selections of loose fireworks under a safe glass top.

These displays were magnificent, and my mouth would water as if I was looking at the most delicious selection of candies. As a boy I would point to what I wanted – a bit like selecting loose sweets. I might have half a crown to spend and get – say – a dozen or so individual fireworks for that money. I would go up with my parents several times in late October to add to my collection, and each time I would know what I needed. I never had the money to buy a big display selection – although Brocks did a small one for five shillings, which I did manage to buy a few times. The fireworks were then taken home and I would place them in one of Mum's square metal cake tins, which were generally the old tins used for biscuits. It's interesting how I always managed to get all the fireworks into this tin (except the rockets) buy layering them and making sure all the space was taken up. I would play on the run-up to the big night by taking them out the tin, inspecting them and then re-stacking the

241

tin. It was some weird, strange OCD I had with the fireworks. Sometimes I wrote down a sequence by which each one would be let off. My mum used to tell me off for taking them out. She said that there would be no powder left in them by the time I go to let them off.

A week before the event my mum and dad would help me make a guy. This would be made by sewing the top of a pair of my dad's old trousers (sometimes pyjamas) to the bottom of an old jumper or shirt. You then stuffed the guy with rolled-up newspaper, made a head from one of my mum's stockings (which would be stuffed with rags), and attached that to the top of the neck of the shirt. The bottom of the legs and arms were tied off with string so the bundles of paper could not escape. Either a face was painted on the stocking or a mask was bought and attached to form a Guy Fawkes face. Then you would have your guy, and he would sit in the living room all week waiting for his fiery demise.

A few days before the night my dad would make a bonfire at the bottom of the garden. He would have saved up rubbish to burn for this for some weeks. This would comprise odd bits from the garden that had dried out. We then only had to stuff some paper inside, put the guy on the top, and that was your bonfire. We always seemed to have lots to burn in those days. People lit fires at the bottom of their gardens on a regular basis. Our dustbins were small, and rubbish seemed to pile up in the shed and outside toilet.

Sometimes the night would be wet, but it never stopped us. We always went out and we always managed to light the fire and let off the fireworks.

Of course it was not just us. Other houses in the street would be doing the same, and several bonfires would be alight at the same time. Baz would certainly be having a few fireworks down his end of the street, and Pete and John would have theirs. One night we heard Pete and John's mum shout out,

"Dad, you forgot the guy. He's still in the outside toilet."

They had lit the fire but forgotten the guy. It always amused us because she always called her husband Dad and never called him by his first name. It reminded me of the Mum and Dad characters in the *Dennis the Menace Beano* cartoon strip.

We would start about half past six and the night might last a couple of hours. What with the bonfire ablaze and my tin box stuffed with explosive I would be champing at the bit to get down the garden. I loved setting off my fireworks. They were all small and manageable. Traffic lights, golden rain, will-o'-the-wisp ... so many different types. Some, like the bangers and the jumping jacks, were a great laugh as there was a certain amount of unpredictability with them. They would later be banned in the UK.

We had rockets and Catherine wheels, squibs, aeroplanes, and the good old Roman candle. There was no real danger, as all these fireworks were small and either made a bright coloured light, loads of smoke and sparkles, or maybe a bang here and there.

One year I did manage to purchase what I regarded as a large firework for two shillings and sixpence. It was called Calling All Cars and had a picture on it of police cars with sirens wailing from them. I always remember the policemen looking menacing as they drove their cars at speed to catch some villain. When we lit this firework as the finale, it shot three squealing banshees into the air. It was so alarming but great fun. Later in life I would relive this same firework with a heavier payload and watch my brother being chased by one stray banshee down his garden.

What fun we had as a family at the bottom of the garden in those days. At the end of our fun it was back to the house to warm up by the fire with some cocoa before bed. The fire would smoulder all night down the garden and would sometimes still be warm in the morning.

Such was my love for fireworks that I refused to throw the empty ones away the next day. They would be kept in the shed for a while until I had forgotten about them, and I guess my dad would throw them in the bin.

That was the more civilised part of fireworks, of course. This was how you were supposed to use fireworks, and the safe way too.

Unfortunately I was also shown another way in which you could use fireworks, and this other way would lead to all sorts of trouble.

Playing outside in the street as we did we sometimes came across the bigger boys who would have some bangers to let off. Bangers in those days were very powerful, and could easily harm you if you got too close to one when it went off. Over a period of time bangers were reduced in power to try and eliminate the possibility of injury if an accident arose. In the end these fireworks were banned completely.

I remember once that one of the older lads in the street had a whole bundle of them with a tight elastic band around them. He had them in his pocket but had shown off what he had. Of course we were up for a bit of excitement, and the older ones were all for showing off what they could do.

There was one time when a boy lit two bangers and pushed them one in each end of his pedal bike's handlebars, and then rode off to this almighty double bang as the fireworks spat out of each end of the bike's handlebars. Another time we went off around the back of the garages with one of these boys and he found an abandoned child's plastic doll. This was then loaded with bangers and blown to kingdom come. All of this was going inside my small brain. I was watching and learning all the time. I was mesmerised by all of this. I began to understand what made the bang with fireworks. It was not the powder inside. No, it was the restriction of gases from the burned black powder. That was what made the bang.

For many a year because of age there was no possibility of obtaining fireworks at all. You had to be around fourteen years old to buy them. If you could find someone to buy them for you then all well and good – but we never did, and so it was going to be a while before we could buy them from the shops.

Bigger Bangs

Baz and I were about twelve years old when I talked to him about something I had seen at home that got me very excited. I described to him in detail what I had seen and then suggested what we should do about it.

My brother had come back from Nottingham University on his summer holiday break and with him was Norman, one of his friends. Norman and Rob were great friends, and as they were studying chemistry at university my ears would prick up when any talk of dangerous experiments. I don't know who mentioned it first, but one or the other decided to perform an experiment outside with some household items from the kitchen.

All this had already fascinated me, and my brother had whetted my appetite further by showing me how you could produce smoke from your fingertips just by rubbing your thumb and forefinger together. This truly was magic to me at the time.

"How could anyone produce smoke and not get hurt?" I wondered.

Rob showed me that if you stripped off the striker from a matchbox and then burned this on a metal tray that the greasy residue left on the metal would smoke if you applied it to your fingers and rubbed them together. Just think how magical it would look to someone who didn't know this. There was nothing in your hands and yet plumes of smoke came from your fingers, but only when you wanted it to happen. I was warned countless times that although this was a great trick the actual concoction on my fingers was poisonous and needed to be washed off afterwards. Years later matchbox strikers were modified and today you can no longer perform this trick ... unless, of course, you can find an old matchbox (but if you do, be aware that it is poisonous).

Rob and Norman raided the kitchen cupboards and found the items they were looking for. Two items were taken out into the garden. I watched in amazement while one product was placed on an old tin to form a volcano shape. Another was then poured on top and mixed with the other.

"It's not working" said Rob. Norman replied,

"Add some water, Rob."

"God," I thought, "This experiment (which was obviously going to cause fire) actually requires water."

A few drops of water were dripped on to the sticky mass. Smoke started to pour out of the mix instantly, and then the whole thing erupted into a huge mass of bubbling, spitting fire. I watched open-mouthed.

"They didn't even light it," I thought. "It just did it on its own."

In truth the reaction that took place was a violent one, where so much oxygen is produced and heat that in the end ignition happens. One product had been a bit stale because it had been sitting in the cupboard for ages – so this was the reason for using some water, which adds more oxygen molecules to the mix to push the reaction into top gear.

Baz listened to me and said,

"Well, how are we going to get this stuff?"

"Simple," I said. "We go to the chemist at the weekend and buy some."

Local chemist shops including places like Boots and Timothy Whites sold (among other things) certain chemicals in tubs and packets.

"This was going to be easy," I thought. We went up to the Bennetts End shops on the Saturday morning. Baz went into the chemist and came out two minutes later with nothing.

"What's up?" I said. "Where's the stuff?"

Baz recited the conversation he had had in the local chemist. As soon as he heard what Baz wanted the guy serving knew instantly what this was going to be used for, and refused to sell it to him.

"Damn," I said. "This isn't going to work."

"Wait a minute," I said. "I have a plan."

"What's that?" said Baz, looking at me in a most puzzled way.

There were two chemists in Bennetts End.

"Go into the other one, Baz," I said. "Just ask for one item in there."

"OK," said Baz. "Worth a try."

Two minutes later he came out with a box of stuff.

"Worked," said Baz. "Easy-peasy."

"Right," I said. "Now all it needs is for me to go into the other chemist where you got refused and for me to buy the other item."

The item I was getting maybe a more normal product, and would not raise suspicions. Another two minutes and I was back out with a small item in a bag.

"Gotit," I said with a huge grin on my face.

"Let's get down to the dell, then," replied Baz. "We need to check this stuff out."

I think we more or less ran down to the dell from there with the goods in our pockets. We could hardly wait. On the ground in the dell we repeated the experiment I had seen my brother perform. As far as I could see we used the same amounts.

"We need some water," I retorted. "We don't have any water…"

Baz looked at me.

"Simple, mate," he said.

He leant over the sticky mass and spat into it.

"There you go: instant water," he said.

It worked, for sure, as the mixture started to smoke – and we shuffled back a bit in surprise. This was fresh stuff, and it really did go off in a violent way… Whooosh… Smoke and sparks and what looked like almost-molten lava poured out of the mass like a volcano erupting.

"Wow," said Baz. "That's really cool."

"Yes," I said. "It's cool, OK, but I wonder what would happen to this mix if it was in a confined space. What if the gases were trapped and could not get out … what then?" I said.

Baz looked at me with one of those looks. Then he grinned the widest of smiles. We walked back to my place from the dell in only a couple of minutes. I said to Baz,

"Wait outside here, mate. I'll nip indoors to see what I can find."

I went inside and found my parents were out shopping, so I had free range to check out all the cupboards. What I was after was a glass pot: a small one with a metal screw lid. I checked in the kitchen and found something that was viable, although it had something in it.

"No matter," I thought. "Just take it anyway. It's almost run out. No one will miss it." I think it was a small jar of dried herbs. I got back to Baz.

"OK," I said. "I've got one," and showed him my find.

"Good," he said. "That's going to make a good test."

We ran back up to the dell.

"Put a measure of product in, then, before I put the other product in," I said. "We've got to be quick here, Baz. As soon as it seems to be going the lid's got to go on, and then you must throw it over into the grass by the bushes. "

"OK," says Baz. I placed some of the second product into the jar too. Baz spat in it and I mixed it slightly with a twig. "OK, that's it," I said. "I can feel it getting warm."

Baz screwed the top on and threw it about thirty yards into the grass in front of us. There were some kids playing over on the top of the bank of the dell. They didn't notice the plume of white smoke running up out of the grass, but they bloody well turned around a moment later. It went off with a booom...

"Jesus Christ," Baz blurted out.

"Oh, my God," I said.

I don't think we expected that result. It was louder than a banger. Some crows up in a tree were squawking hard as they set off out of their roost, obviously disturbed by this explosion.

"I'm thinking we need to get out of here sharpish," I said to Baz.

"Methinks you're bloody right," said Baz as we ran out of the dell, not even going back to see what destruction we had caused.

We got back home and did a check on ourselves. We had not been hit by anything... We just needed to lie low for a bit and not do that again until we were sure we were in a place where it was safe.

"We need more bottles," I said to Baz.

"Yes, we do," he said. "I know just the place, as well. At least, I know where I can get some."

"Oh?" I said.

"Yeah. My auntie is a hairdresser. I can get loads of empty ones from her. They use small shampoo bottles."

"Excellent," I said. "We are in business."

It was a few weeks before Baz got some of the bottles he promised. He got about half a dozen. In that time we had prepared for our next experiment by getting some more of the products. We knew that we had to be careful how we bought this stuff, and so we took it in turns to go into separate chemists for each product so there would be no association between the two items. We also went to different chemists, and one time we walked all the way to the Leverstock Green shops to get one of the items. The Boots down in the town was another option that we used. Once or twice we got asked what the crystals were for, and our answer was that our mum needed them as medication … she was very ill and we needed them.

"What we going to do with these, then?" said Baz.

"Well," I said. "We can go over the fields and use them there … or I really would like to try one in the cut."

"The cut?" said Baz. "What, lob one in the water?"

"Yeah. Why not? It will be watertight when it goes in. It will sink too."

So that was our next experiment. We went down to the canal, set one of the bottles up, and threw it into quite a deep patch of water by the bridge we crossed to go to Apsley. It sank instantly out of sight. We waited and waited … but nothing.

"Damn," said Baz. "The water must have got in."

"I think you're right, mate," I said.

We turned to head back up to the bridge… Thuddd… We looked back just in time to see the water settling back again into the canal. We looked at each other.

"Wow. That was really cool," I said. "The coldness of the water must have slowed down the reaction and delayed it quite a bit."

We looked at the canal as it turned a murky shade.

"We'd better scarper," said Baz.

"I think you're right, mate," I concluded.

We exploded a few other bombs here and there, and always had a stock of the chemicals to use when we wanted.

There was a path that we used to use from the side of the junior school down at the back of the houses. We used this path a lot, as not only was going that route a bit quicker but we also found it interesting. It was a bit unkempt, and in summer you had a hard job getting down it at all. The path was an official one and had a No Cycling sign at the top, but hardly anyone used it because it was so neglected. We liked it because it was like this.

There was a guy about halfway down whose house backed on to this path. He kept pigeons in a loft in the garden. He didn't like kids using this path because we tended to make a noise as we went by. So he would come out and in his own words tell us to bugger off. Baz and I got a bit fed up with him, to be honest. It was winter and the trees were bare. We didn't have much to do, and Baz said to me,

"You know that old git down the back path – Pigeon Man – the one who tells us where to go?"

"Yes," I said. "What about him?"

"Well, don't you think he is due for one of our bombs?"

"Oh, I said. "Yes ... I think you're right.

The problem was that Baz was clean out of bottles, and we needed a vessel to take the mix.

"I'll go inside, Baz, and see if I can find something indoors. Wait here, as I think I can rummage about better on my own," I reassured him.

I sort of knew what I was after, as the idea had come to me a while back. In the sideboard cupboard were some poster paint pots ... all different colours, they were.

"No one is using them. I'll take one that's dried up and nearly all used," I thought.

I took a nice green one. It was manky, to say the least, and I had some trouble unscrewing the top from the glass. The dried paint was really hard and crusted-on. I went back out to Baz.

"There you go ... nice little pot, Baz."

"It's still got ruddy paint in it," retorted Baz.

"Yes, I know. So maybe you won't need to spit in it, will you?" I said.

"OK. Let's go," he responded, with the usual smirk on his face.

We had to be careful down the path, as the winter meant that the trees were bare and we could easily be seen from the backs of people's houses on both sides of the path. What made things quite different that day was that we had had snow in the night, and a thick blanket covered everything. It was cold out, too. There was no sun, and a slight misty fog was in the air. I suspected it was still freezing.

We approached the spot where the guy's garden was. We would load the pot up and then Baz, being the better thrower, would launch it as far into the garden as he could. We began to load the pot up.

"Put a decent amount in," said Baz. "Let's make this one a special one."

"OK," I responded.

So we put the ingredients in, put the rest in our coat pockets, and Baz screwed the lid on and hurled it way up in the air towards the house. It landed on the grass, which was covered in a blanket of pristine snow. It landed on its bottom, as if it had been carefully placed there by one of us. We waited with beating hearts, hardly breathing, and watching the small object thirty yards away intently. When this thing blew we would run, for sure. That was our plan. That's what we had discussed.

What happened next was not what we expected at all. It was not by design, and we had never imagined this. Unlike all the other bottles which had exploded, this one didn't. We watched it, not daring to blink. First it hissed like a puff adder. Then it threw out jets of fire like a dragon, from the sides where the cap fitted the body. It hissed and spat and then it started to spin on the snow. It span and span on the spot. Both our mouths were wide open but speechless. Once it had reached a certain spinning rate it did something we were totally not ready for.

The pot actually took off. The jar actually flew. Baz and I watched as the poster paint pot did a complete circuit of the bloke's garden in the air. It was like a jet helicopter: a spinning top in the air with real flame jets for propulsion. Then all of a sudden, having lost pressure, it came back to earth and settled almost back on the spot where it had taken off from.

"What the bloody hell you think you're doing...?" came a voice from the back door of the house.

"Time to scram," said Baz.

We ran back up the path. We ran so hard, and giggled and laughed all the way to the top. Baz got a stitch through laughing so hard, and I had trouble holding back the tears.

"Did you bloody well see that...?" said Baz.

"That guy's face," I said. "Did you see how red that guy's face was?"

With our hands on our knees we stood at the top of the path, bent forward from the quick sprint we had just done.

"We'd better lie low for a bit, Baz," I said.

"Yeah, but only for a while," said Baz. "This is getting good."

When Baz and I approached the age of fourteen it was possible for us to buy our own fireworks. Leastways Baz could buy them if we picked the right shop, as he looked older than me and was more likely to get served. It was still difficult around Hemel to get what we wanted, and mostly we had to travel to Hemel Old Town and go to a shop called Dinky Dell.

Dinky Dell was a bit of a strange shop that sold a variety of odd things: Meccano, Dinky toys, and knitting wool. For us it was great, as this was the first shop in the firework season to start selling bangers. The guy who owned it was not too worried about who he sold to, which was why we went there. We sometimes bought the odd normal firework there, but mainly what we were after was a box or two of bangers. We loved the 3-2-1 Zero ones that were on sale, and the Thunder Flash and Cannon types. These would be used in different ways to provide a huge amount of mischief for the late weeks in October. As half term was around that time we had opportunities to go certain places and let these off.

Although the obvious thing was to blow things up with bangers we also had other ideas. Bangers consist of a cardboard tube containing black powder. On the top end of the tube (and glued into place) was a fuse length lasting maybe five seconds once lit. You could – if you were brave – light the banger while holding it and throwing it like a grenade. This was fraught with danger, and you could find that you had a banger in your hand with a really short fuse. Some people had lost fingers to these, and we were very mindful of this. We treated these things with respect most of the time but we still did some really stupid things.

I always blame Barrie at school for giving me these ideas. I'm sure he isn't all to blame, but most of the suggestions seemed to come from him. Barrie gave me the idea of making a simple mortar out of the tube from a bike tyre pump. If you unscrewed the tube from the mechanics of the pump you had a nice hard plastic tube with a small hole at one end. The idea here was to drop a banger down the top through the larger hole. The banger would then sit in the tube with its fuse poking out of the little hole at the bottom. You then dropped a glass marble down on top of the banger. You held all this with both hands at a forty-five degree angle with the base on the ground. One person lit the banger and you waited for the bang in the tube. There was enough expanding gas in the tube to push the marble out at quite a speed … in fact it would probably travel some 100 yards or so, maybe more.

Baz and I took all this equipment up to a place called the Lime Kilns. The actual lime kilns were no longer there. What was left was grass, landscaped parkland, and trees and bushes. The white chalk was still in evidence: here and there were some small chalk cliff faces that we could make use of. We used these cliff faces to try out the mortar, using the chalk as a backdrop to view the effects.

Then we really got naughty. From a vantage point on the hill of the Lime Kilns we could clearly see the travellers' encampment known as Elephant Farm. This place was somewhere you just didn't go near. Children were told to give this place a wide berth, as it was a place of trouble. From Baz's and my perspective this looked to be the right place to bombard with marbles. We set the mortar up and fired a few volleys over towards the encampment. They were clearly reaching it, as we heard a few of them hit the tops of the metal caravans parked there. Some activity then started to happen.

"Time to scram," said Baz, and I agreed. We didn't want to hang around with these guys getting upset.

The mortar worked well, and I reported back to Barrie at school that it had been a success. Barrie listened to my tale of bombardment on Elephant Farm.

"I have another idea," said Barrie. "I think it's possible to make something with a bit more punch."

"Oh? What's your idea, Barrie?" I replied.

"I'm thinking we could make a cannon," he said.

Barrie described his idea to me, and when I returned home I set about looking in the shed for a suitable bit of metal pipe. I found some tubing which was about half an inch in diameter, and whose walls seemed to be thick enough to take the explosive pressure. One end needed to be plugged off. I took some wooden dowel and hammered this in until I thought there was no way that the plug could come out. In fact I'm not sure now if this was luck or good judgement but the plug did stay in, and I'm thankful it did.

With one end blocked off I drilled a small hole in the top using my dad's hand drill. The hole needed to be just where the plug ended inside. It took for ever to drill this small hole: there were no electric drills in those days – leastways, we could not afford one. With a small hole drilled through to use as the touch hole the cannon was ready. It was small, only about eight inches in length, but that was enough for what we needed it for.

Baz came around and we set off for the dell, which now seemed to be our own testing ground for all things that went bang.

"OK," I said. "Let's load this up."

I took a banger and broke it in half, as Barrie had instructed. Baz held the cannon up and I poured in the contents of the black powder. This was then rammed down with some bits of newspaper I had brought with me for wadding. Barrie said,

"Don't use too much: just enough to hold the powder in place." Then for ammo we didn't have anything, really, so I put some small stones down it that I found on the ground – and again a bit of wadding, just to hold in place.

"Right, I said. "It's ready."

We laid it on the ground and held it in place with some bricks so it would not move when it went off.

"Baz, hand me a bit of that old cloth from over there," I said.

The dell was always full of bits of rubbish that people had just dumped. Baz ripped some off and we laid it over the touch hole on the top of the cannon.

"Right," I said. "I'm going to light this, and I suggest we get well back."

I lit a match and set the rag alight. We moved back with speed. This was an unknown. The rag burned well and then it started to go out. It had been totally consumed but there had been no reaction.

"Shit," said Baz. "How are we going to let this off? I reckon that hole you've got there is too small."

I certainly had to agree. The hole was no bigger than an eighth of an inch, and I had used the smallest drill bit my dad had got.

"OK, I'll do it," said Baz.

"Do what?" I responded.

"I'll let it off," Baz said.

"How are you going to do that?" I replied, with a look of dread on my face.

"I'll strike a match and hold it on top," said Baz. "Better still, I'll break a match head off and put it on the hole and then light that."

"You're bloody mad," I said.

"Yes," said Baz. "Maybe … but we've got to do this."

Well … I have to say, brave or stupid, Baz did what he said. I stood back and watched at a distance. Baz would not be able to move back quickly enough: I was quite sure of this. Baz lit the match.

"Here we go," he shouted, and he lit the match head on top of the cannon.

It was instant. There was a bang, and Baz rolled back and over his head and landed next to me. The noise was deafening from where we were. The explosion was sharp and quick: much louder than anything we had tried before.

"Are you OK?" I said to Baz.

Baz was holding his head.

"Can't hear a bloody thing," he said. "My ears are ringing."

"We need to get out of here, and fast," I said picking up the cannon.

"What are you saying?" said Baz.

"Oh, come on, Baz," I shouted, pulling his arm and leading him down the slope out of the dell. We didn't waste time getting out and back home.

"How's it now, Baz?" I asked.

"I'm getting it back," he replied, while sticking his dirty fingers in his ears and wiggling them frantically. "I'll be OK."

"I need to look at this again, Baz," I said. "We can't do that again like that."

It came to me quite quickly. It was obvious, really. I had used the black powder from the banger, but the fuse bit of it was redundant and I had thrown this bit away. What if I made the hole in the top of the cannon bigger and then pushed the fuse from the banger into this? If this worked then we would have a nice five-second fuse that would let us get well clear. I started work right away on the upgrade. Cannon mark 2 was ready the next day, and we would be going up to the dump to see my school chums and show them what this cannon did.

Baz and I took the cannon up to the dump and we showed the new mark 2 version to Barrie, who was really impressed. We loaded it up with some airgun lead and aimed it at a pile of tin cans. It just obliterated them all like a shotgun. The fuse modification worked well and enabled us to let it off at a safe distance. It all held together (amazingly) and I'm grateful for that, as of course I realise now that I was playing about with a potentially lethal bomb.

At school I would discuss the makings of things like fireworks etc. with Barrie. We were both very interested in the chemistry of it all. It's a pity in a way that we didn't apply any of this to some academic outlet.

The school didn't help, it would seem, and I'm still amazed today that at one of the assemblies at Bennetts End secondary school the head invited someone from the local Brocks firework company to come and talk to us kids. Can anyone see that happening today? Brocks had a substantial works where the Woodhall Farm estate is today in Hemel. A series of huts in a field comprised the whole industry of firework making. The idea here was that if one hut had an accident and blew up then at least all the other huts were potentially safe. The site closed down in 1971, making way for the new housing estate.

The chap who came to talk to us in assembly actually stood on stage and made fireworks as he talked. He would pour certain amounts of powder into cardboard tubes and then whack all this down with wooden dowels. We were transfixed by all of this. Not only did he show how they made these things but he also let them off in the main hall inside the school. Clouds of toxic smoke would rise from these experiments. To be honest the guy was a complete nutter, but we thought it was rather cool.

Barrie said to me one day,

"I think I have the right mix of stuff for producing a rocket."

"Oh," I said. "What are you using"

"Well, I found that by mixing those crystals you used in your bombs with sulphur I can get a mix that's almost approaching gunpowder. It's not as fast-burning as black powder but it seems to have enough thrust for us to be able to build a rocket using it. I reckon so, anyway."

"Do you want a hand?" I said.

"Sure," said Barrie. "Come around tonight after school, and I'll show you what I have."

We walked back from school that afternoon to Barrie's house down on Barnacres Road. I had never been to Barrie's house before and had never met his parents. When we got there Barrie opened the door and introduced me to his mum, who was at that time unpacking shopping from bags on the kitchen table.

"Have you got my stuff? said Barrie to his mum.

"Yes, love," said his mum. She then proceeded to produce three packets of sulphur and two of the crystals from her bag. I stood there amazed. There were Baz and me having to switch from chemist to chemist to get what we wanted, and here was Barrie's mum just coming back with the weekly shopping piled high with potential explosives.

"Thanks, Mum," said Barrie, as he then escorted me upstairs with the packets in his arms. Once in the confines of his bedroom he showed me what he had constructed so far in the way of a rocket tube.

"All we need to do is fill this with a mix of these two substances and then pack it in tight," said Barrie. "If I only had a pestle and mortar I could grind this stuff down to a fine powder and then it would burn even faster," he added.

We worked on the rocket for some time, ensuring it was packed out and was set up right for a launch in his garden. Barrie held a light to it until it started to fizz. This was the first time I had seen this reaction, and it really was quite something to see. There was a lot of smoke and the sulphur was a little unpleasant, but there was enough thrust to send it up a short way. We spent the time till tea thinking about what might work better, and Barrie continued with this project for some time. I don't think he ever perfected what he wanted, as I think a component was maybe missing from the mix. The fun with all this was the experimentation and seeing what you could do with just a few simple chemicals.

So ... to conclude this chapter. Yes, I still like my fireworks – and no, I don't do anything silly any more. I value my limbs and eyesight too much to try anything stupid. I just wanted to give a further reminder to people that it is illegal to attempt the making of any explosive, and you could easily end up with a prison sentence these days if you try stuff. So don't go there. Leave it to the experts, whoever they may be.

The George

1970-1980

Around the time I was sixteen I started to go to the George pub along Belswains Lane. It was a pub that was close enough to walk to, and also one my parents never went to. They favoured the Boot.

The George was a typical estate-type pub and at this time it had two bars: the public bar and the saloon bar. When we first started going to this establishment we went into the public bar – almost a spit and sawdust place. Rough tables and chairs occupied a small area where you could sit and basically drink what you wanted. A dartboard stood in one corner and a jukebox in the other. What made this pub and this bar a huge draw for Baz and me was the fact it had a bar billiards table. I had seen these tables in pubs before, mainly when on holiday, and they were quite a rare thing.

Bar billiards is (as the name suggests) a billiards-type game played on a table about six feet long and four feet wide. The table has no side or corner pockets. Instead there are nine holes placed around the board for balls to drop down into. Each hole scores a certain number of points. The play alternates between players and your turn ends when you either don't get your ball down a score hole or you knock over one of the strategically-placed mushroom skittles, of which there are three. You use a short snooker cue to hit a ball you have placed near you in a D-shaped area, and this ball must hit another ball before going down one of the holes.

If you wanted a game then you had to place a shilling (or, later, 5p) into a mechanism at the front of the table and pull a lever. The balls would then become available and a fifteen-minute timer would start. You played until a bar dropped down inside the table and stopped the balls from coming back to you. This really was great for Baz and me as it gave us an interest down there apart from just drinking and playing records on the jukebox. We got quite good at it, and eventually someone in the bar suggested we get a team together to play other pubs in the area.

Now I have to say that the George public bar was a kind of a rough old place, and apart from us kids in there it was also occupied by a number of good old working-class navvy types. These guys did a hard manual job during the week, and on a Friday they got paid in cash and would come down to drink and play cards. There would sometimes be a lot of money on the table on a Friday night in that bar, and with the drink too it was quite possible that a fight would break out. Once we saw a guy get thrown out of one of the windows like you might see in a cowboy western. Although it was unlike a film, this was very real. Baz and I never went near the card playing. We could play OK, but we didn't have the guts or the kind of money to get involved in that sort of nightmare.

Although I paint a picture of this place being a den of danger it never was for us. The guys in there respected our space and we actually got on really well with them. We were accepted as part of the crowd in there, and they liked us youngsters being around.

One of the characters in the bar was an Irishman named D. He was a small wiry guy in his late forties, I would guess. D would get a bit drunk at times, and it was very apparent when he was because the song 'When Irish Eyes Are Smiling' would start up. D was quite an extraordinarily flexible guy (given his age) and he had his party trick he liked to do either for entertainment or as a bet for drink.

"I bet you..." he would start. "I bet you I can pick up a matchstick on the floor from between my legs without using my hands."

At this point he would maybe stagger back and someone would have to save him from crashing into some empty chairs or, worse still, disturb the nest of pound notes sitting in the card kitty.

"Yes, D. We've seen it. We know you can do it," we would say.

"I'll shooow you anyways," he would reply. And so the act would start and it was always, without fail, the same performance.

"OK, D, off you go then," we would say.

He would stand upright as well as he could, with his eyes facing to the front. Someone would give him a match from a matchbox and he would hold it in his hand a while showing off the match to his audience. Then he would start to sing 'Danny Boy', and with the song his head would wobble a bit and he would start to bend his legs and slowly drop down on his haunches while singing,

"Oh Danny boy the pipes, the pipes are calling…"

This was not even part of the trick at this point. This was just him setting up the bloody trick. It took forever for the guy to place a match on the floor between his feet.

"From glen to glen…"

He started to straighten back up…

"And down the mountain side…"

Here and there was maybe a wobble at the top as the oxygen hit him again.

And so now after all this the trick was ready to be performed. When you saw this the first time you kind of thought,

"Wow, that's really clever, D," but maybe the third, fourth, and fifth time it sort of got a bit predictable. Someone would shout over from the card table,

"Come on, D. Get on with the bloody thing, will yer?"

D would then do more wobbling with his head as his eyes wandered around his audience and then he would bend over and go down once again, but this time his hands would be clenched behind his back. Down and down he would go until his lips actually touched the floor and he grabbed the match. He was truly a flexible guy and would put any yoga teacher to shame. Coming back up, he would then look around at the audience (match still in his mouth) and sing,

"Ohfff, Daffy bofff, Ohffff Daffy bofff, I lofff youfff sooofff…"

This was the muffled output at this stage: the match interfered quite well with the final line of the verse.

D was great and we all loved his crazy ways, but the problem with D was that he was also on the bar billiards team. Needless to say, after our first game away at another pub we decided that maybe it was always best for D to be the first player to go on and not the last one. He had got so pissed up at the first game we had that there was no chance of him seeing any balls on the table, let alone a match between his feet – which he did attempt to do in front of a quite astonished country pub's posh folk.

"I think we'd better go now," said the team captain. After this we changed the order of play and we managed to win a few games.

Baz drank lager and lime at that time and moved over to lager top a year or so later. Baz always needed a bit of sweetness in his drink then. As for me … I was drinking pints of brown ale which, when I think about it now, makes me shudder. When you ordered a pint of brown ale or light and brown mixed you got a pint glass and two bottles of beer with the tops taken off. Two bottles would give you a decent pint and a bit. I would maybe drink about two or three pints a night, and that would be almost every night. We never stayed at home unless we were really ill. The pub called to us each night. It was our main entertainment. It kept us kind of sane.

The George had an off-licence part to it where the public could come into a sectioned-off bit and get booze to take home. One evening we were down there and one of our crowed had some stink bombs. One of these bombs was thrown into the off-licence bit and we all sat there in the public bar sniggering away. We heard people come in through the door of the off-licence and go,

"Pooo… What the bloody hell is that?"

It was obvious to Pat, the landlady then, who had caused all this. We got banned right away for two weeks.

Two weeks went by really slowly but when we came back we decided to change bars, and so we moved over to the more luxurious and salubrious saloon bar. Pat and Fred who ran the pub eyed us up as we walked in with our tails between our legs. We ordered up some drinks.

"Do you want one yourself, Pat?" said Baz.

"OK, me lovelies. I'll ave a bloody double rum and black on you guys for stinking my bloody off-licence out." She smiled and all was well. Well … it was at least OK until the fish died, that is.

The saloon was much smarter than the public bar: there were nice booths to sit in and lovely red flock wallpaper on the walls. There was a link to the jukebox in the other bar, and a fruit machine was the main source of entertainment in the saloon. In the corner was a lovely tropical fish tank with loads of fish and bubbles inside. We set up camp here and made new friends in this bar with a different section of society. People coming in to this bar were a mixed bunch, but mainly a class above the workforce from the public bar. It wasn't an issue to us, anyway, as we would mix with anyone as long as they were friendly and bought drinks.

Baz and I usually walked down together as we lived in the same street, so often Baz would just come around for me and we would walk across the school field and vault over the gate at the end of Lower Barn. We then skirted around a few roads and slipped down a pathway down towards the Deans shops. Down there we would be joined by a variety of friends we knew: the twins from school, Martin and Neil, Chaz (also from school) and an odd assortment of people who just came and went. Some of our friends would come down in the week and some were more weekend-and-Sunday-lunchtime people like Tina and Gordon.

We had a good time down there, and Friday nights were always a bit special as Pat and Fred decided that a good idea would be to have a disco in the evening. Colin, the chap who ran the local mobile disco, was chosen. His brother Ian worked behind the bar and, I suspect, got him this job in the first place. There was no dancing here, of course – there was no licence – but we could ask for records and Colin would play what we requested if he had the record. This really was the start of the disco era and my introduction to music, which would span my whole lifetime from that point. Up to now music had not really been of interest to me, but the disco scene made an impact on me and I wanted more of that.

I was with Baz one night in the summer, and on our way to the George we went a slightly different route and went down to call on the twins Martin and Neil on the way down. It was only a small detour to go down to Saunders Road. Martin and Neil were tall skinny guys and, although twins, you could easily tell them apart. We had all been at school together from the very start, so we had always known each other. The sixth form had thrown us closer together and now we had all become drinking pals too. Martin and Neil's mum and dad and sister were a great laugh, and were always welcoming to us when we went around there.

On the way down to the George there was much chatter, but Martin and Neil had a proposition to make.

"We think," one of them said, "That we should all go over to the Top Rank next Saturday."

"Yes," said Baz. "That's a great idea."

I was puzzled, to be honest.

"Top Rank?" I said. "What's that?"

Martin explained that it was a disco: a place in Watford where you could go and buy drinks and listen to music... A bit like down the George on a Friday night but one hundred times bigger and better. My head span, to be honest. The words disco, Watford, and bigger wheeled around in my head, making me feel drunk. I was not one for dramatic change, and this sounded like a big, big change to me. Neil said,

"Yep, we can all meet down the George – say – at seven on Saturday, and go from there all in one crowd." I suppressed the panic attack at this point and we marched on towards the pub.

Top Rank

1972
This is what we were listening to at the time:

Chicory Tip: 'Son of My Father'
Gary Glitter: 'Rock And Roll (Parts 1 and 2)'
Slade: 'Mama Weer All Crazee Now'
T. Rex: 'Telegram Sam'
The Drifters: 'Saturday Night at the Movies'
Judge Dread: 'Big Six'
Roxy Music: 'Virginia Plain'

Things had been quite simple up to then: playing cards around people's houses and a trip to the George for a drink and game of bar billiards. But this Saturday we were going to the Top Rank and this would mean traveling on a bus to Watford. It's not like I was frightened by all this, just a bit nervous that we (or rather I) were travelling into new territory. This was the unknown, for sure, but you know how you think on things like this. You kind of tell that little voice in your head,

"Oh, come on. It won't be as bad as you are constantly telling yourself. It will be a walk in the park."

The end result was in fact no walk in any park of any description. It was far from what I could imagine, and if someone with a time machine had gone there and come back and told me the future I think I would have been physically sick on the spot.

Baz and I marched through the double doors of the saloon bar of the George like a couple of gunslingers out of a John Wayne western. This Saturday night out was so special that both of us had new shirts on and our very best trousers and platform shoes. In those days guys wore a jacket and tie and, actually, you would never get into a disco club without these. We looked smart as we pushed open the doors to see the twins already there sitting at one of the booths.

265

They were not alone, though. There were four other guys with them that we didn't know from Adam.

Martin introduced the guys who had also been invited to this little outing to Watford's greatest disco club. These guys all worked either on the railways or in conjunction with it. I always felt a bit awkward meeting new folk.

"This is Vic," sparked up Martin, and I shook hands with a sandy-headed guy about my height with a red and orange tartan jacket on. He had a feathered haircut and blue eyes that looked rather shifty. Vic wore that tartan jacket so much that he fondly became known as Checky Boy to the new gang.

"Meet Bill," said Martin.

"Hi, Bill," we responded. Billy Boy was a taller and lean chap with a slight cast in his eye. His hair was dark and longer than Vic's. You could tell just by looking at Bill that he was no pushover and was probably a bit useful with his fists in a fight. It's interesting how you evaluate people on first meeting them. Usually my hunches were right.

"And this is Cluck."

This was Cliff or Clifford – or Cluck, as he was sometimes called. He was a bit of an oddball and looked a bit like Mark Bolan from T. Rex. His hair was everywhere and he wore calf-length high boots with coloured stars on them. I had never seen a person like this in my life. Where the hell had Martin drummed these individuals up from?

Finally the last of the guys stood up: Eamonn. He was definitely the pretty boy out of the group. Very clean and sharp, with an expensive haircut to match, he was your tall, dark and handsome guy. He would be having girls drop at his feet by my reckoning, and he sure did as well.

What a motley crew this lot was. It was their first time down the George, as none of them lived in our area (their homes being spread over the district). They had to travel down here specially as none of us had a car in those early days. We always had to travel by good old public transport or taxi.

We sat and chatted in the pub until it was time to go outside and wait for the 322 bus to arrive and take us into Watford. Fortunately the bus stop was right outside the George so we could leave it to the last minute to down our pints and walk outside.

It was a warm late summer's evening now, and still quite light. I remember this night vividly as I have played it so many times back in my head. You can't quite understand why you remember some video flashes so well, but this one is obvious. This was the night of many firsts. It was a night when a lot happened to me all in the space of a few hours. It was a night that, try as I might, would never be repeated. My fairy godmother had touched her wand over me that night. You will go to the ball it seemed. Well the rank anyway.

As we sat on the George's pub wall I had no idea what adventure this bus would be taking us on. Although it hadn't been invented or made yet, it was a bit like stepping into *Harry Potter*'s night bus and going off into some magical make-believe land. That's right, as soon as I got on that bus I wasn't in the normal world anymore.

One of us flagged the green single-decker 322 down and we all hopped on the bus and paid the driver the one and sixpence single fare. We sat in the double seats and chatted away. These new guys were great fun. Neil and Martin had been to the Top Rank before so they knew the score, but the rest of us were new to all this. I had no idea what to expect, although it had been explained to me that there were bars and music and a dance floor. The dance floor kind of worried me the most. The only dancing I had seen was the stuff my mum and dad did on odd occasions at the Pontins holiday camp. The vision of mum and dad entwined and gliding around a dance floor in my head was disrupted sharply.

"Banggg…"

I blinked.

"What? What's that?"

"Banggg," said Checky Boy.

"You what?" I said.

"You reckon we might get a banggg tonight?" repeated Vic as he also contorted his face and used some sort of swift arm movement, thrusting his arm up sharply while cupping his biceps with his other hand. He had a huge grin on his face, and by now a few of the bus passengers had twisted their necks around to see what the banggg was about.

Vic's eyes shifted around the bus and then to each of us in turn, and he repeated,

"Do you reckon any of us will get a banggg tonight? You know, a banggggggggg..." The second bang was an octave lower than the first, with an almost guttural sound coming at the last g. A few people smiled and someone leant across to me and whispered in my ear,

"You know ... a shag."

"Ohhh," I let out. "I see." Vic smiled at me and came close to my ear and did a little banggg whisper just for me.

We rolled off the bus still chirping and laughing away.

"Did you see that old dear on the bus when you said 'banggg', Vic? I nearly wet myself," said Cluck.

"Think she thought she was in for some fun," retorted Billy Boy.

"Bit too young for you, Vic," said Eamonn as he pushed Vic with a friendly shove down the road. We all laughed of course until it dawned on me. Girls. Is this all about girls, then?

Top Rank had started off as the Odeon Cinema in Watford and then changed to the Top Rank nightclub. Caters supermarket was beside it and it sat atop all the other shops in Watford high street. Access to it was through a small door at street level and then a very steep staircase to the second storey – which was, of course, above the shops. At the top of the stairs was a box office – a place where you bought your entry ticket. This was all new to me, and I had to be told what to do. Some grumpy woman gave me a ticket after I handed over fifty pence. This was indeed an expensive adventure: first bus fares and then admission charges. I could have had a good night out on what I had already spent, and the night was still young.

We moved through another door and into a wide open space. My eyes flitted about the place, trying to take in all the splendour. It was nothing like I had seen before. The room was huge, with a dance floor in the middle and chairs and tables around the outside of the floor. Then there was a walkway around this and even more chairs and tables set back a bit further. There also seemed to be an upstairs with a balcony looking out over the main floor. Around the outer wall were the bars: at least two, if I remember rightly. Above the dance floor was a glitter ball and next to this was a multitude of lights and ultraviolet strip lights. Only a few lights were on, and the whole place was basically quite dark and felt seedy. I had no idea of course what seedy was at that age, but that's basically what it was. I was excited, I can tell you, and entering the Top Rank was my first of many firsts that night.

"Let's get a drink," Martin called out, and we followed him over to one of the long bars where a number of people were trying to get served.

"Busy, isn't it?" said Baz.

"Yep," I said. "How are we going to do this? A round in here for one person is going to be too much."

That was decided, then, and we each paid for our own drink. I ordered the usual for me: a pint of brown ale. This was given to me in a plastic pint tumbler.

"What the hell is this?" I remarked, while taking a sip of beer from what appeared to be a very scratched-up plastic piss pot.

"It's to stop any trouble," replied Neil. "You won't get any glass in here. It's too dangerous for that … things sometimes kick off in here."

My second first, then: drinking beer out of a disgusting plastic pot which also felt warm to the touch.

We all got our drinks and decided to take one of the tables over. In fact there were so many of us we took two tables. The music was quite loud, louder than I had experienced at the George with Colin Dodds disco. You could talk, though, and we sat there and just took in the view. It was not new just to me. Some of the others had never been here, either, and they too were assessing what was going on and who was doing what. Up on a stage area was the DJ or disc jockey: he had his set-up of two record turntables. One would be playing something and on the other he would be queuing a record up for the next play. My eyes were now getting used to the low light and smoky haze that drifted about. Almost everyone in there smoked, including us. I guess they must have had some extraction vents to get rid of the smoke. Around the dance floor were tables. Some had parties of guys like us and others had all girls. It seemed that everyone was eyeing everyone else up, like some mass cattle market. Again I thought,

"This is about girls, isn't it? This is why we are here. Oh, hell. Girls..."

We had a couple more drinks and were enjoying ourselves just sitting and listening to the music being played. It was a mix of old and new stuff, but was generally from the top twenty. Some girls were out on the dance floor and dancing around a ring made with their handbags in the middle. Some people now think this is a joke, but it did actually happen. Part way thought the evening the disco stopped and the stage revolved around to present a band to the audience. It was nothing special, really – and although we liked the novelty of hearing a local band live for the first time, we really liked the disco. Another of my firsts that evening: a live band. But there would be more to come ... much more.

We were well-oiled by the time the disco came back. It was getting on for about eleven o'clock now and the place was chock-a-block with people. Then it happened. One moment I was sitting with a brown ale in my hand, the next I was on the dance floor. It had only taken a few notes from one record and Neil shouting at us and that was it.

"Come on, come on, come on, come on, come on, come on, come on ... I say," sang Garry Glitter.

"Get up on the floor, all of you," shouted Neil. "Get up now."

"Do you wanna be in my gang, my gang, my gang? Do you wanna be in my gang? Oh, yeah," Gary continued.

By this time we were all up. Baz, me, Neil, Martin, Vic, Bill, Cluck, and Eamonn.

This was yet another first – maybe the one I dreaded the most, in fact: dancing. What the hell was I to do?

"Come on," said Neil. "I'll show you. We all do the Stomp. OK?"

"The Stomp? I'm thinking. What the fuck is that?"

So the spectacle began with this group of young guys standing in a circle and stomping our feet on the floor in time to Gary Glitter singing,

"Do you wanna be in my gang? Oh, yeah."

The "Come on, come on" bits were the best, because we really stomped so hard on the floor with our heavy platform shoes that the needle on the record deck actually skated across the record and ended the music instantly at one point.

"Cut it out, guys," was the response from the stage as the disc jockey attempted to find the place the needle had jumped from.

We continued nonetheless with more stomping, and Neil showed us his rock and roll moves by tucking his thumbs into this trouser belt. He started making some forward-jerking movements with his upper torso.

"Come on. Do this too," shouted Neil. We all followed in some sort of animal frenzy. One of the lines – "Who'd ever believe it?" – was quite right. We must have looked a bloody sight, all right. Who would bloody believe it? But we were totally oblivious to our surroundings and what people might be thinking, which was probably,

"What a bunch of twats."

The record came to an end. Some of the guys sat down. Neil, Martin, and I stayed up, for some reason, as the next record span with a gentler beat. I quite liked this, to be honest. I didn't think I would, but it felt kind of good to be up there dancing … kind of powerful. Now I had to kind of use some of my own steps to dance to what was being played.

To the side of us was a girl on her own. She spotted us and joined in our little group. She had a lovely smile. She was a petite girl, and very pretty indeed. Neil went and sat down. This was not stomping music and I think he had had enough of the current, more sedate slow record.

For some reason Martin and I started to dance around this girl as if locked in some sort of competition for her. We orbited her like moons around a planet. My head was swimming. What was going on here? Is this normal? I stayed with it, and if Martin used some fancy moves then I would challenge him with my own naff ones. She looked from me to Martin and back again, as if trying to make some choice. Her eyes wandered to me and it was at this point that Martin realised he was runner-up. He went and sat down, smiling at me as he left as if to say,

"You won, mate. She's yours."

"What the hell is happening?" I was asking myself inside. "Why me?"

It was me and the girl on our own on the dance floor. Well … not completely on our own, but – let's face it – the comfort blanket of my mates was gone. We danced together for a bit longer and another record started. I could see my chums back at the table. They were watching me with interest. I saw the red tartan outline of Vic, and I swear I saw his arm rise up violently and his mouth articulate the word he had used on the bus. God … the bus ride. That all seemed all too far in the past now.

I was spinning around and around on this dance floor holding the warm body of a girl close to me. She smelled really nice and I was wondering if I had put enough Brut aftershave on that evening. Did she really like me? Why me, for God's sake? Why not Eamonn? He was far more attractive.

No one had given me the manual of what to do. I had no idea, and my naivety showed to this girl. P grabbed hold of me and drew me in close. We were now dancing a slow dance with a sort of too-fast beat playing. We span around and around in some form of giddy embrace. At this point I stopped counting the number of firsts I had added to my list. First girl, first dance, first embrace... Where the hell was this going?

"Are you gonna buy me a drink, then, handsome?" she said, looking up at me with the loveliest of faces I had ever seen. She had big wide brown eyes and a huge grin on her face. She was fair-haired and had thick red lipstick on.

"God," I thought. "Lipstick… What's Mum going to say…?"

"Sure. I'll buy you a drink," I responded. "What do you want?"

"Port and lemon, please," she replied.

"God," I thought. "How posh." I don't think even we had a bottle of port in the sideboard at home. I didn't want to stop the closeness and the spinning on the dance floor. It sort of felt comforting, but we had to stop. It was getting silly.

"Come on," she said. "I'll sit here and you get the drinks from the bar. I'll still be here when you get back, you know." She smiled again. I was in love, that was for sure.

I went to the bar, passing a few of my new mates along the way who were still boozing away at the original table. Vic was missing and Eamonn was chatting up another girl on one of the other tables. I got to the bar and ordered a half for me and this port and lemon thing. I had time to think about all this and think what might happen next.

"Do I have a plan when I get back to her? No … but just take it easy, and take her lead. She does seem to be in charge here," I thought.

I took the drinks back to P, who was sitting on a lonely spare chair that had been separated out from the rest of the tables. As I approached she spotted me and stood up.

"One chair?" I said.

"That's OK," she replied, with that huge cheeky smile she had. "You sit down and I'll sit on your lap."

"Oh, my God," I thought. "Oh, my bloody God…"

Now I don't know if any lucky flying bird had shat on me that night on the way in or I had happened to touch a chimney sweep on the bus, but things were happening in this place at lightning speed. Four hours ago I had been sitting in the George almost as a child just out of nappies, and here I was with a woman who was now asking

me to sit on my lap. What was going on here? Wake up. Wake up…
But, no. This was no dream. This was as real as it gets.

I sat down, and P sat on my lap as she said she would. Her arms instinctively crept around me and she looked into my eyes.

"What's your name, fella?" she asked in a soft voice.

"Er … everyone calls me Dick," I replied, more nervous now for mentioning the D word.

My heart was pumping fast now and the rest of the room was now a blur. It was just me and her in that room now, and nothing else mattered.

"I'm P," she said, without me asking. She then did something I knew she would do all along, but even though I knew it was coming the event poleaxed me nonetheless. She kissed me on the lips and it was the most magical of moments I had experienced up to then, even surpassing the time when my dad showed me the new air rifle he had bought me. It was even more magical than unwrapping my Johnny Seven at Christmas. One kiss is all it takes. I wanted more, and she knew it too.

"I like you, Dick," she said in soft tones close to my ear. It was me this time who instigated a kiss, but this one was rather deep and sensual. I heard some woohoos from behind me but I carried on.

"You're good, Dick," P confirmed as we both came up for air. Of course I was in love instantly and I was putty in her hands, but I didn't care. I would have jumped off a cliff if she had asked me.

We drank our drinks and kissed some more, and she explained that she lived in Hemel and was here with her best mate. She didn't know where her mate had gone, but she thought she might now be with a guy as she had now been gone a while. We had another slow dance and sat down again. I could not take my eyes off her. She was mesmerising.

Was this my first real girlfriend? Had I really come to a disco and pulled without trying? Is this normal? Would this happen every week? The answer to all those questions was of course a deep resounding no, but I didn't know it yet. I was still on cloud nine.

"Here she is," said P.

"Who?" I asked, as I strained to turn my head in her direction without us both falling off the chair.

"My friend. Here she comes." A much taller and full platinum blonde was striding towards us with a little guy on her arm.

"Hold on a minute," I was thinking. "I know that... Oh, no," I thought." No... Nooo..."

"Banggg," came the retort from the little guy in the garish tartan jacket on her arm.

"How you doing, Vic?" I replied, trying to ignore his vulgar expression and apologising to P for the outburst. "This is my mate Vic," I said.

"That's a turn-up," said Vic. "You and me pulling the same couple of birds like that. What are the chances of that happening? Banggg."

"Zero," I thought, but then this was the strangest of nights I had ever had in my life.

"Look, you guys," said P. "I have to go, you know."

"Go? Go where?" I said.

"I have to go home. I'm expected back by half twelve. My dad will go mad if I'm not back in time."

"Well, I'm staying with Vic," said her mate, with a happy "I've scored" sort of face.

"Shit," I'm thinking. "What now? Do I offer to take her home? Do I stay with my mates? What now? Where's the rule book? Oh, help..."

"OK," I said. "I'll take you back home." P smiled but I guess she knew what she was doing. "I can't let you travel back on your own, can I?" I said.

She was too cute to just leave to walk the streets of Watford alone. I might have been new to all this but I had been brought up with some manners, and I knew this was the expected thing to do.

We said our goodbyes and Vic remained behind with her friend. We left the Rank and walked out into Watford high street. It was now chilly outside, as it sometimes can be in late summer.

"Oh God," I thought. "I didn't bargain for this. I was hoping us mates would all go back together and now I have this girl to look after." I was an adult for the first time. I was taking charge of someone who needed help. It felt good, and my confidence began to grow. I could now do anything as long as P was on my arm.

She had a furry jacket on. I doubted that it was real fur for one minute, but with my arm around her it felt like a real one to me. I knew where we had come in from on the bus in a general sense and assumed that there would be a bus stop on the other side of the road. There was, as it happened, and a few couples were already waiting. It wasn't long before a bus came along: the 322, which would take us back to Hemel.

"Thank God for that," I thought.

P lived in Adeyfield, and although I knew where that was I thought that it wasn't going to be a good walk from where the bus would set us down. My plan was to get off the bus at the top of Durrants Road and walk down to the taxi rank, get a taxi there, and take her home by car. This I did – and we kissed some more, both walking down to Apsley and in the taxi. She got out outside her house, whispering to me that she could not bring me into the house that night ... a peck on the lips, and she had gone.

I eventually got home and went to bed. Mum and Dad had long gone up and I heard the snoring coming from their room. I had a hard job getting to sleep that night. P was in my head. I wondered honestly if this had all been a dream. New friends, discos, warm beer, girls, dancing...

I finally got to sleep and woke up late on Sunday morning. My clothes were still on the bed from the night before. I reached over and took my shirt and smelled it. P's scent was on my shirt. It hadn't been a dream, then. It had been all real.

That Sunday morning I woke up realising I had a girlfriend. Me, for God's sake, with a girl. I felt in my jacket pocket and pulled out a matchbox with writing on it. It was her phone number. I needed to keep this really safe. I was as excited as anything, and after breakfast I didn't waste any time phoning her and asking her out...

I had a date. She would see me tonight down at the George. Excellent.

That week was a funny old week for me. My relationship with P lasted about six days in all, because when it came round to going to the Top Rank on Saturday again it was not me taking P to the disco. No. It was Billy Boy. In fact the following week after that it was Neil, and the week after that I think it was even Eamonn. I learned something that week. You can kind of trust your friends with all sorts of stuff. They will help you out when times are bad, and even step in and punch someone's lights out if need be. They will stand by you to the bitter end, but for God's sake keep a bloody eye on your bird because as sure as eggs are eggs they will steal your bloody bird off you as soon as your back is turned.

I think the funniest thing that happened that week was that I took P to the Hemel pictures to see a film called *The Devils*, a Ken Russell special. It was an X film of the worst kind. I had no idea who Ken was: all I was interested in was getting P on the back row of the cinema. My plan was a firm one in theory, but I hadn't quite reckoned on old Ken's film-making. P was physically sick from what was shown on the screen. We had to walk out about halfway through. My appetite for putting my tongue down P's neck had subsided somewhat and I just took her home.

P drifted off and I never saw her again at any club. You always remember your first kiss. It's as important as most things in life. You remember where you were and who you were with, and it's a significant milestone.

A Job for Life

1972-1973

After I left school, having had a really easy time in the lower sixth at Longdean, I had no idea what I wanted to do. Does anyone really know at that age what they want? I had left with not very much as far as qualifications are concerned. Basically I had eight or nine CSEs, one of which was an O level. This was not very inspiring at all. I sat down with Dad one evening and we discussed some options.

The school was useless. They had career officers come in, but I have a hard time remembering what they actually did or said. Nothing, I suspect. Unemployment was low, anyway, so getting a job was not going to be too difficult. It was just a matter of trying to find the right one for you.

People still thought then that a job was for life. In other words what you trained up to become would be what you did for all your working life. In fact it might be possible to work for the same company too for 50 years. Of course those times and thoughts on life were disapering now and a job for life would be something of a rarity.

I'm quite sure that my dad did the legwork on the entire job searching, because he actually found something for me. I have no idea where the job prospect came from. All he said was,

"You have an interview down at the Dacorum College with a man who owns a private television rental company. I'll take you down there, so don't worry. Just be yourself and be well mannered."

And so it was that we went to the college and my dad showed me to this guy from a company called Weatherhead's who had come all the way over from Woburn Sands to interview me. He said to my dad that he could sit in on the interview. How odd all this now seems ... that you would sit in a room having a job interview with your dad sitting there. If someone today said to me,

"Can I bring me dad in with me for an interview?" I might just burst out laughing.

In those days there were no CVs, so the guy asked me lots of questions about electronics and what I was interested in. I explained that I had been making things out of the Philips Electronic Engineer's kits for a few years. He seemed impressed by my answers and my dad chipped in once or twice when I looked a bit lost. Then the interview was over, and the man made no secret of the fact that he thought I would make a good apprentice. I was in. I had had one interview and I had a job.

"You start in a week's time," said the man. "Report to the shop in Berkhamsted at nine a.m. on that Monday. We will send you the apprenticeship details in the post."

I was over the moon. I had no idea how much I would earn … maybe £20 or £30 a week … I would be rich. No such luck, of course. The paperwork arrived and I remember looking at this paperwork for many an hour. It detailed, among other things, the pay scale for each year that I would work, starting at £10 a week for the first year and rising a pound or sometimes two each year. Seeing the next five years of my working life mapped out in exactly what I would earn was a little soul-destroying. I would also work every Saturday and have half a day off on a Wednesday, and I would have two weeks paid holiday a year. All of this was a daunting prospect. School had been a breeze. What was this going to be like?

Still … it had to be – and I would be doing something of a trade, which would be far better than my counterparts working in factories. Having said that, my mate Baz was already working at Abbot Print and he was earning at least twice what I would be earning. It didn't sound fair then, but it sort of worked out in the end for me. Nothing stays the same for long in life, and you learn that things happen along the way that can't be planned for.

Weatherhead's had their shop smack bang in the middle of Berkhamsted high street. Dad took me over there the first day and showed me the bus route for my return in the evening. I would be using a bus each day to get there and back – which was no big deal, really. The shop was an old building: in fact, when you looked at it from the outside it was wonky and bent. It had been made up of maybe two or three buildings at some point, and it commanded quite a presence in the high street. Weatherhead's was a top-end TV and audio specialist. It specialised in TV rental, mainly, both high-end and at the lower end of the scale.

I walked into the shop as nervous as hell on that first day. How different this was from school: this was grown-up stuff now. I was considered to be a man. An attractive man in his thirties stood at the counter of the shop and I approached and introduced myself.

"I'm Richard Blackshire," I said. "I'm starting work here today."

The man smiled. He was young and tall, too, with tight curly hair. He wasn't what I expected: I was expecting someone much older, someone maybe more mature for this type of shop.

"Come along with me," he said, and took me past the office at the back which turned in on itself to face a narrow, steep staircase. "You will be working in the workshop most of the time," he said.

The landing at the top had several rooms coming off it. All the floors were wonky and uneven and made you feel as if you were drunk as you walked.

"How strange," I thought. The man had to duck a few times as the ceiling was also uneven in places. It was like walking through the crooked house featured in one of my old nursery stories.

We walked into the workshop. This was a longish room with a door at each end and a tiny window to the right which let in the only natural light for the room. Two men were standing in this room. One, a tall chap with flame-red hair and bright blue eyes, stood directly in front of me. He had a white coat on with a W on the top pocket and a few pens and other tools poking out of the top.

"This is Tony," said the man. "He is the engineer here, and you will be reporting to him for all your work." Tony gave a half smile and shook my hand. I had to admit that he looked a bit scary, but the whole situation was scary.

"This is Les," said the manager as he turned to face the second man. "He does all the domestic appliances for us. You know, like hair driers and vacuum cleaners."

"How do?" came the retort from a man who must have been in his sixties. He had slicked-back jet-black hair and a fag hanging out of his mouth. When he spoke the fag just stayed stuck to his lip as if stuck there with glue. All the time I knew Les he always seemed to have the same fag stuck to his lip.

"Hi," I said. Les continued to poke things into some vacuum cleaner he was mending.

"I'll leave you to it," said the man, and he was gone in a second.

That was it. That was me starting work – earning my crust, so to speak.

"What would they get me doing?" I thought. "I know nothing."

Tony was a man of few words in those early days. I didn't quite know if it was shyness or what it was. He was in his forties, I suspect, and wasn't married. He lived with his mother in a block of apartments in Berkhamsted. You kind of had to get to know Tony before he lightened up.

The approach here was that I would go around with Tony to people's houses, and basically learn about fixing TVs. I would carry the tools, and if something was needed from the van then I would go and fetch it. Initially I would be allowed to take the back off the TV, but would not be allowed to do anything else till I knew what I was doing. The first day felt strange as Tony said very little to me, but he was very kind and caring all the same.

As time went on our bond and relationship grew stronger. It took some time to get off the ground, but I really loved working with Tony. He was a lovely, really kind and sincere guy who really should have had more in his life than he had. We used to laugh a lot in the van about all sorts: mainly the customers we had just visited but sometimes the staff in the shop, who really were a mixed bunch.

I didn't drive, of course, and Tony did all the driving in the little green Morris Minor van. As time went on Tony showed me how to do specific jobs on the television sets at the houses we called on. I got used to an approach of finding out what the problem was very quickly. With four calls in the morning and four in the afternoon you had to evaluate very quickly whether to fix the fault or take the TV set back to the workshop. We had loan sets in the van, which we would lend to people while their set was repaired. There was a lot of lugging about of TVs. Colour TVs were no joke. They took two people to lift them as they were huge, and full of glass tubes and valves. Sometimes we had to go up several flights of stairs carrying something in excess of eighty pounds in weight. It was no surprise that this lifting would take its toll on my back in time. We would be given our jobs in the morning and then set off in the Moggy Minor (as we called it then). Tony would analyse the best route to take to get to each house in the most logical way. We would then be gone for the morning. After a few weeks I managed to get myself a few tools and my own toolbox. I felt like a proper TV engineer then.

Friday came around – and Friday was pay day, even though Saturday was a working day. I was handed my first very own pay packet with real money inside a brown paper envelope. I waited till lunchtime to open it. I looked at the slip. It said nine pounds-odd. I had not done a full week yet, and so my first pay was less than I would normally get. Still, nine quid was like a stackload of money compared to the fifty pence pocket money I had been getting. I knew full well what I would go and buy first with my wages. I wanted a cigarette lighter that I had seen in the high street: that's what I would buy.

Mum wanted a contribution to my food and board from me from now on, and she said that £1.50 a week would be acceptable. It always seemed a lot to me, but in hindsight I now understand. I just hoped that that money helped them a little, as they didn't have very much at all.

Our patch for house calls to fix TVs was mainly around the Berkhamsted and Tring areas. It was always an interesting day, as one minute we would be visiting some palatial gaff way out on the Ashridge estate and then the next minute we would be in some dirty, dark dwelling in the depths of Berko. It really was chalk and cheese, and I saw the insides of some remarkable dwellings during those couple of years I worked out of the Berko shop. It always surprised Tony and me that if we ever got a tip from a customer it would almost always be from the more working-class families: this was surprising, really. We got offered tea and coffee at some, and sometimes we really got teaed out by the time lunch came around. A quick drive back to the shop for the toilet was often needed.

Tony and I didn't have much time to look at the TVs that were sitting in the workshop for repair: we were out most of the day on calls. So how Weatherhead's dealt with this was that once a week an engineer and his apprentice would turn up from head office in Woburn Sands. Brian was the engineer's name, and Brian was a TV genius. Brian and his apprentice would work on the whole backlog of the sets whose problems we could not fathom out. They took back any they really struggled with to head office.

Two weeks into this job I was informed that I would be attending a training week at the head office in Woburn Sands. I had only just got over the shock of working when the prospect of going away from home for a week on my own for the first time hit me. I found this another daunting prospect, as I had never ever been away on my own. How would I cope? Woburn Sands sounded a huge distance away. Was it on the beach I wondered?

My dad took me over on the first day of training at Woburn Sands. I had my bag packed and some money in my pocket. I was dead nervous. I had no idea what to expect and, really, I was still quite immature. The week-long course would consist of lectures each day and some fault-finding on TV sets. Those attending had a mix of abilities. Some had been with the company a while and then you had me who had been with the company only a couple of weeks. How was I going to compete with the rest of the apprentices? This was no level playing field, and there was to be a test at the end of the week on Friday morning. Oh, hell...

The head office was like a mansion and stood in its own grounds. Our lectures were in grand, high-ceilinged rooms. We listened to all sorts, including semiconductor theory and fault-finding on TV sets. All the guys were nice there, and the guy leading the course (who was the guy who had actually interviewed me) understood that I was new to all this. I did, however, find the whole thing very stressful. I wanted to do well but I still knew very little. I took a lot on board but I had problems finding the faults on the TVs when the tests came around.

The other issue for me, of course, was that I was staying on my own in Woburn Sands at one of the pubs near the railway level crossing. No one else was staying over so I spent all the evenings on my own. I hated it, to be honest. This was way outside my comfort zone, and Friday could not come around quickly enough.

When Friday came and I had my bag packed up at the house waiting for my dad to pick me up, I really felt quite angry. You might think I would be happy it was over – but for this young man (who was very immature still) all he could manage was a massive stroppy mood, so much so that my trip back to Hemel with my dad was almost in complete silence. I was so damn stroppy all the way back. I just could not wait to get back home and get my arse down the George to meet up with my mates. We drove in darkness as it was now November time, and passed through Dunstable. I remember my dad commenting on something as we passed the foot of the Downs. He said to me (and this stuck so firmly in my head),

"Look up there, lad."

He was pointing to where the California Ballroom was. "You would probably like it up there, you know. There's music and dancing and bands." How damn right my dad was, but he had a stroppy kid in the car who just grunted at this. However, I ignored his advice and it would be a year or so before the words California Ballroom would appear again in conversation.

Another few months after the dreaded course I was told that I would now be going to college for day release to go on a City & Guilds course in TV electronics. None of this had been explained to me at the interview, and it fazed me a bit when I was told. I thought I would be learning all I needed from Tony, but this was not to be. The course I would have to attend was run from Welwyn Garden City, which was miles away.

Thank God my dad knew everything about public transport. He helped me out no end in these times. He knew exactly what I needed to do – and actually the 314a bus from the Boot pub would take me all the way there, almost to the door. But – Dad being Dad – he made sure I knew what was what, and he drove me over there on the first day and showed me the bus stop to go to on my way back. That bus trip once a week took an hour each way. The double-decker took ages as it lumbered up through Hemel to Leverstock Green, then towards St Albans, Hatfield, and Welwyn. It stopped countless times along the route but only once did it let me down, when it stranded me in St Albans.

At this time my life seemed to be about buses. I had my daily bus to catch in Apsley opposite the Fountain pub each morning. I had a choice of two buses: the Green Line bus or a more local double-decker. I stood at that stop every day, sometimes in the rain and cold, wishing the bus would come. There was no cover there, as it was a request stop. Sometimes the bus didn't come and I would then walk along to the bus station at Two Waters and grab an alternative one coming out of the station. Mostly I was on time for work and I never got told off. The college day was much the same. Waiting for the return bus in winter at the bottom of Lemsford Road was not a pleasant experience. It was mostly dark and cold and there was no shelter. You just wished and wished for that bus to come, willing it to come around the corner and save you from the cold.

Weatherhead's wanted me to be able to drive.

Weatherhead's had a master plan up its sleeve, and at no point did they hint at what they wanted me to do or become. Once I could drive everything would change.

In Cars

1973-To Date

Cars warrant a section, I think, because without a mode of transport almost everything we did as teenagers would have been hopeless. As a family my brother was the first to buy a car: it was a Morris Minor 1000 cc.. It was an old second-hand car (of course) and had its problems, but we thought it was fantastic. The family actually had a car.

This opened up possibilities for the family, and although it was Rob's car he used it to take us to places we would not have ordinarily gone to. This was the early sixties, and the road was still relatively free from being cluttered by cars. Hardly anyone had a car. It was still a luxury item, but as things got better for people after the war people started to acquire certain luxuries such as cars. The rise in the standard of living was slow at first but gathered pace through the sixties, as with items like televisions, fridges, and washing machines British homes started to enter the modern age. A car was still expensive, but for many it became essential for carrying out their work. As my father was essentially a salesman in the paper trade, making him as mobile as possible was an obvious choice. For years he used public transport, trains, and buses to get him to places. He would maybe see one or two customers a day, but with a car this would all change.

So it was that in the later sixties my dad obtained a lovely two-tone Ford Cortina Mk 1 Super with automatic transmission. Boy, this was a car and a half. Rob took me out in it a few times without Dad and showed it some pace. For the time in the 1960s this thing flew like a bat out of hell. It had a 1600 cc. engine and a Borg-Warner gear box with its three automatic gears. When you kicked the accelerator pedal down the car would just push you back in your seat.

So we were a two-car family, and the street also suddenly became full of cars. Some parked along one side of the road while others had to park on the hardstanding between the pavement and the road. Hardly anyone had a garage in those days, and there were certainly no garages next to people's houses: this was a road of council house. If you wanted a garage you paid the council to rent a garage around the back of the houses in the garage forecourt.

Now cars then were certainly a different kettle of fish to what we know today. Cars then frequently went wrong and you had to know how to fix minor mechanical issues yourself. Cars failed and cars rusted, and it was either fixing stuff on the engine or patching up the bodywork. Both Rob and Dad had a cardboard box in the shed. In each there would have been spray paint, car filler, glass fibre, oxide undercoat paint, brushes, trowels, metal gauze, and rust inhibitor. At least twice a year they would be out in the street pulling off rust lumps from the car body panels and sanding down rust bubbles on the surface. You had to get in there quickly and deal with the rust before it really took hold. They would be out there days patching up, rubbing down, painting undercoat, and then applying several final sprays of paint from a can. The results were variable: some held, and some lasted another year before a lump of rusted metal and filler would just drop out on to the road.

On Rob's Moggy Minor he once had a perforation of rust holes around the front lights. There was so much rust here that the light assembly almost fell out. There was nothing holding it in.

If it wasn't patching your car up then it was fiddling with batteries, points, plugs, air filters, etc.. The timing of the engine was controlled by something called the points, which basically opened and closed and let power through to each spark plug. These small, cheap devices were prone to problems. The gaps across the contacts needed constant resetting – and you were forever out under the bonnet with feeler gauges, setting the small gap that was needed. And if it wasn't the points then the plugs needed taking out, cleaning, and resetting with the feelers. Winter was the worst time. I don't know how many times I woke in my bed in winter to the sounds of someone trying to start their car. I used to lie there thinking,

287

"Come on, fire now," and, "Nearly, nearly … it's almost there."

Then suddenly you would know the battery was flat and that would be it. Batteries just didn't last – and quite frequently Rob and Dad would bring their car batteries in out of the car, connect them to a charger by the fireplace, and set them off bubbling all night while they charged up from the mains electricity. In the morning you then had the task of taking the battery to the car, connecting it up, and then seeing if the car would start. Cars got too cold sometimes in the winter, and Rob and Dad would sometimes leave an old overcoat over the engine at night to insulate it from the cold and frost. Dad used to tie something to the steering wheel so he didn't forget that a coat was under the bonnet before started up.

So where did I come into all this? Well … I was working at Weatherhead's in Berkhamsted and was asked by work to start to take driving lessons, which I did. Dad then surprised me one day. He gave me the keys to the Cortina and some L-plates.

"Wow," I exclaimed. "Driving lessons with you?"

"Yes," said Dad. "In your own car."

"What do you mean, 'My car'?" I exclaimed.

"I mean it's now your car, son. I'm getting a new one though the company. This car is now yours."

So it was that I was now the proud owner of a car.

Now owning and driving an automatic and then going and having paid lessons in a manual car was problematical. It took me ages to learn to drive. I just could not get the gears to work for me. I have no idea how many lessons I had: it just went on and on for ever. I failed my first test in Berko. I hit the curb while reversing down a hill. But I passed the next test and, boy, was that a day to remember.

I'm not sure anyone can quite describe the feeling you get when you pass a driving test. It's almost on a parallel with sex … it's that release … that realisation. I passed, and I was sooo happy. The instructor drove me home. He said it would be a good idea for me to just calm down.

I got home. My Cortina was parked outside as it usually was and I ripped the L-plates off and went inside to tell my parents. I had my tea but was constantly looking out the window at my car. It really did feel like my car because now I could get in it at any time and drive. I actually felt like an animal must feel when it's let out of a cage. I sat and ate my tea, thinking,

"I can go anywhere now. I can go to the coast … anywhere. "

The phone rang. It was the twins.

"How did you get on, mate?" said Martin.

"Passed," I said. "I bloody passed"

"Right," said Martin. "We'll expect you here at seven, then. You can take us down the George."

I didn't mind, of course. They just wanted to be part of my happy news. I got in my car all alone. I wasn't sure who in the street was watching me … maybe no one, but maybe everyone. God, it felt so strange in a car on your own with no one to tell you to put it in gear or,

"Do this. Do that…"

You're on your own. You're empowered now to drive a potentially lethal machine. I started up the Mk1 and shoved the column-changer gear selector over to reverse. The car thumped as the box selected the right gear.

"Here we go," I said to myself. "I'm free at last."

Certainly the car changed everything for me. It changed my world in an instant. I had wheels now and I could be places when I wanted, and not when others chose to take me. Some friends became better friends because I had a car. Some girls liked me more because I had a car. It didn't matter much to me what other people's agendas were. I had my car and I owned it outright: it was mine and I could do what I liked to it.

Of course, I furnished it as soon as I could with the best radio player I could afford. I needed music in my car, and this had not been a priority for my dad when he owned it.

My lovely maroon and grey two-tone Cortina lasted me a few years before it was apparent that it was on its last legs. Cars never really lasted much beyond ten years in those days. I had to get rid of it and I managed to sell it in the paper for a few quid. I was sad when it went, probably the saddest I have been when selling a car. However, she had done me good service and seen me through some important years, taking me to work and college and doing me proud.

I needed another car and thankfully I had saved up some money to get my first car that I bought with my own money. Dad was a bit unsure about what I chose but to be honest I had to get something, and I had a limited amount of money to spend. Thankfully what I got turned out to be a good car in respect of its mechanics and the rust situation.

The cactus-green Triumph Herald was an estate car with a 1200 cc. engine. This was a different beast from the Cortina. This time I had a manual box and a nice wooden dashboard. The car was more basic than the Cortina. It wasn't as fast and it wasn't as comfortable but it was a sex wagon on wheels... As it was an estate I had to think about what I could use the space for in the back. Luckily Auntie Elsie had some nice plain carpet offcuts at the time, and I used one of these to furnish the back of the estate. It looked comfy in there. In fact it looked like you could have a party in the back ... perhaps even sleep in it.

The Herald was great but it needed some care in driving. The wheels and how they turned were a bit strange to get used to but I managed it, and it saw me through yet another part of my interesting days of girls and the Cali. The car didn't go fast, and if I went on the motorway then sixty was your limit. There would be vibrating past this point, to where you just didn't feel safe. Sixty was top whack but it was nice to drive, and I loved its stubby little gear shift on the transmission tunnel. It felt a little like a sports car.

I never had a car for very long: maybe a year to eighteen months, and then it was changed. That's just how it went then. I had a string of cars after the Herald: a Ford Zodiac, a Mk2 Cortina, a Mk 3 Cortina, and the terrible Vauxhall VX 1800.

Apart from the Vauxhall VX all my cars seemed a good purchase and did me well.

More Tails from the Rank

1973

This is what we were listening to at this time at the Top Rank:

Eddie Kendricks: 'Keep on Truckin''
Ike & Tina Turner: 'Nutbush City Limits'
James Brown: 'Get Up (I Feel Like Being a) Sex Machine'
James Brown 'Make it Funky'
David Bowie: 'Space Oddity'
Barry White: 'Never, Never Gonna Give Ya Up'
Marvin Gaye: 'Let's Get it On'
Stevie Wonder: 'Superstition'

From that first outing to Watford and all the excitement that went on, Top Rank became a must for a Saturday night. Forget the George or cards with the family or whatever was going on. You had to be going to the Rank. "Be there or be square" was the motto, and everyone we knew wanted a slice of the cake.

Our little club expanded, and at times there were quite a few going on that 322 bus: sometimes as many as ten of us would leave from the George pub and sit on the wall by the bus stop. Although we always got the bus from outside the pub our return journey was almost always the train back late at night, usually the last train too.

I loved the Rank with all its different aspects. The night was, of course, always about having fun and trying to pick up girls. I wondered what had happened on that first night. It was so easy. Had I picked up a girl, or in fact had she picked me up?

I used to watch Bill and Eamonn out on the dance floor. They had all the talk: all the blarney and the blag they needed to get who they wanted. Bill had some strange chat-up lines in those days just to get in conversation with the girls and get the ball rolling. It's all about confidence, of course, and going in there and just speaking up. In fact it probably didn't matter what you said.

291

One of Bill's classic ones – I never understood how it worked – involved walking up to a girl on the dance floor. Bill would be smiling at her.

"Hey, babe, has anyone told you that you have dandruff on your shoes?"

The girl would look down in stunned silence at her shoes, maybe reflecting back to when she got dressed to come out. Had she forgotten her panties? Bill then would smile again.

"Only kidding, babe. Fancy a drink?"

That was it. The net closed, and off Bill would go with some stunning bird on his arm. Could I do that? Erm, no. I lacked the front and the confidence that Bill had. I would need a different approach.

On subsequent visits to the Rank I had more time to explore the floor area and walk around the areas downstairs and upstairs fully. I wanted to understand where all the best vantage points might be for chatting up girls. Upstairs was very dark, and it seemed to be a good place to take a girl if you had pulled one. There was some seating around the balcony area and over at one side there was a glass dance floor which, apparently, they could light up. This was never in operation on a Saturday, and I suspect that it was used at other times in the week. It was dark and dead here, with dark walls and no one around. You could lose yourself in this area if you needed to. I walked around up here for a bit one night and found what looked like a door towards one of the back walls.

"What's this?" I thought. "Maybe an extra loo ... or a secret room?"

Maybe the Rank had another area you could go to that no one had found. Had I indeed found the secret entrance to a special place in the Rank?

"Hold on," I thought. "I can hear noises coming from the other side of the wall. Hey, what's going on in there? There are people in there."

I pulled on the handle. It was stiff, as if either something was holding it shut or pulling from the other side. I pulled even harder, and the door swung open silently on its hinges.

"Hey ... fuck off, will yer?" was the unexpected retort that came out of the darkness.

"Bill? Bill, is that you in there?"

"Dick? Is that you, Dick?"

"Yeah ... it's me, mate. What are you doing in there, Bill?"

I was stunned, to say the least. I could not see far in but this was certainly Bill's distinctive voice, now a little calmer now he knew it was me.

"Dick, mate ... have you got any more condoms?"

"You what?" I said. "What are you doing in there, Bill? Are you having a wank or something?"

Then I heard another noise, some shuffling, and a girl's voice for sure.

"Oh, Bill ... come back in, Bill ... Bill, I'm sooo hot for you."

"You got someone else in there, Bill?" I said, with a grin on my face.

Bill came over to the opening but didn't come out from what was obviously a large broom cupboard-cum-store room. His trousers were unbuttoned and he was holding them up with one hand. There was also a large bulge in his underpants.

"Look, have you got any rubbers, mate? I used all mine up. She's a fucking nympho..."

I got my wallet out and opened it to reveal the pristine Durex package.

"In case of emergencies break glass." That's what it should have said on my packets. This was an emergency OK ... and so the glass was broken and I handed Bill the packets.

"Here you go, mate. Have fun."

"Thanks, Dick. I'll buy you a pint later, mate. Now close that fucking door."

It was not long before my other schoolmate Chaz wanted to come down to the Rank and try his luck. Chaz was good fun but he could be a bit awkward at times. He tended to be late arriving places or he forgot things like his fags or we needed petrol when we needed to get somewhere quickly … or his car fell to bits or his bike would not start or his flies were undone. You name it, and Chaz was prone to it. But he was a good best buddy for quite a time and I ended eventually being best man at his wedding.

Chaz usually brought along his friend from his road in Kings Langley. Graham was a great guy to have around. He was bright and had the knack of keeping Chaz in check as well as the rest of us when we ran adrift and got stupid. A few others teamed up with us and the mix of anyone going out on a Saturday changed from week to week. Baz had dropped out somewhat as he had become loved-up with a bird from Hemel. Neil and Jim (another good mate, who was from his ice cream round) had met two birds: Karen and Carol were their names. Carol went out with Jim and they eventually ended up marrying. Neil dated Karen for a bit, and then it seemed that she preferred his brother Martin. When Martin signed up for the Royal Navy he asked Baz if Baz could keep an eye on her while he was away at sea.

"Oh, yes. Sure I will," said Baz. He kept an eye, OK … a bit more than an eye, I would say, because it wasn't long before they were engaged. You can see how things changed around with girls in those days. Nothing stayed the same for very long at all.

Chaz and I went out every Saturday night to the Top Rank. There were always a few of us and we always started off getting a table and some drinks. We liked to get a good table near the dance floor where we could spot any potential crumpet, as we called it. Girls and guys were the same, and it wasn't long before the term cattle market was born to describe the activity at these establishments.

The disco music played. There would be an Elton John number or maybe Slade and then your usual Gary Glitter, although at one point the DJ refused to play Gary Glitter because of the stomping. In fact his records became so damaged that some would not play even if no one was stomping. The toons (as we called them) were your usual current top twenty chart stuff and a little older sometimes, with the odd old Beatles record thrown in. DJs were always mindful that the success of an evening depended on people dancing, and so certain records were known as floor fillers – in other words, records that would guarantee getting a good percentage of the kids up dancing.

Slade had just finished, and the next toon started to play. A thumping beat with a defined hard back beat was evident. Those who had just danced to Slade and 'Get Down and Get With It' left the dance floor. A different set of punters walked on from the tables. This floor change was purely down to the music, and I noted that these people were dressed slightly differently to us.

"What's going on?" I said to Chaz.

"I don't know, to be honest with you. It's something different, for sure."

In front of us were three girls dancing with a young skinny black guy. The black guy was really moving and using some really complicated footwork. His legs were a blur as they kind of twisted in and out of each other in a speedy repetitive way. Michael Jackson had not yet perfected the signature style of dancing we would become familiar with later (he was only fifteen at the time) but if one had been able to see the future one would have noted the similarity between what this guy was doing and Michael Jackson, the soon-to-be master of funky footsteps . In fact much later in life I would understand that the guy singing on the record would be the guy who would influence Michael Jackson the most.

The girls dancing in front of us were not doing the usual melodic trot from side to side as was usually the case with the chart toons. They were in a sort of line and they were dancing these strange set of steps in unison.

"What is it, guys?" I let out to the party at our table. "Who is this?"

"James Brown," said Jeff from behind me. "He's a black American singer and he does all this funk stuff."

"Funk?" I said. "What's funk?"

Chaz and I sat there transfixed by what was going on, as the singer went on about being some sort of sex machine and getting it up. That night the funk entered both Chaz and my soul for good. The music and the beat were infectious. We were listening to what was known as "on the one beat". We wanted more. We needed to learn more. We craved the funk.

"We need to collar those girls, Chaz," I said as Chaz was now searching in his non-crush-proof Kent fag packet for the elusive last fag. Jeff piped up,

"I'll do it."

Jeff went over to the girls, who had stopped gyrating now and who were standing on the edge of the floor watching the black guy. Another toon had started immediately on from the last. It was 'Make It Funky', another James Brown number. The rhythm was even sharper, and the very fit black guy went into even faster steps and at one point reversed what he was doing in an instant.

I saw Jeff chat to what looked like the youngest of the three girls. She nodded and talked to the others, who then looked around and came over to our table.

"You're a star, Jeff," I thought to myself. Jeff was good at chatting up girls and he had the nerve to just go over and do the talk and the trapping. It was always the opening gambit that Charlie and I didn't like. Jeff was a master at it and probably even more successful than Bill, at times.

I could see now that the one talking to Jeff was indeed two or three years younger than us. She might have been as young as fourteen but she had a big chest, and that's what probably got her into the Rank. She didn't really look her age in the dim lighting. The other two smiled at me and Chaz.

"I'm J," said the ringleader, "And these are my two sisters. We're from North Watford. Where you boys from?"

We talked openly about what we liked and the girls explained about the dancing and funk music. They explained that this was what they liked and that there were other funky bands, but nothing much was played at the Rank apart from some James Brown. The toon had finished and the black guy walked off as David Bowie started up with 'Starman'. The black guy was not with these girls at all, and didn't bother to come over afterwards. His attraction was just the dancing, which he had performed and executed with precision and power.

J attached herself to me: she was the oldest of the sisters. She had an attractive smile and a cheeky way: she was just a normal girl from North Watford. Chaz seemed to hook up with the middle sister, who was slim and attractive. So it seemed we had scored for the night, thanks to Jeff. I remember thinking,

"Thank God Vic is not here on this night." I'm not sure he could have contained himself.

The night was a good one. We all got on well. We danced to the fast ones and slow-danced to the smoochy ones. We chatted and drank and had a bit of a kiss and cuddle at times. J and I even went upstairs to the quieter area for some private talking and kissing. We sat on the floor up there with our legs out right next to Bill's secret cupboard, and talked and laughed till it was time to go home.

"Hey, why don't you all come back to our place for coffee?" said J, once we had got back to the tables. "It's only up the road – and Mum and Dad will be in bed, for sure."

"Sure," I said. "That sounds great."

My head was full of brown ale and the scent from J's perfume. If she had suggested jumping in the cut I would probably have gone along with it.

"Is anyone else up for this?" I asked my two chums. They both were, of course, but I had this nagging feeling in the back of my head. Booze is great for having a good time – but then it suppresses other things too, like logic.

We all set out from the Rank. It was gone midnight by this point and I had no idea where we were heading ... somewhere in North Watford – but I didn't know where North Watford was, anyway, and I don't think any of my mates knew either. It was a bit of a walk to The Harebreaks from the Rank – but we were young and, really, distance was never an issue to us. This was an adventure and we were with our new-found birds.

We arrived at the road the girls lived in and were told to keep the noise down as their dad would not be best happy if he was woken up. The house was quite basic, with simple furnishings. There was a fireplace with stacked-up fag butts in it. We were made welcome by the girls, who indeed made coffee for us in what seemed very humble surroundings. This was all a bit different from what we had in Hemel, but we were never ones to pour scorn on those who maybe didn't have much money. Jeff and I were from working-class backgrounds and lived on a council estate. Chaz, was more middle class. We all accepted anyone and anything different with a smile.

We drank our coffee and chatted for about an hour. Then it dawned on us ... how the hell would we get back from here? The last bus and train would have gone by now. We had two options: either stay the night or walk back to Hemel from The Harebreaks. In fact we only had one option, because the girls said that Dad would not take too kindly to seeing all these guys in the living room when he came down for his morning cuppa. The way Dad was portrayed we didn't want to meet him either.

The three of us got up and said our farewells to the girls. Some lingering kissing went on with hand-holding, till fingers parted and we were out of the door.

We walked outside on to the pavement of the long road that is The Harebreaks.

"Which way do we go, guys?" I said, with a sense of, "Oh, shit. Where are we?"

Luckily Jeff had some idea as to what direction to head in. I'm not sure if it was more luck than judgement but walking up The Harebreaks took us to the A41, and it was then quite easy to see the route back. I have subsequently calculated that it's nine miles from where we started back to my house, and that does not include the walk from the Rank to the girls' house. We were all wearing big platform clodhoppers that night, as we always did and – as you might expect – this was not the sort of footwear to be wearing to walk a distance of nine miles.

It started off OK, but by Hunton Bridge our feet were as sore as hell. We stopped many times for rests and, at one point – when we hit the traffic lights by one of the train bridges – one of our party had the bright idea of stomping up and down on the road to see if the traffic lights would change. Oh, what a great idea that was. When I eventually walked up the ash path, the final part of the marathon, I was a lonely figure for sure. It was just getting light and about four o'clock in the morning. I had not been able to contact my parents to say what was happening. God knows how worried they actually were. I got in and went straight to bed, exhausted.

Chaz and I dated the girls by seeing them at the Rank each Saturday. I'm not sure that there was any other way we could have seen them. They would sometimes ring me on the phone at home and once my dad answered the call. Later in life he confided in me that they (Mum and Dad) were both worried as to what was going on with these girls. For me it was just an adventure, but I guess I know exactly what they were worried about. Every parent must be.

As we didn't drive we could never see girls easily, but on one occasion Vic persuaded his mate – who was older than us, and married – to drive over to North Watford one evening and meet the girls in a pub. We were told to meet up in the Verulam Arms (as it was called then). It was a largish estate-type pub and quite packed out. The four of us sat at a table waiting for the girls to arrive.

We sat drinking our pints and just taking in the scene, as you do in new establishments you visit. The pub was really busy, and a lot of people were talking in quite a loud way. I don't think we were even aware that anything was wrong, as none of us had picked up on the commotion in the corner. I'm not sure who saw it first, but when we did all our faces were filled with horror.

A guy staggered past our table knocking into it slightly as he passed, and there was quite clearly a knife sticking out of his back. Our driver took charge.

"Guys, we get out of here now."

We didn't need telling twice, and we hopped it out of the side entrance and made it to the car that was parked over the road. Then things happened quickly, and just as our driver started the car up the police arrived.

"That was lucky," Vic said. "We would have got mixed up in that if we had stayed." I don't think we ever went back there after, and I'm not sure that we saw the girls again either.

I used to go to day release college at Welwyn Garden City at that time, and a group of guys I met there became my mates from college. We used to chat about this and that when we went for our mid morning tea. I used to go on about the Top Rank and how good it was to the other lads there. The other guys, who were from around the Kimpton and Codicote area, said that they went to the California Ballroom – which was, in their humble opinion, the best too. It was like a bit of a joke among us, because I would argue that where I went on a Saturday was the best and Tony and his mates would justify their Saturday trapping place. There was of course only one way to settle this. Tony said,

"This week, right … we will drive down to Watford to your Top Rank this Saturday, but on the following week you need to get your arse over to the Cali."

In fact this was a good idea from Tony but Tony had a car, and while it was easy for him to get to Watford how the hell would we get to Dunstable?

True to their word the guys arrived that Saturday, and we met them at the Rank. They were impressed and had a good night, meeting my mates and integrating really well. We all got on fine, and it's interesting how guys just get on and spark off in a good way when meeting new people.

"This place is really cool," Tony said. "We will deffo come down here again."

I think one or two of them pulled that night, and that was always good for morale with the lads. As we said our goodbyes Tony said,

"I'll see you at college in the week, mate … and remember you're coming to the Cali next Saturday."

As they left my head was obviously in deep thought as to how to get to the Cali. Chaz came over to me and said,

"I think I have a solution to this. Let's ask Graham, my neighbour. He has a car. We need to chat him up and maybe bung him some money, but I reckon I can get him to take us to Dunstable."

That was our plan, then.

The Practical Joke that Backfired

1972

Before we leave the era of the Rank completely, there was one incident that happened one night which should not be missed out.

We normally got the 322 bus into Watford in the evening but our return was almost always on the train because it left that bit later, and we knew that we would be able to stay to the end of the disco. Staying to the end at the Rank (and at any disco) meant you were guaranteed the slow dance, as it was always played last thing. Also, getting the train back meant that we could all stay together as a group. Some of us would get off at Apsley and some at Hemel station. Getting that last train back was the perfect end to the evening.

On this occasion a problem arose. We got to Watford station to find the ticket office shut. Normally there was always someone to sell us our single return back. Although it fazed us a bit it didn't stop us walking on to the platform and hopping on to the last slow train from Euston to Bletchley. We thought nothing of it, to be honest. We had been drinking and there was a lot of merriment and bravado on the carriage that night as we settled down in our seats. It was the late-night last train and it was full of lads like us, talking and messing about. I suppose to the general public we might have looked a bit intimidating but we were not like that at all. We were just enjoying ourselves.

Someone had got a loo roll out of the bogs and had chucked it down the carriage like a streamer. Someone threw it back up, and there was an endless loop of tangled bog roll passing over the passengers' heads and passing under the seats. We thought this was so much fun, but it had to end as we approached Apsley station. We said our goodbyes to those going on, staggered up the carriage, opened the door, and stumbled out into what can only be described as a scene from a horror movie. The lights, noise, and merriment ceased in an instant as soon as the carriage door slammed shut. Humanity was inside the train, and we were no longer part of it.

Four of us stood on the platform for a minute, adjusting to the darkness. It was foggy, and the mist enveloped the whole station like something from a Jack the Ripper scenario. There was no one on the platform but us – at least, we didn't think so. The train had left now, and I could only just make out its single red warning light as it disappeared into the darkness. We were left in total silence.

"Hey," whispered Chaz. "We've got no bloody tickets, have we?"

"Nope," I said, feeling in my pockets for the tickets I knew were not there. "Never mind," I said. "There doesn't seem to be anyone here."

"Nope," said another of us. "There is someone there. See that light halfway down the other side? That's coming from the exit. The office light's on, for sure."

"We are going to get stung here, for sure…"

These wise words came from someone in our group who knew of stations and railway dealings and ticket offices and inspectors. Not having a ticket would not be an excuse, and all hell might be to pay here.

"Look," said the voice of reason. "I'll go down, like, to where the light is. I'll see who is on, like, chat 'em up for a bit … you know, be friendly. I'll keep 'em talking and you guys can climb over the fence. It'll be easy. It's foggy, anyways. Give me 'arf a min to get down there, and then get over the fence. Make it snappy, like, cos I won't be able to keep 'em talking too long."

He was gone in a flash, and we had no time to discuss the whys or wherefores of this sure-fire plan. We had no bloody tickets and we were standing on a ghost platform getting cold. The station would now be closed up. That was the last train: we had to act quickly.

"OK, let's go," I said. The biggest of the three of us gave Chaz and me a bunk-up over what was quite a low fence. It was probably about five feet high and nothing, really, that we could not scramble up – after all, we were quite fit young men. We all made it over, and

303

found ourselves on the other side of the station in the area where people would turn their cars around after dropping passengers off. There was no one there, thank God. There were no security cameras in those days. They hadn't been invented.

"OK," I said. "We still need to get past the opening into the station where the ticket office is."

Whoever was in there was bound to see us if we just walked past.

"We need to run, guys, OK? Run like the wind and don't look back," I said.

So we ran and we pelted down the slope of the road that leads up to the station. As we ran I could hear something. There was some banging and crashing but we ran and we ran until we got to the bottom road, and even then we didn't stop much. Where our other friend was remained a complete mystery. In fact we would not find this out until the next day, when the police turned up at my house.

Mum and Dad were quite cool when Mr Policeman called at 18 Lower Barn the next evening. I was not so cool, of course. I had no idea really why he was here. I was marched into the dining room to talk to the officer, and Dad stayed in there with us with his watchful eye on events.

The policeman asked me questions about the night before, about the station, and about what had happened. I told them all I knew, expecting to get some sort of fine for ticket evasion. But the ticket – or lack of it – was not the issue here. I had no idea till the policeman told me that the events that had taken place involved our friend and the station master and the departures board: one being used against the other, it would seem.

"Oh," I said. "I didn't realise."

Dad said,

"What happens next?"

"Well," said the copper. "We have already charged your son's friend, so this is really a formality." As soon as the copper had gone I got on the phone to Chaz to warn him.

Chaz was in the middle of the street talking to our other friend when the copper's car came around the corner in his car to interview them both. The copper wound down his window.

"Been tipped off, have we, lads?" It seems that the guilty look on my two mates' faces in the cop car lights was enough to say that they had been warned of the visit.

The *Gazette* called it *The practical joke that backfired*. We didn't have to go to court and I think our friend just got a telling-off and a fine. Needless to say, we kept out of trouble after that. Well ... nearly, anyway.

California Ballroom

1973

This is what we were listening to at this time:

Harold Melvin & The Blue Notes: 'The Love I Lost'
The Isley Brothers: 'That Lady'
The Temptations: 'Hey Girl (I Like Your Style)'
Ohio Players: 'Funky Worm'
David Bowie: 'Life on Mars?'
Roxy Music: 'Pyjamarama'
Hot Chocolate: 'Brother Louie'

Tony had convinced us that it was a good idea for us to experience each other's disco clubs on a Saturday night. After visiting our Top Rank it was therefore our turn to go to the Cali.

Chaz had chatted up his mate with the Ford Escort, and we had arranged to meet down the George and to go from there. We could only take five people – and that included the driver – so Chaz, Billy, the driver, and I – along with one other chosen from our usual party – would be going. The rest went on the bus as usual to the Rank.

This was exciting to be going in a car on a Saturday. It felt posh … upmarket. We felt special as we crammed into Graham's small Mk1 Escort. We chatted and laughed as we drove along the Leighton Buzzard road out of Hemel and then turned up right towards Studham and the Downs. I was thinking,

"This is exciting, for sure … but the Rank…"

I loved the Rank. I felt a little homesick to be going somewhere else. In fact I felt a bit cheated out of my Saturday.

"Oh, well," I thought. "It's just one Saturday. You will be back at the Rank next week."

The drive is all countryside and I had no real idea where we were going, although Graham seemed to know exactly where we should be heading. He was a very bright young man, and I'm glad he was in charge on that night.

The flat part of the Downs road soon turns into a steep hill as it approaches Dunstable. As we sped down the hill and Graham used the gears to slow the Escort down we could see some bright lights at the bottom.

"That's it, guys," said Graham. "That's the Cali, for sure."

Graham pulled into a parking space only one or two away from that familiar Ford Anglia or Angle Box, as people sometimes called it. It was Tony's souped-up pride and joy.

We were early in relation to the opening times, but we were bang on the expected time Tony said we should get there for. Tony wanted to meet us and take us in. He wanted to show off the place and just make us feel at home. We looked up at the Cali. It was huge, as far as we could tell. It was dark now, but we could see the outline of the building.

"Is this all the Cali, then?" I said to Tony.

"Yep. This is it, guys. This is all the Cali," said Tony.

Tony introduced his friends once again but we had all met at the Rank the previous week. There would not be any issues here as we had all bonded well at the Rank, and new friendships had been struck.

"Let's go in, then," said Billy, eager to see what the crumpet might be like in Dunstable.

We walked down to the lower levels, where the entrance was. The Cali seemed to have several levels and buildings, all blending into the rise that meets the Downs. It was massive. There was already a bit of a queue starting and we could see many teens walking up from Dunstable from where a strange-looking odd building stood.

"What's that?" I said to Tony.

"Oh, that's the Windsock pub. It's kind of a meeting place some people go to before they come here."

This strange building had two points in its roof and what looked like a ski jump in between. It looked unreal, futuristic, and exciting.

307

"We can go for a drink in there some time, guys," said Tony. "That's if you come back."

He had a grin on his face. He bloody well knew, didn't he? It was a knowing grin – the grin you get when someone just knows. Tony was enjoying this far too much.

We entered the main ticketing area where a ticket office stood and a large cloakroom was also situated.

"It all seems nice so far," I said to Chaz and Billy.

"OK," said Tony. "Gather round." This was starting to feel like some sort of tour guide's outing at a stately home. We huddled around Tony and he started his tour.

"Right," he said. "Off to the right here is Devil's Den, but we won't be going in there just yet. We'll go straight up to the main floor and off to the Hillside Bar for a drink."

"Hold on," I said to Tony. "Are you saying that this place has more than one dance floor?"

"Sure, it does," said Tony, with a smile. "It has at least two dance floors and four bars, all separate."

"What?" said Billy. "Are you saying that there are four fucking bars in this place?"

"Yes, I am," replied Tony. "Did I not tell you this before?"

No, he had not bloody told us any of this, and he bloody knew it. He had kept the secret of the Cali quiet until he could show it off. He had even said at the Rank how nice it was there, and he must have known in his heart that what he would be showing us was far beyond what the Rank was.

We followed Tony up two flights of stairs till we entered a huge open-plan dance floor. The lack of people at this time meant that we could look around and take in the scene that presented itself. There were no tables here like at the Rank and no seating near the dance floor. It was all wall-to-wall and wall-to-stage areas for dancing. Around the walls, and covering every inch of wall and ceiling space, were panels which displayed projected moving oil images. It was bloody magical. I could not take my eyes off it. The whole wall, all three sides, was a living mass. Splodges of oil in all colours were projected on to the walls using special projectors. Tony said,

"Oh, yeah. Oil projectors … You won't have seen them, before will you?"

With our mouths still open and looking in wonderment we tried to say,

"No."

It's difficult to describe that night, really. You kind of know what you like, and it becomes the norm for you … and then someone shows you something else – something better. It's like jumping from one cliff edge to another. You're safe where you are, but you know really you need to jump over to another place. The Rank was my safe cliff edge and I felt secure there. Where I was jumping to was awe-inspiring. This place was just amazing … an Aladdin's cave.

Tony took us up to the Hillside Bar, which basically took us around the back of the stage area where a bar opened up into a long extensive seating area. The bar was maybe twice the length of the one at the Rank and took up the whole length of the room. There were chairs and tables along it, with booths you could sit in. We got a drink, which lasted all of fifteen minutes, before Tony said,

"OK, we're off now."

"Where?" said Chaz. "We only just got here."

"The Vista bar," said Tony.

Off we went, again following Tony's lead, back out across the dance floor to where we had come in, then up another flight of stairs to yet another bar.

"God, how big is this place?" I thought.

"Let's have a quick half in here, I think, chaps – cos we've still got more to go, and I want you on your feet for the night and staying out of trouble."

A swift half was downed in the Vista bar. We went back out of the Vista bar and up yet another staircase which took us much higher … and now we were away from the music we could hear on the main dance floor. Tony announced,

"This is the Pool Bar."

"Wow," said Billy. "Fucking ace ... pool tables."

There was indeed a large number of pool tables in a very large area serviced by yet another bar. I understand that the Pool Bar used to be called that because in the past it had serviced a real swimming pool outside, which had fallen into disrepair. Now the Pool Bar was filled with pool tables.

We actually had never seen a pool table before. It was very American, and we had never come across the likes of this. The odd bar billiards table was all we had seen.

"Is there more? Is there more...?" cried Chaz, in tones of disbelief.

"Well," said Tony. "This is about it ... but we not yet been to Devil's Den, have we?"

So we had another swift half in the Pool Bar and we were then taken all the way back down to the lobby, where there was another entrance into a dark place with the title of Devil's Den written across the door. We went into a much darker and more secluded place. There were red devil faces around the walls that seem to glow in an eerie way.

"What gives with this place?" I said.

"Well," said Tony, "The main dance area and disco is, like, for your run-of-the-mill chart stuff and soul music. "Down here," said Tony, "Is much darker. This is the place to come if you like funk and if you like jazz funk too, and the more – let's say – non-chart side of soul."

I looked at Chaz and Chaz looked at me.

"This is our place, then, Chaz," I said. "This is where we will be."

"Oh one more thing," said Tony.

"Each week on stage there will be a first class soul act playing live."

Chaz and I could not speak now we were stunned.

"OK ... that's your tour, guys," said Tony. "What do you want to do?"

We chatted a bit and Chaz and I decided to stay in Devil's Den for a bit. Billy and Graham and our other mate wanted to go and play pool. So we left the others to it and said we would meet up later. Graham told us to be outside by the car at twelve – no later, or he would be leaving without us.

Chaz and I got a drink and we sat at the back of Devil's Den for a bit watching the world go by. This area had its own dance floor and DJ. A small bar served drinks and the tone in here was much more laid-back than the other bars. It was like you might expect a jazz club to be: dark and smoky, and it seemed to attract a certain type of clientele. The girls' fashion in this bar was more outlandish and extreme. It still followed the current trends but focused more into a fashion scene all of its own just for Devil's Den.

It's strange, because if someone mentions seventies disco fashion then one immediately thinks of the film *Saturday Night Fever*: bright, garish jumpsuits made of satin material with ridiculous flared legs, and men in white suits. In actual fact there was none of that here at all. The film industry seems to have warped our sense of what people wore at that time. That film came out at the end of the seventies and, really, its effect went more into the 1980s.

During the early to mid 1970s the girls and boys wore flared trousers, but in the main these would be in quite muted colours. Trousers – which would be tight at the top – would be high-waisted, with sometimes four or even five buttons high on the waist. The shoes or boots would be platform, of course. For the girls boots might be white and wet-look, with a block heel. Some of the soles on men's shoes then might be the crêpe-sole style. The higher the shoe or boot the better, of course. Men wore shirts with funky designs on, and one of my favourites was one with a pattern of little robot dogs. Shirt collars were always worn outside the jacket: this was also part of the fashion.

To get into a disco or club you usually had to have a jacket on, and jeans could definitely not be worn. Men also wore those terrible-looking tank tops – a tight sleeveless jumper with heavy patterns across – over their shirts. Another look the girls had – and this seems to have been a bit of a uniform in Devil's Den, in particular – was the back-split pencil skirt. This would be worn with a tight fitting T-shirt with maybe a glitter design on the front. T-shirts would be tucked inside skirts and trousers. Nothing hung out in those days, and everyone was super-slim.

Another fashion item then for the girls – and a big hit with the boys – was hot pants. These were tight, high-cut shorts which would show loads of leg but enable a girl to dance freely and safely. This was a far cry from the image portrayed by John Travolta in 1977. When we saw it we thought the film a huge joke – almost a comical parody of what we knew.

Tony was right about the music in Devil's Den. James Brown was played, for sure, but all the American funk and jazz funk imports were also played. These were toons we didn't know but stuff we would soon own, for sure. Devil's Den was perfect for us. It was as if it had been made just for us two. No "Ground Control to Major Tom" here, or Elton John, or Mud, or The Sweet, or any of the other chart churn stuff. This was raw funk in here, and over a period of time we would become expert in all music relating to funk and jazz funk.

When we came to leave that night a very rude awakening took place. I had forgotten all about the Rank in those few hours. I was in love with this place. I had jumped to another ledge. The problem was that we had no bloody dependable transport to get here.

The issue got ten times worse because soon after our first trip to the Cali there was a notice in the local newspaper. It spelled out the death of the Rank. It would be closing for some considerable time and it was uncertain as to what format it would take when it did eventually reopen. It would still retain some form of disco/nightclub. The new place was to be called Baileys, we heard.

We counted down the weeks we had left. There were about four weeks of the Rank left, and then that was it: we would be high and dry. It soon came around, of course, the last night ever at the Top Rank Watford ... and there was a huge party there with a massive crowd. We all went and we drank and danced till the lights came up at twelve midnight. Everyone was sad to see the closing, and I suspect maybe a few friendships dissolved that evening.

The Rank was indeed a special place, and what took over from it was nothing like what had been before. When you change something you rip the soul out sometimes, and that's what happened to the Rank. Just its faint memories live on. One aspect of the Rank that did live over into Baileys when it opened was the little old lady who sold the fags. She had her own broom cupboard and a hole in the wall you could buy your fags from. When Baileys started up there she was again, sure enough: the same broom cupboard and the same hole in the wall. It was like they had renovated the whole place around her.

Chaz and I were sad of course very sad. This had been a great place, but we had another place to go to now as long as we could get some transport. Chaz had a plan, of course: not a great one, but a plan that would work for a while.

Here is a list of the bands we saw at the Cali at the start of our adventure along with admittance price:

Sweet	80p
Junior Walker & the All Stars	£1
Edwin Starr	80p
Hot Chocolate	£1
The Drifters	£1
Suzi Quatro	£1
Sparks	£1
Mungo Jerry	50p
Average White Band	50p
10cc	50p
Jimmy Ruffin	£1
The Chi-Lites	£1
Osibisa	80p
Desmond Dekker	60p
Mud	£1

The Return of Fred

1972

In life you often meet up with people more than once. It just happens like that, and it's not always by design. It's just that your paths cross over. So it was that Fred made his presence known for a time down the George. He had actually lightened up a fair bit from school, and the controlling part of him was now non-existent. I was drawn to him once more like some stupid moth caught in the light from the moon.

One night down the George it was one of those non-event evenings, possibly a Friday or Saturday, where for some reason the Cali was not on and Chaz was probably on holiday. I was down there on my own.

Fred came in and over to me and we chatted.

"Fancy making a bit of a night of it, mate, and going for a bit of a pub crawl?" he suggested.

I looked at him with narrowing eyes.

"Yes, why not?" I thought. "It's better than staying in the George all evening. There clearly is no action here tonight."

"We could drive down to Kings Langley and leave your car there and get it tomorrow morning," he added.

At this point I was beginning to see why he had collared me. Fred could not drive.

"OK," I said. "I'm game. Let's go."

So we drove to Kings Langley and we had a few drinks that night in a few of the establishments. It got to about eleven o'clock and we started our walk back along the main road. We weren't pissed, you understand … we had had a bit, but we were not drunk and falling about. We were just a little jolly and in a nice place.

Halfway along the main road between Hemel and Kings Langley there is a bus stop. It's one of those nice wooden olde worlde ones. I think it had a nice thatched top to it.

"I want a piss," exclaimed Fred as we got parallel to it.

"OK, Fred," I said. "Go inside and have one, then."

Fred went in but before he could get his wiener out he tripped on a bit of wood sticking out the side of the shelter.

"Fuck you, you bastard," Fred shouted at the wood, and began to kick it a few times.

"Take that, you fucking cunt."

"Hey … take it easy, Fred. Have a piss and let's get going."

So he did. We left the shelter and started off again, unaware that we had been watched by some do-gooding dog walker out late at night.

We didn't get too far. We just got to the Red Lion pub and were turning along there towards the back lane when two police cars came screeching up to us. There were two coppers in each. I was bundled into the back of one car and Fred was pushed into the other. It all happened quickly, but in those few seconds between Fred seeing the police and us getting arrested Fred's brain had already formulated the story we should give them. He told me this story quickly as if he knew we would be separated and questioned later. I was shaking like a leaf.

Fred assumed that the reason we had been arrested was because he had been seen pissing in public. That, unfortunately, was not the issue here.

A strange evening in Hemel police station then took place, with me first watching Fred get charged and then photographed with mug shots like you see in the films. I was thinking,

"Hold on a minute here … all I wanted was a quiet night down the George, and here I am in the police station with bloody Fred."

I had to write a statement, and the police said I could be called as a police witness against Fred. I was still very mystified as to what was going on here. I mean … yes, people do have a piss sometimes in the street. Yes, maybe it's wrong, but involving the police? This was crazy. It wasn't till Fred was charged that I understood a bit more.

Fred was being charged for vandalising the bus shelter. There was nothing about urinating.

"Vandalising?" I thought. "There was no vandalising here."

Fred had tripped over some wood in the shelter and then kicked it, but he wasn't doing further damage. In fact the bus shelter was already in a state, having already been vandalised.

I got home late that night, as the police episode had added another two hours to the night. My parents were already asleep when I got back, and they had no idea where I had been and what had happened. In fact I never told them anything, not even when the letter arrived telling me I would have to appear in court.

The day of the court case arrived, and I remember that I had a splitting headache all that day. This was madness, as Fred had done nothing wrong. Some bloody dog walker had made an assumption about our little act in the bus shelter and put two and two together to make five. I had to have the day off work for this court case and I must have made some excuse to my parents as to what I was doing.

It was, to say the least, a frightening experience to feel you were in this situation where you had to be questioned against your mate. Fred was questioned, then I was questioned in the dock. Both of us had to swear on the Bible to tell the truth and nothing but the truth. Then a third person (a representative from the bus company) was called. It seems that the police had asked for a full report on the condition of the shelter to ascertain what damage Fred had done. It didn't look good for Fred that the bus shelter had already been in a real state, and now it all seemed to be a formality that Fred would take the hit for something he had not done.

Thank God for British ineptitude, that's all I can say. When the bus company was asked to report on the shelter it was clear right away that the inspector had visited and reported on the wrong shelter. In fact they had got confused and assumed that it was the one on the other side of the road. This one had no damage.

As soon as this information was heard I saw, while looking around the room, a number of people sighing in disbelief. Even before the judge passed his judgement the newspaper reporter had got up and left. There was no story here, for sure.

Fred was of course not found guilty, which was just as well because he and I had not done anything wrong anyway. The whole episode was a complete misunderstanding. We went to the pub afterwards and got pissed.

California Dreaming

The California Ballroom was first opened on Saturday night 12 March 1960 from 8 p.m. till 12 p.m. The bill poster's heading showed its full name at the time: the California Pool Ballroom, as this establishment had its own outside swimming pool. On the first night of opening the singer Ronnie Carroll topped the bill. He was an Irish singer who was married to another well-known celebrity: Millicent Martin. This first opening evening was for charity, and the proceeds went to the Old People's Welfare charity. I suspect after this that the money went into other pockets. The price on that night was 7/6d, or seven and six as we used to say (about 37p in today's currency).

When we arrived at the Cali in the early seventies there had already been changes made to the place. The pool outside was no longer in use. It had been in operation since 1935 but people wanted modern heated indoor pools, so outside ones became unpopular. Another pool had been constructed inside the Cali but by the time we started going this indoor pool area had been converted to the lower entrance area and Devil's Den.

The Cali was a ballroom – a traditional one, at the time – and so the entertainment tended to revolve around the top ballroom bands of that time. Some of the well-known bands playing were Kenny Ball, Humphrey Lyttleton, and Bert Weedon.

As the sixties progressed the emphasis in music started to change with the more modern times, and although primarily the Cali was still used for ballroom dancing the likes of the modern bands were creeping in – for example The Dave Clark Five, The Barron Knights, and Roy Castle.

By 1965 we had The Kinks and The Hollies playing, and Manfred Mann. Times had changed and ballroom was no longer popular with the young. Pop music was where people wanted to be. The Who, Tom Jones, David Bowie, The Bee Gees, and even the great Stevie Wonder all played at the Cali. The place was rocking in the sixties, and every week there would be some band on who everyone knew. When the 1970s arrived the Cali had changed yet again. Aligning itself with the now in-vogue beats of disco, its emphasis was largely based around black soul music and reggae ... enter Chaz and Dick.

Black bands in the United States were having a tough time. If you were black and in the States you might still be considered a second-class citizen. Prejudice against black people certainly didn't help music sales. Black music in the States was mostly listened to by black people. But here in the UK, and specifically at the Cali, things were completely different. There was a great love for the soul and funk bands from the US – so much so that bands were happy to come to Britain and tour.

The Cali saw a band play every Saturday, and mostly these were bands resident in the United States. These bands were playing to a huge fan base of mainly white youngsters. This aspect turned the whole soul music industry around. The UK and Europe to an extent was where you could make it if you were a black soul group.

Sometimes at the Cali a group of northern soul guys and girls would turn up. One guy we knew from school was Reg Stickings. He really did seem to be into the scene in a big way. We used to watch as these dancers span and somersaulted and twisted and jived with precision. It was a totally different scene from what we were into, and the music was different too. Although we appreciated what these guys did we kind of couldn't get our heads around the music side. I have no doubt in my mind that if we had liked the music then a different direction would have been taken. Maybe, just maybe, that great book Reg Stickings wrote later in life would have been a little different and would have featured a couple of other oddball characters from Hemel Hempstead.

Back to the Cali

1974

Here is a list of the bands we saw then and the admittance price:

B.T. Express	60p
The Equals	60p
The Coasters	70p
Clem Curtis & The Foundations	£1
Pan's People	60p
Limmie & The Family Cookin'	70p
Harold Melvin & the Blue Notes	£2
Barry Blue	£1
Alvin Stardust	£1
The Detroit Emeralds	£1
The Three Degrees	£1.50
The Glitter Band	£1
R. Dean Taylor	£1
Jimmy Cliff	80p
Jimmy James and the Vagabonds	60p
Ben E. King	90p
Cozy Powell	£1
KC and the Sunshine Band	£1
Leo Sayer	£1
Carl Douglas	£1
Four Tops	£2.50
Gwen & George McCrae	£1.50

I met up with Chaz on the Sunday after we had been to the Cali for our first visit. It was our usual Sunday lunchtime stint for an hour before we went home for our traditional Sunday roast dinners. There were a few others down the George, and as usual Pat and Fred the owners had put out the usual bowls of crisps, cheese, and pickled onions on the bar for the locals. Some who came down considered the bowls to be fair game and to be their breakfast. In fact most of us would have tumbled out of bed maybe half an hour before, arriving at the pub still with sleep in our eyes.

There was loads of chatter, of course. It was mainly people asking about the Cali: what it was like and what went on. I was more interested in what Chaz had to say. He had hinted that he had a plan of action, and until I could get him on his own I wasn't going to say anything.

Certainly Chaz's friend Graham could drive us there, but we could not rely on this for too long. Graham was a great guy, but I got the impression that he wasn't that interested in discos and dancing.

"Come over here, Chaz," I whispered. "What's your bloody plan, then?"

"Well," he said. "I've been thinking. We're in a bit of a fix here getting to the Cali. There is no public transport so we have to use what we have, yes?"

"Yes," I said. "So what are you saying then? We walk…?"

"No," said Chaz. "We go on my motorbike…"

Now … I have to explain. Chaz had a Honda 90 motorbike. It was not the fastest thing on two wheels, but he had transport and it got him around to places. Not only did he have this bike, he had also passed his bike driving test and could carry a passenger on the pillion. However, one thing really, really worried me about Chaz and the bike – and that was his sight. His eyesight was like Mr. Magoo's. What troubled me further was that he insisted on wearing a crash helmet with a visor that was a smoked brown colour.

"We what…?" I blurted out.

"We go on my bike," he repeated. "It'll be simple. I'll pick you up. I have a spare helmet. It will be easy."

My face must have looked a picture, to be honest. Chaz's plan was indeed doable. Crazy though it was it was achievable, and I could not think of anything else we could do. We were desperate, and that meant desperate measures.

"Look," I said. "My mum and dad have a huge issue with motorbikes, and me going on yours needs to be kept secret. OK?"

"OK," said Chaz. "I'll ring you first, and then meet you at the end of the street and pick you up by the phone box."

So the plan was hatched. We talked some more about the logistics of it during the week but basically we knew what we had to do to get to our prize place. It was the only way and, as expected, Graham had cried off with the car.

Now if any of you know the route from Hemel to Dunstable over the Downs you will know that even in these modern times that it's not a great set of roads to travel on at night. It was around October time when all this took place, and we would be travelling in the dark with unlit roads at times. I had never been on the back of Chaz's bike before and so had no idea what to expect, but it had to be done at any cost.

I met Chaz at the end of my road as expected. He handed me a helmet, which I strapped on. I had my clubbing gear on and a coat over the top. Thank God I had brought a coat. We headed off, and I clung on to Chaz for dear life. Could he really see anything through that smoked Perspex visor? We got through town easily and then on to the Leighton Buzzard road. It was dark all right, and the beam from the Honda's front light was the only thing lighting anything up. All I could see was the road ahead for about thirty yards and some of the grass verge on either side, but that was it. It was cold, too, and I used Chaz as a windbreak. God, this was bloody awful.

"Are we going to die out here?" I thought.

Chaz drove about fifty mph along that twisting Leighton Buzzard road, which had claimed a few fatalities in the short time we had been alive. Soon we came to the right turn to take us up to Studham and beyond. I have no idea how we managed to get there. Chaz drove OK, but I think we got lucky. It was pitch black over the Downs, and all I could see at one point as I looked over Chaz's shoulder were loads of moths streaming into the headlamp.

The lights of the Cali appeared in the distance.

"Thank God for that," I thought, trying to forget that we still had to get back after the night had finished.

We arrived and cleaned up as best we could.

"God, Chaz," I said. "We both smell of bloody exhaust smoke and fuel. How are we going to pull like this...?

"Sorry," said Chaz. "It does leak a bit, but it's the only way we can get here."

When we got inside the Cali I realised that there was a nice black grease mark right across my light beige flared trousers.

"Chaz ... look at these. Your bloody bike ... we stand no chance tonight." And as sure as eggs are eggs we didn't pull that night because both of us looked as if we had been on the back of a bloody motorbike all night.

I don't recollect much about the trip home. It had been a wasted evening: no bloody birds, messed-up bloody trousers, and we stank of two-stroke... The trip back was cold and it had turned foggy but we got home without an accident, which I still consider a miracle. I got off the bike at the end of the road.

"OK," I said. "That's it. We need another plan, Chaz. Get your bloody thinking cap on."

Once again while we were down at the George drinking on the Sunday lunchtime – with cheese and onion free for all – we talked long and hard about the night before. The usual post-mortem took place.

"What are we going to do?" said Chaz. He had to admit that the bike option was just not going to work.

"I'm going to start driving lessons next week," said Chaz.

"That's great," I said. "But what do we do in the short term till you get a car?"

We sat looking into our pints, doing some deep thinking. Even if we scored at the Cali and brought out some nice-looking birds they would just laugh at the sight of a Honda 90 sitting there. It was hardly a passion wagon.

I was deep in thought and scanning the bar aimlessly.

"Hold on a minute," I said. "That guy over there ... it's Les, isn't it?"

Les was a local in the George and quite often came over to talk to us. He had been to the Rank with us a couple of times too. He had been going out with one of our old school chums, Tina. They had split up but he still came down to drink. Les was about a year younger than us, having just turned seventeen. The strange thing was that I had this notion that I had seen him drive a car.

"Les," I shouted. "Over here, mate."

Les left the one- armed bandit and came over to the booth we were occupying.

"Can I get you a drink, Les?" I said. Les nodded enthusiastically.

"Chaz, get Les a drink, mate," I said, not taking my eyes off Les and keeping my smile going.

Chaz got up in a huff and went to the bar while giving me that "Why me?" look.

"Les, I understand that you can drive a car. Is that correct?" I said, in the nicest, jolliest voice I could muster.

"Yes, I can," he said. "I passed my test soon after my seventeenth birthday."

"Do you have a car, Les?"

"No," he replied.

"I thought I had seen you driving one," I said.

"Oh, yes. I drive my dad's Avenger. I'm insured for it and he lets me take it out whenever I like."

"Oh…," I said, trying to keep calm.

Chaz came back with a half pint.

"Les, mate, how would you like to come with us next week to the Cali in Dunstable?"

This was make or break time. Would he take the bait?

"You know, Les … that Cali is full of mouth-watering crumpet," I added. His eyes lit up at the thought of women. "You know, Les, those Dunstable girls … they sure are cute."

His mouth dropped open.

"Yes," said Chaz. "They're really easy to chat up unless you've got grease stains on your kecks."

I gave Chaz the "Shut up" look. This was going well: better than expected.

323

"I'm fucking up for that, guys. As long as you guys chip in with some petrol we can do this easily."

"Phew…" I let out a sigh of relief that must have been heard by the entire pub. I sat back almost exhausted.

Les, Chaz, and I made up a good team for quite a while. Les took us over to the Cali a large number of times and we paid for the petrol. He was a great mate, and he really did get us out of a fix. The three of us would be unstoppable at the Cali now. The A team had arrived.

The Boys Do Holiday

1974

It had to happen, of course: the lads' first holiday away. Chaz, Les, and I wanted to go away somewhere on the south coast. It would be the first time I had been on holiday without my parents.

"What is this going to be like?" I thought. It had to be fun or a disaster. There was never any in between with us. It was Les who suggested it, and really I have to give him a lot of the credit. He really did come up with some good ideas in those days.

"Where are we going then, Les?" I said to him as the three of us sat huddled around one of the tables at the George.

"I reckon," said Les, "That we have to go to a holiday camp. It's going to be the easiest for us. There'll be no cooking, and it's about as cheap as we're going to get it."

"OK,"I said. "How are we getting there?"

"Car," said Les. "I've already tapped my old man up for using the car for a whole week. You guys give me some petrol money, and we are in business."

I had no idea where we were going but Les had done some research, and Chaz and I left him to it. He must have sent for some brochures from Pontins, because a week or so later he was back down the pub and we were discussing locations to go to. I have no idea how this came about, but it was decided that we go to the Isle of Wight and to Puckpool, just outside Ryde. I left it to Les and he booked the whole thing up. It would be just under twenty quid each for a week's stay, a tidy sum in those days – but we had no food to pay for, and the beer in the camp would be cheap. We would be rolling in birds there, for sure. It was going to be a bloody awesome adventure.

We set off in Les's dad's blue Avenger towards the south coast. None of us had been this far before on our own, and thank God Les's dad had a map in the car because it wasn't clear to Les where we should be pointing. One of us had to map-read, and again this was a new activity to all of us.

We had gone down to catch the ferry at Portsmouth on the Friday evening after work. We had packed a small bag each with just the essentials inside: toothbrush, smellies, condoms, and the odd spare pair of underpants. Not much else would be needed.

I have no idea how we found the ferry port in Portsmouth because even today I have difficulty, and I now have satnav. But we found it and got the tickets to go over to the Isle of Wight that evening. It was early evening when we drove into Ryde town, and we parked and got some fish and chips and sat on the seafront with a couple of bottles of beer. Ryde's a nice seaside town, and it all felt rather pleasant just sitting there with my chums. I turned to Les.

"Les," I said, "We're booked into the camp tomorrow – Saturday. Right?"

"Yep, that's right," replied Les.

"So, Les, what are we doing here now?"

"What do you mean?" said Les. "We are here, aren't we? We just drive into the camp in the morning."

"OK, Les, but where are we bloody sleeping tonight?"

"In the car, of course," was the no-nonsense, almost "Why are you asking?" reply.

Chaz and I looked around at Les.

"You are joking, aren't you, Les?" said Chaz.

"Well, have you got a better suggestion? Cos, as I see it, it's the car or the beach tonight."

We went off to a pub – and then at about ten thirty walked back to the parked Avenger that was situated on the esplanade, but a little way from the pier and the main attractions.

"So who is sleeping with who tonight, then?" giggled Les. "Cos I'm going in the driver's seat. Are you two homos going in the back?" he joked.

"Chaz, you go in the back," I said. "I'll be OK in the passenger seat, I reckon, with the seat back a bit."

So it was that three guys attempted to sleep in the car overnight in Ryde. Chaz suggested that the windows should be open a crack or we might all be dead in the morning through lack of oxygen. Les said it had nothing to do with lack of air and more to do with some other odour. By the morning I think he had a point.

That night has to be one of the most uncomfortable nights I have ever spent anywhere in my life. Restless sleep, or getting any sleep at all, was the main challenge of that night. Even today when I visit Ryde I look at the spot where we parked the Avenger with a certain amount of distaste. I sometimes think that one of those brass plaques should be screwed to the wall there saying,

"Here is the place where three stupid amigos slept the night and nearly gassed themselves on their own farts."

I have no idea if anyone saw us in the car that night. The windows were fogged up, anyway, and I would think that anyone passing would probably see three guys as a possible threat.

We awoke about seven. It was light outside, and the smell in that car just told you we needed to bail out.

"I need to get out of here, guys," I said. "I need to stretch my legs and have a piss somewhere."

I left them to it for a bit, and went over the road and had a fag looking out to sea. It was going to be a great day today. We were going to have so much fun, but right then I felt like the Devil himself had been sitting in my mouth all night.

We got some breakfast in Ryde and then headed off to Puckpool, which was a short ride from Ryde (if you will excuse the pun).

We got ourselves booked in and got the keys to the chalets. We had our own separate one each, all side by side in one row. These small huts had a single bed, a loo, and a washbasin, and not much else. There was no shower and no bath. If you needed a bath or shower then there was a wash house to do all that, but hey… Guess what? We didn't bother. We had Brut and we had Hai Karate to smother any smells. We were never going to be in these huts long, anyway, so it didn't matter to us that much. We were going to do a bit of sleeping and, with some luck, maybe the odd bird might come back for coffee – which of course was not available in the hut, either. (I think the phrase "Come back for coffee" means something else.)

Pontin's was a laugh. It fed us and it had some entertainment and cheap beer for us, but we quickly realised that these places were family-orientated and the available birds were in fact few and far between. We needed to get out of the camp, to go under the wire and seek out something along the lines of the Rank or Cali.

Our best night of all was when we drove out to a club we had been told about. The Carousel Club was way out in the sticks somewhere. It no longer exists and I can't even find any reference to it these days. It wasn't a big place, but it was just what we were looking for because it was playing good music and was also full of crumpet. We had our best trapping clothes on and we looked the business. It didn't take us long to get in with some girls and, luckily, they were from the camp we were staying at. Bingo: we were in here. They had got a bus out to the club and – of course – us lads being kind-hearted we offered them a trip back to camp at twelve midnight. So that was six of us in the car going back … three in the back and three in the front … work it out.

I'm not sure what else we did that night, as it's just a blur. I know it was fun, and in the morning we had a hard job getting Chaz to wake up and answer the door to his chalet. Bang, bang, bang … Les persisted in knocking to wake the dead but there was no answer.

"I'm not having this," said Les. "You've got your knife on you."

"Yes," I said. "But what are you going to do?"

"I'm going to take the bloody door off," was the reply.

I'm not sure who was more shocked, to be honest … us? Or Chaz, when his door just fell out of the hole it was blocking and hit the ground with a huge crash? Les had unscrewed all the screws out from the hinges. Chaz stood there in his underpants, looking out. By now there was a small crowd behind us.

"Are you coming to breakfast?" I said to Chaz.

"Yep. Give me a minute to get me togs on," was the reply. We went to breakfast and left the door propped up against the hut.

"We'd better put that back," I said, "When we finish brekkie. They're not going to be best pleased when the chalet girls came around to clean."

We left Puckpool quite quickly on the following Saturday. We had to be out early anyway but we needed to get off early for our ferry ... and also someone had written something on the sign at the front entrance to the camp.

It was sad to leave, but we all turned our heads as we drove out of the camp to see the large picture sign that showed a family having fun on the beach ... and above it, the new title for the holiday camp. Some idiot had had the smart idea to cross out the first P in Puckpool and replace it with an F.

The three of us never went on holiday together again but I did return to Puckpool a couple of years later with Baz, and we had a stonking week there.

Further Education 1972-1975

My college days were to be a complete giggle, if I'm to be honest. It was only one day a week and the course of City & Guilds TV and electrical mechanics was going to take three years to complete all three parts and an extra fourth year for colour TV and advanced electronics. One day a week was manageable and actually a bit of a welcome break from the shop and the outings with Tony. Although I went to Welwyn Garden City College, it was not the main campus I was taught at. Oh, no. Where my course was run from was a small set of buildings more like a school, set about half a mile from the main college.

This small sub-college was situated on Applecroft Road. It's no longer a college but a school. My early days here were unexciting, and initially a bit of a drag. There were a few who went there at the start who really didn't want to study. They messed about a little too much, and in some respects it still felt a little like school. They were not that interested in electronics, and one wondered why they had chosen a job in that particular trade. It didn't take long, maybe one term, before things shifted around a bit and people left and new people came in. At this point college became better and the people who attended with me were skilled, knowledgeable, and mature. For three to four years we all became quite a close gang.

It's interesting how people just seem to pop in and out of your life, and for me the one person who performed this stunt a number of times was my good friend Jim. Out of all the places Jim my old school mucker turned up at was this college. We had not spoken for quite a long time, so it was a huge surprise when one day he just walked into class as bold as brass and announced he was joining the course.

Once the dross had dropped out of our class we really had a good selection of guys to converse with. One of these guys – Tony – was to become a close friend for quite a time. Tony drove a sporty Ford Anglia and it really was his pride and joy. Later he sold it and got

330

himself a nice Ford Cortina 1600E. Tony having wheels was a godsend, because it meant we could go out at lunchtimes to the pub. This made a huge difference to the day, and we all packed inside the car and drove off to our favourite pub for a toasted cheese and ham sarnie. In fact it was the first time I had ever come across such a culinary delight. It was a new thing in the seventies, and we loved them.

Tony had a couple of mates at the college too. One was Dave, who was also in our class, and there was another in a class where they learned about wiring houses. Having these guys around at lunch and break times was a great laugh. Good times were had and happy memories were made.

Tony was the guy who was instrumental in eventually introducing me to the California Ballroom. We would sit in his car and he and his mates would be sounding off about how good the Cali was and the girls there. I would counter this with how good the Top Rank was and how the Cali could never compare. Of course in the end Tony won the battle outright.

We had a guy in our class who always seemed to be messing about. He was one of these mischief-makers who would be for ever flicking stuff or talking or acting up, and it really got on everyone's nerves. Then suddenly he went off sick and we were told that he might not be back for the whole term. We had no real idea what was wrong with him, and we had almost got to the point where we thought we might never see the poor bugger again. Then out of the blue he came back. He had lost weight and we all checked him out when he walked in. There was a small scar on the guy's forehead – a thin line running down from his hairline. He was quite open about it all and explained that he had had a brain tumour, which had been removed. We all sat open-mouthed as he explained his illness and the procedure that had taken place. Well, it was just amazing how different this guy was from that point on. His personality had completely changed through this illness, and for the better too. I guess it's not often that you can say that illness does people a favour, but in this case it had. He was the nicest of guys you could ever want to meet and this change in him made him very likeable. He did extremely well at his studies after this and went on to complete the course with high marks.

Each year there would be an exam – one you had to pass, otherwise you would be out. Parts 1, 2, and 3 had to be completed before you could consider yourself an engineer. I passed mine and then went back for more punishment to do colour TVs and advanced electronics. This I also passed in my fourth and final year. I remember the day I came out of that final exam. It was a bright sunny day, and we had taken our exam in the main Welwyn College building. We all massed outside as one gang and we had a few pictures taken of us all: the last meeting of the college gang. Most were going off to the pub to celebrate, as is customary in these events. It was midday and we had the rest of the day to ourselves. But I didn't go. No, I had something else on my mind. I had the works van with me and I had a little girl waiting for me over in Stopsley, in Luton. No ... I had a woman on my mind now, and the pub was not on my radar for that day.

Dunstable Days

Life seems to be full of little twists and turns, mine being no exception. You think you have things all set out nicely and tidily, with an easy existence. Plain sailing, they call it ... until a big wave comes along and tips your bloody boat over.

I could now drive a car, and in fact I was driving my own car now to work at Berkhamsted. This was much better than getting the bus. I could get up later and get home quicker. The car made a huge difference to my life. Even college was better, as now I could drive I didn't have that God-awful bus ride each week. I could drive into college and sit in the car park alongside my mate Tony ... no more cold nights at the bus stop. However, as soon as I could drive the world changed for me too.

Weatherhead's told me that I would no longer be working at the Berkhamsted shop, and that I would now be based at Dunstable. I would be allowed to use the company van to drive back and forth – and go to college, even, but not use it for private use. I would also have a pay increase too, as this was seen as a promotion in a way. I was now in the third year of my apprenticeship, and I kind of knew enough now from Tony and my day release to be able to work as a proper TV engineer. Whether I was ready for this was another matter. This is what Weatherhead's had decided would happen.

I had no idea what went on at the Dunstable shop, which wasn't much further to travel to than the Berko one. I arrived there, clueless, in my car and parked around the back yard. The shop was bigger, with a manager in charge of the shop along with two lady assistants and a young boy who was the junior shop assistant. The manager was a tall, kind soul with a soft voice. I later learned that he used to be in the police force, but you would never have thought it from how he looked and acted.

I was escorted down to the workshop, which this time was on ground level and near to the vans in the yard. Inside were four guys:

two young lads – Steve and Vas – whom I later learned were first-year apprentices, Mike a guy a bit older than me who was a qualified engineer, and an older guy who was the domestic appliance engineer. What was all this about, then?

It seemed that there was no TV engineer resident at Dunstable. Whoever this had been had left some time back. All that was left were two young lads in their first year who basically knew jack shit and could not drive. Mike had been brought over from one of the other branches to help out, the same as I had.

This workshop had a big problem. It had a backlog of TVs that needed fixing. The wooden rack shelving had a number of TV sets waiting to be fixed. In addition the job cards kept coming in each day for more repairs at different addresses.

It was at this stage that I realised exactly my purpose at Dunstable. I was to be the new Tony here. It would be me who would now be going out as the engineer with my own first-year apprentice. It would be me who would schedule the work, drive the van, and fix the TVs. I had come from a situation where I didn't really need to think each day with Tony about. I sat in the van, drank tea, got some tools out of the van, and stroked the customer's dog …that sort of stuff. And now I was in charge. I was top dog, or was that the dog's bollocks? I was not too sure.

Mike was senior to me, and he kind of organised the situation initially. We would both have to go out as two squads to reduce the number of jobs outstanding as calls. After we had cracked this and got the calls manageable I would go out, and Mike could remain back at the workshop and get this backlog of TVs fixed. It was a plan, for sure, and a sound one.

Mike ran a minivan that was as cool as hell. Vas seemed to have already chosen Mike as the engineer he wanted to go out with. I had Steve with me as my assistant. Talk about my comfort zone being vaporised instantly. I was in the deep end and gasping for air … here I was as a TV engineer, going to go out to fix TVs in a town I knew nothing about with a young lad who I had only met for five minutes in a van I had never driven.

"How much more difficult can this get?" I thought.

The Morris van we had was brand new. It was nothing like the Moggie Minor I had driven a few times with Tony after I had passed my test. This van was in fact easier to drive, which was a benefit for me as I needed all the help I could get. I was still a new driver fresh from the pass I got from my second attempt at the Berko test centre. We got in the van and I started up the more powerful 1300cc engine. Steve had the cards for the jobs with the addresses on. I said to him,

"Well, where the fuck are we?" smiling at him to break the ice. Steve said,

"There is a map here in the glove compartment. It covers all of Dunstable. I'll look up the addresses and tell you where to go."

So that's what we did. The map was our saviour in as far as it ensured our morning went without too much trouble. Steve was eager to learn from me as much as he could. I did well in ensuring that all but one TV that day was fixed, and only one had to come back to the workshop. Mike had done his TVs super-quickly and had got back and started turning around the backlog. When we got back mid morning for a cup of tea the old domestic appliance guy had already made us one. What a treasure he was.

That day was a long and hard day. We worked hard and I really felt I was now earning my money, for sure.

What was great about this job was that I was working with some young people, and that made all the difference. It took a few weeks for Mike to clear down the sets that had piled up, and the racks were now empty. Mike could go back now to the shop he worked from and leave me and the two apprentices to our own devices. We would have the pleasure of either Mike or SuperBrian once a week to fix the really hard stuff, but basically I was now in charge of the workshop and the work. I had just turned nineteen.

One day – and not long after starting at Dunstable – I had a bad accident in Eaton Bray. I was travelling along the main road at school time when some woman decided that she would just drive out into the road in front of me. I jammed on the brakes and I heard Steve say something, and then it all went crazy and dark for an instant. I probably was travelling a little over the thirty limit but not much: at least, when the police measured the tyre marks they didn't think I was over the limit. I did hit her hard all right, because I knocked her front wheels clean off. She was OK and so were we.

The van was a write-off – a total write-off – but it wasn't my fault, and so as far as work was concerned it was not an issue. I had a day off for the shock which affected me the next day, but I was back after that to continue.

When I got back to work from my little accident I was told that I now had to drive something else. I was marched outside to the yard and there, in the place of my lovely Morris van, stood an old Moggie Minor. Vas could not stop laughing at this turnaround in what I now had to drive.

When Mike left things changed around. Vas, who no longer had Mike to go out with, wanted to now go out with me on the road. Vas saw me as the cool prospect to be with, so he talked with Steve about this and negotiated a switch-around, whereby Steve stayed back at the workshop and got on with a few things while we went out together.

What a bloody team this was now. Vas and I were the kind of mix you really didn't want to happen. We were an explosive couple of teens who really looked for fun at every opportunity. It's not like we didn't work hard, because we got the job done and had the whole art of driving around the area at top speed and visiting houses down to a fine art. I have no idea what people must have made of us, because we must have looked incredibly young at the time. Would you really have let these two guys in your house? I had long, almost shoulder-length hair and Vas always had his aviator sunshades on and looked like someone from the Mafia.

Vas thought it was a great laugh when I happened to find back from the company laundry a white engineer's coat with the W on the pocket stitched on the wrong way around. Instead of a W it looked like the M similar to the one used by the Mothercare children's and baby clothes shops. I liked this rebel version of the white coat so much that I took it home for my mum to clean so I could always keep it as mine.

While Mike was at the workshop he had shown Vas a trick he would sometimes do in the minivan while driving about. The vans then had no steering lock on the ignition key: in fact the ignition key slot was in the middle of the dashboard and was basically accessible to both driver and passenger.

Vas and I were driving along the Luton road on the way to a job in Luton town when Vas said,

"Hey, Dick. Check this out." He leant forward and switched off the bloody ignition on the van.

"Vasss, what the fuck are you doing, man?" came my immediate cry as the Moggie lurched and lost power but kept going with the forward momentum.

"Watch," said Vas. After only five seconds had passed he switched the ignition back on and the Moggie Minor lurched forward once again. It restarted and gave a tremendous bang from the back of the van.

"Fucking hell, Vas. What the hell was that, man?" I said, while gaining back control of the power to the van and quickly looking around to see what disturbance we had caused.

"Shit, man. What did you do there?" Vas explained that Mike had shown him that – if you switch the ignition off – the fuel pump still pushes fuel through the engine and into the exhaust pipes. When the power is returned the whole bloody lot ignites in one almighty backfire.

We laughed all the way to that job, and on the way back I tried it again.

"Hey," said Vas. "Look at those girls coming up on the side of the road. Do it now."

I let the clutch in and turned off the ignition, only to switch back on as we passed some likely-looking girls walking towards Dunstable. Banggg. Vas could hardly talk through laughing.

"Did you see that blonde tart?" he said. "She almost fell in the bush."

We used the backfire trick now and again, but didn't overplay it. One of the best ones we found was from coming over the top of the Downs on the steep hill that descends down to where the Cali stood. If you switched off coming down this hill you didn't lose speed, as the steep one in ten hill kept you going so you could pump fuel in for longer. This was our favourite place to fire one off – until, that is, we came over the top of the Downs and Vas said,

"Do it." I said,

"I'm not sure, Vas. This doesn't feel right today." I had this feeling that this might not be the right time to be doing this.

"Do it, man," retorted Vas. "OK I'll do it myself then," said Vas, and he switched the key to its neutral position. The van still sped down the hill, gathering speed in silence.

"On now, Vas. Not too much, mate."

"No, let it ride a bit. Let's have a big one."

"Now, Vas. Now." Vas switched on just as we were nearing the last curve of the downward hill of the Downs.

BANGGGGGG … it was like a grenade going off.

"Bloody hell, Vas. Is the exhaust still on?" I shouted. The corner came and I dropped a gear for it. Then my face changed colour…

In the Cali car park was a police car, and a copper was standing at the edge of the road beckoning us to drive into the Cali.

"Fuck," we both said in unison, as I indicated and slowly drew level with the policeman. I wound down my window on the tiny green van.

"Anything wrong, constable?" I asked.

"Sirs," he said, "I could hear you coming down the hill just now. Is there anything wrong with your vehicle?" he enquired, with his lips sort of pursed as if he kind of knew what us jokers had been up to.

"I think the mixture's a bit rich, officer," I quickly replied.

"Yes, that's right," said Vas.

"Shut it, Vas," I whispered out of the corner of my mouth. "I'll get it sorted when we get back to the yard, officer, if that's OK," I added.

"Lads, this is a routine check we are doing today so we are stopping people at random. I just need to look around the van and then you can go," the officer said.

You may well guess that that was the very last time Vas or I let off any bangs from the Moggie again.

Vas and I seemed to get the giggles sometimes when we were visiting people's houses. It kind of got so bad sometimes that I had to send Vas out to the van to get something imaginary just so he could let it all out in the confines of the Moggie and come back in composed again. It was the customers, you see: they just tickled the young immature minds of these two TV engineers.

One of the funniest situations I saw once – and yet it was not funny at all, really. We were around this couple's house and were fixing a colour TV. The lady of the house had shown us in and taken us to a very large living area. It was a very posh house indeed. She explained the fault and said that her husband would be in in a while to talk to us, but she added that we should not be too disturbed because her husband had had throat cancer and spoke a bit differently from the rest of us.

"Oh, boy," I thought, where is this going.

We didn't know what to expect. Neither of us had come across anyone before who had no voice box, so when the poor chap arrived in the room I really thought I might be sending Vas out for parts really, really quickly.

Vas and I were sitting on the floor. We had found the fault and I was instructing Vas on how to solder a new replacement thyristor to

340

the power supply board of the colour TV. The customer talked to us and bent over to see what we were doing. The hole in his throat which he seemed to be talking through whistled air in and out ... so much so, and so near to Vas's head, that I could see Vas's hair blowing up and down as he spoke each sentence.

"Oh, my God," I thought. "This is going to freak Vas out in a minute if I don't do something." I stood up and faced the guy and explained what we were doing. The guy straightened up away from Vas, and this took the pressure away from my young apprentice. Vas didn't move. He just got on with the job, but I could tell he was freaked out by all this. He said afterwards that he didn't think he would be able to go back there again if we needed to go.

Vas was always coming up with new ideas we could do for a bit of a laugh.

"Things we could use to make the day a bit more enjoyable," were his words.

I had recently bought a portable cassette machine from the shop at a bit of a discount. I liked to record music from the radio and the old Philips one I had was not working so well, so I bought a new one. When I took it into the workshop Vas immediately said,

"We can have some fun with this, you know, Dick."

"What do you mean?" I said. "What's going through your young mind, Vas?"

"Well," he said, "You know when we go into customers' houses and we have these stupid conversations with them about what's wrong with their TVs? Well, we could tape the conversations."

"Oh, and how do you think we are going to do that then, Vas? Aren't they going to be just a tiny bit suspicious if we have a tape machine in the room with us and you are poking it under their noses?"

"No problem," said Vas. "I have thought it out. We have two toolboxes, right? Yours and mine ... yours we use to do the work. Mine's a dummy, right? We take all my tools out of mine and put the machine inside it, right? Then all I have to do while you're fixing the problem is to stand by the customer with my toolbox, right...?"

341

I have no idea where all these things came from, but each time Vas came up with a prank we seemed to bloody go along with it.

"OK, OK," I said. "Let's try it out, then."

We had some practice runs in the workshop using the concealed tape machine in Vas's toolbox, and then taping Pete the domestic repair guy when he came in. It seemed to work.

"So let's try it for real," said Vas.

So we went out one day and I remember it very clearly. We both went to the door and I rang the doorbell. I had my heavy toolbox in my hand and Vas had his held under his arm. I guessed this was so it was higher up to catch any speech. The door opened and we were told to come in.

What happened next was bizarre, to be honest. I struck up my normal conversation with the customer, asking questions about the TV before I switched it on … then next to me was Vas holding his toolbox under his arm very awkwardly, as if he was holding a ventriloquist's dummy. As the customer moved about to point at switches and parts of the TV and the aerial socket, so Vas would follow with this little rabbit hutch under his arm. I was thinking,

"The customer is going to ask in a minute why this guy is hugging his toolbox in this way, because it looked the most unnatural thing for anyone to be doing."

So it went on all day: me talking, and Vas trailing around with my recorder in his toolbox. One or two were interesting, as some of the customers were already angry over the service and speed even before we got there. For these customers Vas would chirp up a bit more in the conversation to try and get a bit of gentle banter going that we could record. I would not say he was trying to stoke the fire, but once or twice he did respond with,

"Well … we have been really busy today, so I'm sorry … we just had to put you at the bottom of the list." Another time when one of the customers asked why we were late, Vas said he had had to go to his dad's funeral first and so things had got a bit delayed. Oh, my God. Sometimes there was no stopping Vas.

When we got back to the workshop we took the machine out and rewound the tape. Oh … did we laugh, or what? We laughed so loudly that they heard us in the shop area and the manager came to check things out. In he came bursting through the swing door, ducking his six foot six frame as he entered.

"Anything wrong, guys?" he said, looking suspiciously at each of us in turn and looking very much like John Cleese in *Fawlty Towers* when he knows the hotel inspectors are about.

I could hear Pete the old boy in the corner of the workshop trying to stifle a laugh by using his tobacco pipe as a dummy. There was just this loud sucking noise coming from it as the spit went back and forth within the pipe as he tried to conceal his laughter. The manager looked at Pete in disbelief, clearly wondering how such a thing could make such a musical tone.

"No, no, Mr Smith … It's nothing at all … just a joke Vas told. That's all," I said with two fingers crossed behind my back.

We didn't use the tape machine much after that as it kind of got in the way, and anyway I wasn't going to keep such an expensive bit of kit at work all the time just for the odd laugh.

Life was kind of good at Dunstable. It was close to my beloved Cali, and I sort of felt like I belonged there. Berkhamsted never felt like this. Being on the high street of Dunstable, you had access to all manner of shops and pubs. One of my favourites was F. L. Moore the record shop, which sold all sorts of records. What was more interesting for me was it that stocked the latest import labels from the USA. These records had no small hole in the middle, and so when you played them you had to use a plastic filler disc in the centre. Imports were more expensive, of course, but if you wanted the rarer toons then you had to fork out a bit more money. My record collection grew at a fast rate during this time.

Music was important, of course, but the old Moggie Minor van we used for work had no radio in it at all. We had no entertainment while we raced around Dunstable. Vas said to me one day,

"We need some music in the van. Have you got anything we can use?"

"Well," I said, "I have an old tranny at home. It's a bit big, as it's one of those radios you can pick up aeroplanes and taxis on."

"Bring it in," said Vas. "Let's see what we can do with it."

So I did bring in this lump of a radio, and these two electrical engineers constructed the neatest, most fantastic car/van radio you could ever imagine ...... nope, that was not the case at all.

The only way the radio would work was if it was near the roof, way up near one of the side windows. So Vas got some metal chain and just chained it to the side of the van. That was it: that was our van radio. If we went around a corner fast then Vas would most likely get hit by the tranny as it span wildly about. The other thing that caused us problems was that the radio was directional. So it was fine if we were pointing up or down Dunstable high street, north or south, but heaven forbid if we had to go to Luton or towards the Downs. We always tried to pick our route so we could keep as much as possible to the area where the reception was good. This sometimes meant going miles out of our way just so we could hear our favourite toons.

At this time in my life everything seemed to be working well. I had a fun job, a girlfriend, and my weekends and evenings were good times too. I enjoyed my times at Weatherhead's in Dunstable. The guys there were fun to be with and there was really no stress in my life.

Christmas was always a busy time at Weatherhead's, right up to the last few hours of Christmas Eve. We worked the whole day, right up to 5 p.m.. If someone had a faulty TV on Christmas Eve then basically they were going to be without TV for the whole of the holiday period, so we were always on standby right to the last minute to go out and deliver a loan set if required. OK, we had some food and drink in the shop, and in between calls we had some merriment – but we all looked forward to the time of getting out of there and starting Christmas for real with friends and family.

For me starting Christmas began as soon as I was out of the door and in the Moggie, firing it up and shooting down the short alley on to the main high street in Dunstable. I remember once I was really in the party mood. Someone had given me a big fat cigar and a can of beer in the shop and I still had a party hat on while winding my way around the lanes back to Hemel. I swigged the beer and puffed the cigar and sang to myself as I drove. I would be back home by six – and by seven I would be back out on the road again, heading to Dunstable for a special session at the Cali.

I worked at Weatherhead's for around four years: two at Berkhamsted and two at Dunstable. My monthly wage there was a little over £100 towards the end. I was qualified now: I had my City & Guilds full advanced engineer credentials.

An advert in the paper from a TV company called Vision Hire held the carrot firmly out in front of me. I went for an interview and it was, as they say, a no-brainer. The money would be doubled and then some – and I would be working in Aylesbury, a new place with new people. I would also get a brand new estate car, all paid for.

Weatherhead's could never compete with an offer like this, and so I handed in my notice to the manager at Dunstable. It was a sad day when I left. There were many friends whom I would never see again, and I had good times too with those guys. All the staff in that shop were lovely – the guys and the ladies. Everyone treated you well, and it was how you really want work to be in life. When I left everyone clubbed together and bought me a flashy ballpoint pen and ten number six fags. The fags were Vas's idea, of course.

California Trapping

1975

Here are the bands we saw then and the admittance price:

Kool & the Gang	£1.50
The Hues Corporation	£1.50
Rufus featuring Chaka Khan	£1
The Tymes	£1.50
Chairmen of the Board	£1.50
Steve Harley & Cockney Rebel	£1.50
G.T. Moore and the Reggae Guitars	N/A
The Stylistics	N/A
Hamilton Bohannon	£1.50
Smokey Robinson	£1
Fatback Band	£2
B.T. Express	£2
Donald Byrd & the Blackbyrds	N/A
Mac & Katie Kissoon	£2

With Chaz and Les in tow the Cali awaited what could only be called the three amigos of the discotheque world. We all had cars now, and took it in turn to drive each week. Of course it wasn't just the three of us going. Vic, Bill, and Baz often came, and so of course did my mates from college. Included in this, of course, was my great new workmate Vas. There was always a crowd of us there. We were going to take the Cali by storm, for sure. It was always our Saturday entertainment, no matter what else was happening around Hemel.

Saturdays were the main night, and the Cali always had a main act playing on stage in the main hall. Whoever it was would do a main stint for maybe one and a half hours. Before that and afterwards the disco would play toons, and here was your chance to maybe get a dance with a pretty girl. I always had a master plan in my head for trapping girls. How could we fail?

One night I sat Les and Chaz down in the Hillside Bar. It was early and things were just getting off the ground in the main hall. The floor in the bar was still relatively dry of beer and we settled down to a couple of pints of beer from the obligatory plastic beakers.

"Right," I said. "This is my master plan. You know when a slow record comes on and guys rush to get a dance with a girl." Both looked at me and nodded.

"Well," I said, "I've been thinking. The whole operation is flawed."

Blinking, Chaz said,

"And why is that, then?"

"Well," I said. "It's like this. You've got bunches of girls out there all dancing around their handbags, right?"

"Right."

"They dance and they look around and are eyeing up the guys as much as we are eyeing them up, right?"

"Right." The two nodded again in agreement.

"Right," I said. "So we all agree, then. The problem we have when a slow one starts up is that they see us coming."

"They bloody see you coming a mile off," said Les to Chaz, with a wind-up grin on his face.

"Come on, guys. This is serious," I retorted.

"Right. Now this is my plan. If we come around from the rear and approach them from their blind side they'll have no time to think about accepting or rejecting a dance from three smoothie guys."

"Who are the smoothie guys?" said Chaz.

"Us, you doughnut," I retorted. "Now they are more likely to just go with it, aren't they?"

"So what you're saying, then," said Les, "Is that we use some form of military manoeuvre to get a snog and a grope."

"Yes," I said. "It's foolproof."

I said to my two comrades that I had seen girls chat among themselves as we approached and decide before we got to them. It was usually a big "No". Sometimes it was a more positive "No" or "Fuck off dickhead.

"Girls assess," I said, "And make a decision before we even get to ask."

"Right," I said. "Have you two got this now? When the next slow one comes on, we go. OK? Circle around the back quick and get stuck in. OK?"

"OK," responded the two conscripts.

We sat and talked about stuff, mainly girls and music and cars: the sort of things guys talk about when out. Then from in the main hall I heard the next toon about to start. The first few bars were all it took, and I knew it was a slow one.

"Gooo…" I shouted at them like some caustic sergeant major drilling his troops. Les got up but Chaz still had the beer to his lips.

"Nowww… Chaz. Nowww…"

"But I've still got half left," replied Chaz.

"Fuck that. Now shift your arse. Nowww."

Chaz got up, helped by Les's hand, and beer spilt everywhere as we half knocked over the table in pursuit of the master plan. We near ran down the short corridor that ran between the Hillside Bar and the darkness of the main floor. Even in that short time girls were dancing with guys and our choices were getting reduced every second.

"There," I said. "There is a bunch right at the back."

Four girls were in a line with no one near them.

"Chaz, you come with me. Les you go wide right. Go, Go, Gooo," I commanded.

We got into position behind the girls, and I was quite sure that even our speed had not been spotted. We were like the silent panther in the jungle creeping unsuspectedly up on our prey … disco ninjas with our silent stealth slippers on. Well, OK … maybe not that stealthily.

"Do you want a dance, love?" I said to one of the ones in the middle. She looked around at me with a smile. Her face was a picture: a rather spotty picture, as it happens.

"She really should use cream," I heard myself say as I awaited the answer. "God, love. You're quite ugly, aren't you?" my inner subconscious was interjecting. I started to wish at this point that a

"No" would come. Chaz had been rejected already but I saw Les had got stuck in.

"No, fanks," came the reply, with a smile that didn't help the completion. "Me and me mate are going to Devil's Den now." I heard my mind snap in with,

"Yeah, that's probably the best place for yer, love."

"OK," I said. "Thanks," and walked away.

Chaz had waited for me, and we walked back to the bar.

"Do you think my pint will still be there?" he said.

"Maybe, Chaz. Maybe. We've got to get this chatting up thing sorted, mate."

Les had his dance, but was then told that he was no longer needed as his partner was joining her mates. So five minutes later Les was back in the Hillside Bar with his dejected pals. Les sat down.

"Hey, Dick, next time you have any bright ideas like that maybe you could factor in things like steering away from the local leper colony. It's bloody dark out there. You just don't know what you're chatting up."

The chatting up bit was always a bit of a mystery to me. Some of our crowd were really, really good at it and then there was us. Selection and rejection are funny things, and if you get a few rejections over a period of time then your confidence starts to suffer. Les, Billy Boy, and Baz usually had no problem with chatting to girls – and getting them, too. In fact sometimes girls were falling over themselves to get to get to these would-be Casanovas. It all felt so unfair. I kind of understood after a while that no real master plan was ever going to work unless it involved a certain amount of upfront bravado. I was kind of shy and obviously lacked that confidence to just say what I would like in front of a girl. I had no real notion of how you might just go up to a girl and talk. Billy Boy could use almost any chat-up line you could think of, and I have already explained one of his more bizarre ones.

Of course, it wasn't all about girls. We were there for the music too: the toons that were played and the big bands we would see. If we didn't get a dance in an evening we still had a good night out, and basically that was all good in our books.

After a few weeks of going to the Cali we tended to not venture far and settled in the Devil's Den bar, and only gravitated to the main hall when the band was on or when we thought a slow one was going to be played there.

Devil's Den was different from the rest of the set-up. Situated on the ground floor, it was a small disco that played import music. This was largely funk and jazz funk, the sort of music Chaz and I liked. Les was a bit indifferent on the music side, but he liked the atmosphere in Devil's Den and tended to stay with us.

One night in Devil's Den it just all fell into place. Isn't it strange when things happen when you just don't expect it? We had been in there a while and had just got a drink at the bar. Les spied some girls in the corner: three or four of them in a group. Les just went over and chatted and asked if we could sit down with them. He hadn't told us his plan, hadn't informed us of his manoeuvres: he had just gone in quite brazenly. I had to admire his approach. I longed to have that confidence he had: that sort of magic I thought it must have been.

Les came back to his two rookie mates.

"Guys, they said we could sit with 'em."

"You what?" I said.

"They are OK, mate. We can go join them. They are cool. They even look tidy."

Chaz looked at me.

"Come on then," I said. "What we waiting for?"

The girls seemed quite comfortable with us, and I found myself sitting next to a lovely-looking girl with short wavy brown hair and a lovely smile. It was always hard to tell what anyone really looked like in the Cali, especially in Devil's Den where it was really quite dark and seedy. Sometimes you might get a girl outside after the disco or see her on a date in the daylight and think,

"My God. Was I really with her last night? Is this the same person?"

Part of it was the dark and part of it was what we called the beer goggles effect. Every girl looked fantastic after a few hours of drinking.

My girl had a T-shirt top on with a sparkly design on the front and some high-waisted black trousers. Her shoes were the obligatory stacked-up platform type. She had red lipstick on and blue eyeshadow. She was a slim size ten girl, I would think, but nearly every girl then was about that size. I asked her name and asked where she lived.

"Luton," was the reply. I then asked what she did and she said she was still at school.

"Oh," I said.

"It's OK," she said. "I'm in the sixth form. I'm old enough to be out drinking."

We had a lovely night that night in Devil's Den. I danced with her and she smiled back at me constantly. We sat and chatted but I had no idea what was going on with Les and Chaz. They were still there and I got the impression that Les had scored too, but Chaz maybe had not.

Apart from meeting up with P at the Top Rank on that fateful night this was the only other opportunity since where I felt I had had a hand to play with.

It was time to go and my new friend got up.

"How are you getting back?" I said.

"My dad will be outside," she responded.

"Oh," I said. "OK," and then I had some inspiration. "Can I have your phone number, do you think?"

"Yes, of course you can," she replied with that smile on her face which I knew I would remember for a long time.

"Oh, God," I thought. "Where's a pen when you need it?"

"Don't worry," she said. "Give me your matchbox."

I dug in my pocket and pulled out the matches I used then. L dug in her handbag and pulled out her lipstick.

"Here," she said, and she wrote her short Luton number on the box.

She kissed me on the lips and then left. She turned once more by the door to look back at me and give a small wave, still smiling of course. That was it. She had gone, and all I had in my hand now was a box of matches with a thick red number written upon it. I was now back with Les and Chaz. The lights were back on now and the evening had finished.

"Do I have a girlfriend?" I said. Les said,

"Yes, I think you do, mate. I really think you have done it this time. Well done."

Girls

I phoned the girl I had met in Devil's Den the next day. I sat on the bottom stair step in the hall of my house and dialled the number. Who would answer? In fact was it the right number? What might she say? All these things passed through my anxious mind as my fingers slipped through the holes in the dial-type telephone we had. This lovely mustard object was now going to link me to Luton and the girl of my dreams.

Her mum answered and I felt my guts go heavy. I asked to speak to her daughter and she immediately said,

"Hold on a minute. I'll get her for you." The pace of my heart quickened, and the anticipation of hearing her voice was almost impossible to bear.

"Hello" I heard at the other end.

"Hello," I said back.

I could feel her smile down the phone. You just know it sometimes. Her voice had a warm tone that was both reassuring and comforting to hear. It made me feel confident, so I asked if I could take her out that week.

"Yes, of course you can," she replied. "I'll give you my address."

I came off the phone and Dad came out of the living room.

"Hope you're going to put some money in the box, son. You were on the phone ages..." he said. There was a wooden box by the phone to which you were supposed to contribute if you used the phone. I stuck 5p in and thought that would be about right.

The date would be exciting. I had to do some research, as I didn't know where exactly she lived. It was outside my TV repair sector, but I had maps in the van which would tell me exactly where her road was in Luton.

I would guess that everyone has the feelings I had as I set out in the Herald to drive up the M1 to Luton on what really was in all honesty my first real proper date with a girl. I was excited and nervous at the same time.

I remember that night very clearly. It was late in the year, and when I arrived it was getting a little dark. Thank God for my map, because her house was in a relatively new area near to the Vauxhall car works. The house was modern, and unlike our house. You could just tell this was privately owned.

We had a good evening that night and went to a pub way out in the country. We didn't sit in the pub at all. We got our drinks and sat in my car. We wanted to be private and alone, and as it was getting dark outside it felt sensible to sit in the car. I think we were lost in ourselves, because I drove off back from the pub with the empty glasses still in the car ... something of a trophy, I guess.

This girl from Luton was my first real love, and we lasted for about six months or so before the fateful day came when she rang me at home to say it was over. Ironically, I was sitting on the same step at home with the phone to my ear as I had when I first rang her. It took me a while to get over this parting but It didn't take too long to get back out there trapping, as my dad would say. There are, of course, always more fish in the sea.

All the girls I dated I either met at the Cali or the George or some other club in the district. In a way I got lucky with the girls I managed to trap and go out with after my friend from Luton. I never quite knew where I was driving on first dates to see these new girls. It was always a matter of getting the map out and looking up the address. To my amazement I arrived many times at addresses to find that my date actually lived in some palatial residence. Well ... let's say a house far removed from the council one I lived in.

Chaz and I picked up a couple of girls together many times, so this made a repeat date easy as we could just take one car and pick up the birds (as we called them) from where they lived. We once picked a pair of girls and got their numbers, of course, and made arrangements to see them in the week. They came from Luton from the Farley Hill area. near what's called The Ring. We later found out that this area was a bit of a dodgy part of Luton. To me it just looked normal like any council estate.

Chaz drove his big Vauxhall up the M1 and I navigated us to where this rough estate was.

"OK, Chaz," I said. "Pull over here."

"Why? Are we here, then?" he retorted.

"No, we're not there yet, but we need to get sorted out first."

"What do you mean by sorted out?" he replied.

"Look, Chaz. We have both been smoking in your smelly car, right? That's not going to help us with the hope of a night of passion in your car, is it?"

"Nope, I suppose not," he said. I got a bottle of Brut cologne out of my jacket pocket. "Here. Spray this about a bit. It will mask any nasties you might have."

We sprayed ourselves until the whole car stank like a tart's boudoir. We then had to open the windows before we gassed ourselves.

"Right," I said. "Now shove this in your gob."

"What's this?" said Chaz in total puzzlement at the white object in my hand.

"It's only a bloody mint," I said. "Don't worry. It's not a Mickey Finn. "

So we both sat there for a couple of minutes sitting in a fug of Brut and sucking mints on the outskirts of Farley Hill.

"Right. Are we ready then?" I said.

"Yep. Let's go," said Chaz, and restarted the Cresta.

We enjoyed our night out with these girls and also many other nights too. One of my favourite dates was another trip out with Chaz, and this time it seemed that we had picked up a couple of girls who lived in Trowley Bottom near Flamstead ... talk about posh. Chaz lived in a nice house in Kings Langley, but where these girls lived was like another world. We met the girls in the pub there – the lovely Rose and Crown, which is no longer in use. What a shame. What a lovely summer's evening that was, in such an idyllic setting. The girls were great, and I must have managed to keep mine for all of two weeks before she packed me in.

It never lasted long with me. I don't know if it was me or my Brut aftershave or Chaz or what, but the girls came and went like the wind. A few weeks with a girl was a huge achievement: they just were not that interested in a longer-term relationship. Baz, on the other hand, was always in love – up to his neck in it. Baz was always, it seemed, engaged or going steady. Sometimes we didn't see him for months and months, and then he would just pop around my house and say,

"Are you going to the George tonight, or are you going up the Cali?"

I once dated a girl who lived with her parents as part of an old people's home in Dunstable. That was a fun night when I arrived there and found I was in this huge complex of pensioners. We had a great night in that night, and raided the kitchen stores when we got peckish. Where people live is so random at times, it seems, but it makes the date so much more exciting. You just don't know who you're chatting up.

It is interesting to note that while all this dating and womanising was going on I never brought any of them back home to meet my parents. I'm not sure if I felt ashamed of where I lived or who my parents were. It was a very long time before any of my girlfriends came back to 18 Lower Barn. Those who did where usually the ones who would become long-term girlfriends.

California Closing

1976-1979

Here are the bands we saw then and the admittance price:

James Brown	N/A
People's Choice	£1.50
The Trammps	£1.50
Bobby Womack	£1.50
The Miracles	£1.50
Brass Construction	N/A
War	N/A
Ohio Players	N/A
KC and the Sunshine Band	N/A
Heatwave	£3
J.A.L.N. Band	£1
Archie Bell and The Drells	£2
Tavares	£2
Hi-Tension	£2
Showaddywaddy	£3
Rose Royce	N/A
Sylvester	N/A

There were some great acts to be seen during 1976, and one of the highlights – of course – was seeing the great Godfather of Soul James Brown. You could move down the front by the stage and see this black guy work with only a few feet between you. I'll never forget this night, as it was absolutely one of the best act nights we ever saw.

There had of course been so many other bands over the years who had also been brilliant, and I always felt so privileged to see these bands each week. Soon it would be drawing to a close towards the end of 1979.

It was a gradual decline that took place. In 1977 the business was sold off to a businessman who made some substantial changes to the format of the place. There were to be more discos at night, but fewer bands played in the main hall. The hall was used at weekends for the new craze of roller disco, and we went once or twice to twist our ankles while listening to the latest toons. I always found these outings a bit strange, to be honest. Here was a place we had frequented in the dark. It had a soul, for sure: after all, it had been playing soul music. Here we were in the daylight with the lights on going around and around on a sprung floor which was meant for dancing on, not roller skating on.

A skate park was constructed outside where the old outside pool used to be. This was for kids, and served the growing interest of the time of jumping over things on a board with roller skate wheels attached. This was something we were not interested in at all.

They opened up the main hall for functions sometimes, and at one point the whole hall was filled with pool tables for an event.

Devil's Den had been renamed as Dido's nightclub, which was something Chaz and I hated.

All these changes didn't do anything much for revenue, which continued to decline. It was stated that the Queensway Hall in Dunstable had picked up numbers and this was now where the kids were going.

There was always a bit of a bunfight going on between the owners of the Cali and the residents of the houses that looked on to the place. The Cali was there well before the houses but like all things in life, of course, people complain once they get their feet under the table. So it was that pressure was applied to the council to do something about the noise and disruption at night from the Cali.

A company from Luton applied for planning permission in 1979 and eventually, after a year, planning permission was granted.

The last ever packed-out party took place on December 31 1979, a night I attended. Within days the bulldozers moved in and tore down what was this iconic place. The Cali was dead – but not forgotten, of course.

In its place now are houses: an estate of bricks and mortar which don't entertain and don't thrill an audience every Saturday night.

How stupid we sometimes are. How short-sighted we become when money is a concerned, and people want change to satisfy their needs.

At least I have those memories and those lovely nights of fun, watching some of the best acts in the world. I'm pleased I was there then to witness it all.

Here are the other clubs and places we went during that time:

Tiffany's Nightclub: Dunstable
Sands: Luton
Scamps (The Living Room): Hemel Hempstead
Batchwood Hall: St Albans
Spider's Web: Watford
Unicorn Club: Leighton Buzzard
King Langley Services Club: Kings Langley

In Conclusion and to Close

The end of the book has finally arrived, and I need to wrap up a few loose ends here. This book has been a very strange journey indeed. It's been fun to reminisce and remember those nuggets of memory you thought you'd lost: to overturn the odd stone and see what festers beneath.

I think that those people past the age of fifty understand a little of how life tricks you over a period of time. Not only does the memory get a bit flaky, but it also warps and plays tricks too. Looking back at the years gone by has been like playing those black-and-white movies in my head. Some of it has been so scratched and faded it's almost been impossible to know what actually happened. However, I have had some help along the way of course.

I would like to dedicate this book to a whole host of people: those who have helped me in life, immediate family and friends, and especially my old school chums, who have been brilliant in contributing some of the stories here.

All the people in this book that I have mentioned I do love dearly without exception, and I do appreciate so much their input into my life.

When I was a small boy with a very curious mind I often wondered what the future might hold. At times there was some speculation (of course) from the media, as to what this future vision might be. It was quite clearly understood that as we were living through the atomic age in the 1950s that things would change big time. Things in the future would be different: they would be better, brighter, and faster.

People thought that it wouldn't be long before we had cars that would hover in the sky. They thought work would be done by robots and that everywhere you looked would be pleasant and green, even more so than at that present time. More leisure activity for the family would mean more green parks to play and walk in. People in the future would always be happy and free from stress and worry. There would be no more illness, and medical operations would be simplified and always successful. The utopia that was the future was very vivid in our minds because behind us were the two world wars with their death, destruction, and misery. Looking forward to the new space age and all it brought was a positive step forward that everyone wanted to endorse. Maybe more importantly, we all thought there would be no more wars and no more killing.

Of course improvements have been made but there is nothing like the visions we were given during the fifties and sixties. It's a lesson for us all, I think. What we think the future will hold is sometimes far from the truth. What does happen is usually totally unexpected.

So will man ever land on Mars? Will cancer be cured for good? Will a solution be found for global warming? Will *Doctor Who* actually run out of lives? I suspect that I won't be around for some of these but I certainly hope that the young people of today dream and make aspirations and visions about what they see the future holds. It's the only way we move on.

I had to stop writing this book at some point and a natural end seemed to be around the time I reached my early twenties. Of course the stories go on, but there are not enough pages left to cover everything. So we must, I'm sorry to say, come to an end.

On a final note I will travel back in time to the first section of this book, where I described a vision I had in the back garden on that sunny day with a blue sky. If you remember … I reached up with my small hand stretching so hard to reach the objects that floated there. Red, blue, green, and yellow balloons floated high in the blue vista. The children from the school had been allowed to set off some balloons with name tags on. I could see the tags attached to the bottom of each sphere. I reached up, of course, but the balloons were too high and out of reach. I wanted them. I wanted them so badly.

Through life I have at times tried to reach the unobtainable: the impossible balloon that's way out of arm's reach. The lesson that day taught me that you might try and fail – and sometimes you become dejected – but to try is always the best thing.

Always try your hardest at everything you do. Try and fail sometimes ... but try, and you may succeed most of the time. Have fun, my dear readers, and have a fruitful life. May the funk be with you.

Acknowledgement

There are a few people to thank in part for their help with writing this book. Some for their input into the stories and some for providing lovely photographs. I have received much encouragement and good wishes along the way from both friends and family. It's a big general thank you to all involved.

I would first like to thank my brother Rob for his anecdotes pictures and inputs from those times before I was born. Filling in the gaps so to speak was very helpful.

I would like to say a big thank you to my old school mates; those I am still in touch with, who again have given me some additional stories and just been there to remind the old grey matter of certain fuzzy facts from the past. Thanks in addition Jim for some of your photographs they are priceless.

My illustrator has been most patient with the task of constructing fantastic drawings from my feeble descriptions and sometimes very badly drawn sketches. Although I can watercolour paint my draft input doodles have been a real challenge to my patient artist. Thank you for your help and contribution.

I have to also thank those people that have been around me through my life and have directly and sometimes indirectly contributed to the events in this book. Baz and Chaz to name just two of the main characters and co-stars of the book. Barrie and Terry who I still have contact with and can't thank enough for just being there.

To one of my main teachers Mrs Evans who gave me some wonderful pictures she took at the time back in the 1960s. Thanks Mrs Evans you are never forgotten and sorry I got wet in the watercress beds.

Mum, Dad you are up there somewhere and looking down, I hope you like the content I know some of it will be a shock. Sorry. You're always in my thoughts and thanks for putting up with me at times.

All friends, family, my wife Sandra, ex work colleagues you have all wondered what this is about and now you know. Thanks for reading.

Readers, you bought this book on the pretext it might entertain. Well I hope it has and that I made you laugh in places. That was my intention.

Last but not least, Reg Stickings. If I had not read your fantastic book on Northern Soul, then mine would never have got started. Thanks Reg I owe you a pint.

14139387R00203

Printed in Great Britain
by Amazon.co.uk, Ltd.,
Marston Gate.